Microsoft® Access® 2013

Step by Step

Joyce Cox
Joan Lambert

PUBLISHED BY
Microsoft Press
A Division of Microsoft Corporation
One Microsoft Way
Redmond, Washington 98052-6399

Library of Congress Control Number: 2013931601
ISBN: 978-0-7356-6908-6

Printed and bound in the United States of America.

First Printing

Microsoft Press books are available through booksellers and distributors worldwide. If you need support related to this book, email Microsoft Press Book Support at mspinput@microsoft.com. Please tell us what you think of this book at http://www.microsoft.com/learning/booksurvey.

The example companies, organizations, products, domain names, email addresses, logos, people, places, and events depicted herein are fictitious. No association with any real company, organization, product, domain name, email address, logo, person, place, or event is intended or should be inferred.

Acquisitions Editor: Rosemary Caperton
Editorial Production: Online Training Solutions, Inc.
Technical Reviewer: Rob Carr
Copyeditor: Jaime Odell
Indexer: Joyce Cox
Cover: Microsoft Press Brand Team

Contents

PART 1

Simple database techniques

2   Create databases and simple tables   53

3   Create simple forms   91

4   Display data   115

5   Create simple reports   135

PART 2

Relational database techniques

6   Maintain data integrity   157

7   Create queries   197

PART 3

Database management and security

Introduction

Over the years, Microsoft has put a lot of effort into making Access not only one of the most powerful consumer database programs available, but also one of the easiest to learn and use. Because Access is part of Microsoft Office 2013, you can use many of the techniques you use with Microsoft Word and Microsoft Excel. For example, you can use familiar commands, buttons, and keyboard shortcuts to open and edit the information in Access tables. And you can easily share information between Access and Word, Excel, or other Office programs. *Microsoft Access 2013 Step by Step* offers a comprehensive look at the features of Access that most people will use most frequently.

Who this book is for

Microsoft Access 2013 Step by Step and other books in the *Step by Step* series are designed for beginning-level to intermediate-level computer users. If part of your job involves entering data in or producing reports from a database designed by someone else, this book will help you understand the behind-the-scenes functionality of the database. If you are tasked with the maintenance of an existing database, you will learn important techniques for ensuring data integrity. Although we don't cover the macro and VBA functionality that enables experienced developers to create full-featured database applications, we do touch on more advanced topics such as controlling access and preventing problems.

Examples shown in the book generally pertain to small and medium businesses but teach skills that can be used in organizations of any size. The databases you create and work with are desktop databases, designed to be used in Access 2013 on a local computer. Access 2013 has powerful new capabilities to enable more advanced users to create applications, called *Access web apps*, that are stored as SQL databases on a Microsoft SharePoint 2013 site and can be viewed and manipulated through a web browser. Because of the behind-the-scenes requirements of these databases, we briefly describe them but don't cover them in depth.

Whether you are already comfortable working in Access and want to learn about new features in Access 2013 or are new to Access, this book provides invaluable hands-on experience so that you can confidently create and work with many types of desktop databases

How this book is organized

This book is divided into three parts. Part 1 explains how to get data into a database, either directly by entering it into tables or indirectly by using forms; and how to get information out of a database, either by displaying it on the screen or by printing it in reports. Part 2 discusses ways to ensure that the data in related tables is accurate, how to use queries to extract data from related tables, and how to create forms and reports that use related tables. Part 3 covers more advanced Access techniques, including securing the database and customizing the program to fit the way you work. With this three-part structure, readers who are new to the program can acquire basic skills and then build on them, whereas readers who are comfortable with Access 2013 basics can focus on material that is of the most interest to them.

Chapter 1 contains introductory information that will primarily be of interest to readers who are new to Access or are upgrading from Access 2003 or an earlier version. If you have worked with a more recent version of Access, you might want to skip directly to Chapter 2.

This book has been designed to lead you step by step through all the tasks a beginning-level or intermediate-level user is most likely to want to perform with Access 2013. If you start at the beginning and work your way through all the exercises, you will gain enough proficiency to be able to create simple databases and work with more complex databases created by experts. However, each chapter is self-contained, so you can jump in anywhere to acquire exactly the skills you need.

Download the practice files

Before you can complete the exercises in this book, you need to download the book's practice files to your computer. These practice files can be downloaded from the following page:

http://aka.ms/Access2013sbs/files

IMPORTANT The Access 2013 program is not available from this website. You should purchase and install that program before using this book.

The following table lists the practice files for this book.

Chapter	File
Chapter 1: Explore Microsoft Access 2013	GardenCompany01.accdb
Chapter 2: Create databases and simple tables	None
Chapter 3: Create simple forms	GardenCompany03.accdb
	Logo.png
Chapter 4: Display data	GardenCompany04.accdb
Chapter 5: Create simple reports	GardenCompany05.accdb
Chapter 6: Maintain data integrity	GardenCompany06.accdb
Chapter 7: Create queries	GardenCompany07.accdb
Chapter 8: Create custom forms	GardenCompany08.accdb
	Hydrangeas.jpg
Chapter 9: Create custom reports	GardenCompany09.accdb
Chapter 10: Import and export data	Customers.xlsx
	Employees.txt
	GardenCompany10.accdb
	ProductsAndSuppliers.accdb
	Shippers.xlsx
Chapter 11: Make databases user friendly	GardenCompany11.accdb
	Icon.ico
	Logo.png
Chapter 12: Protect databases	GardenCompany12.accdb
Chapter 13: Work in Access more efficiently	GardenCompany13.accdb

If you would like to be able to refer to the completed versions of practice files at a later time, save the modified practice files at the end of each exercise. If you might want to repeat the exercises, save the modified practice files with a different name or in a different folder.

Your companion ebook

With the ebook edition of this book, you can do the following:

- Search the full text
- Print
- Copy and paste

To download your ebook, please see the instruction page at the back of the book.

Get support and give feedback

The following sections provide information about getting help with this book and contacting us to provide feedback or report errors.

Errata

We've made every effort to ensure the accuracy of this book and its companion content. Any errors that have been reported since this book was published are listed on our Microsoft Press site at oreilly.com, which you can find at:

http://aka.ms/Access2013sbs/errata

If you find an error that is not already listed, you can report it to us through the same page.

If you need additional support, email Microsoft Press Book Support at *mspinput@microsoft.com*.

Please note that product support for Microsoft software is not offered through the addresses above.

We want to hear from you

At Microsoft Press, your satisfaction is our top priority, and your feedback our most valuable asset. Please tell us what you think of this book at:

http://www.microsoft.com/learning/booksurvey

The survey is short, and we read every one of your comments and ideas. Thanks in advance for your input!

Stay in touch

Let's keep the conversation going! We're on Twitter at: *http://twitter.com/MicrosoftPress*.

Simple database techniques

Chapter at a glance

Tables

Explore tables,
page 28

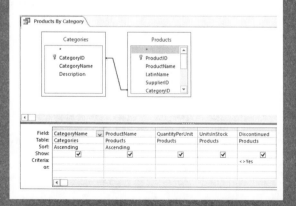

Forms

Explore forms,
page 33

Queries

Explore queries,
page 38

Reports

Explore reports,
page 43

Explore Microsoft Access 2013

1

IN THIS CHAPTER, YOU WILL LEARN HOW TO

- Identify new features of Access 2013.

- Work in the Access 2013 user interface.

- Understand database concepts.

- Explore tables, forms, queries, and reports.

- Preview and print database objects.

This chapter introduces Microsoft Access 2013 and is designed to serve different purposes for different readers, depending on prior knowledge of this program and other Microsoft Office 2013 programs.

- If you are a beginning Access user, you might want to skip the lists of new features and start with "Working in the Access 2013 user interface."

- If you have used other Office 2007 or Office 2010 programs but have not worked with Access before, you might want to skip down to "Understanding database concepts."

- If you have upgraded to Access 2013 from Access 2003, you might want to read as far as the end of "Working in the Access 2013 user interface" and then skip to Chapter 2, "Create databases and simple tables."

- If you have upgraded to Access 2013 from Access 2007 or Access 2010, you might be interested in the new features that have been introduced in this version of the program, but you might not need to work through the exercises in the rest of this chapter.

Throughout this book, you'll be working with databases that contain information about the employees, products, suppliers, and customers of a fictional company. As you complete the exercises, you will develop an assortment of tables, forms, queries, and reports that can be used to enter, edit, and manipulate the information in a database in many ways.

In this chapter, you'll get an overview of the new features in recent versions of Access to help you identify changes if you're upgrading from a previous version. You'll explore the program's user interface, and the concepts and structure of data storage in Access. Then you'll look at database objects such as tables, forms, queries, and reports, while learning about Access features and functionality that you'll explore in more depth in later chapters. Finally, you'll preview and print database objects.

PRACTICE FILES To complete the exercises in this chapter, you need the practice file contained in the Chapter01 practice file folder. For more information, see "Download the practice files" in this book's Introduction.

Identifying new features of Access 2013

Access 2013 builds on previous versions to provide powerful tools for all your database needs. If you're upgrading to Access 2013 from a previous version, you're probably most interested in the differences between the old and new versions and how they will affect you, and you probably want to find out about them in the quickest possible way. The following sections list new features you will want to be aware of, depending on the version of Access you are upgrading from. Start with the first section and work down to your previous version to get the complete picture.

If you are upgrading from Access 2010

If you have been using Access 2010, you might be wondering how Microsoft could have improved on what seemed like a pretty comprehensive set of features and tools. The new features introduced between Access 2010 and Access 2013 include the following:

- **Access web apps** You can still create powerful database applications that are stored locally or in a central location. But if your organization is running Microsoft SharePoint with Access Services, you can now create a web form of a database that anyone with the correct permissions can view and manipulate from a web browser. Judging by the amount of effort Microsoft is putting into Access web apps, it is likely that this sophisticated evolution of the web capabilities introduced with Access 2010 will be the wave of the future, at least for larger enterprises.

- **Windows 8 functionality** Access 2013, like all Office 2013 programs, is a full-featured Windows 8 application. When it is running on the Windows 8 operating system, it not only has the sleek new Windows 8 look but it also incorporates the latest touch technologies designed for tablet and mobile devices.

- **Starting screen** Access opens to a screen that provides easy access to new database templates, the databases you recently worked on, and locations where existing databases might be stored.

- **Cloud access** When you connect your Office or Access installation to a Microsoft account (formerly known as a Windows Live account) or a Microsoft Office 365 account, you have the option of saving desktop databases "in the cloud" to a SharePoint document library or a Microsoft SkyDrive site, so that it is available when you are not at your desk.

If you are upgrading from Access 2007

In addition to the features listed in the previous section, if you're upgrading from Access 2007, you'll want to take note of the following features that were introduced in Access 2010:

- **The Backstage view** All the tools you need to work with your database files, as opposed to their content, are accessible from one location. You display the Backstage view by clicking the File tab, which replaces the Microsoft Office Button at the left end of the ribbon.

- **Customizable ribbon** Create your own tabs and groups to suit the way you work.

- **Unifying themes** Add pizzazz to database objects such as forms and reports by applying a professional-looking theme from a gallery of options.

- **Web databases** With Access 2010, companies with employees and clients in different geographic locations can make their databases accessible over the Internet in a web browser. (This technology is still available in Access 2013, but it has been superseded by Access web apps. An Access 2010 web database cannot be converted to an Access web app.)

- **Navigation forms** Offering the sophisticated browsing techniques people are accustomed to using on websites, these forms provide an essential navigation tool that can increase the usability and data security of any database.

- **New database templates** Creating common types of databases is easier when you start with a template. The database templates that come with Access are supplemented by those made available by a community of database developers through the Office website.

- **Application parts** Add predefined database objects to an existing database. In addition to various types of forms, several Quick Start parts are available. For example, adding the Contacts part adds one table and associated queries, forms, and reports.

- **Enhanced Layout view and layout controls** It is easy to make design changes in Layout view while viewing the underlying data.

- **Enhanced Expression Builder** The layout of the Expression Builder dialog box has been refined to make building an expression more intuitive. In addition, a feature called IntelliSense has been incorporated to display options based on what you enter and to provide syntax guidance.

- **Improved conditional formatting** You can use data bars to add at-a-glance insight into the data in Number fields.

- **Ability to export to PDF and XPS files** When you want to make a report or other database object available to people but don't want them to be able to manipulate it, export the object in either PDF or XPS format. You can optimize the file size for printing or publishing online.

If you are upgrading from Access 2003

In addition to the features listed in the previous sections, if you're upgrading from Access 2003, you'll want to take note of the following features that were introduced in Access 2007:

- **The ribbon** The user interface organizes the most common commands for any database object into tabs and groups so that the appropriate commands are immediately accessible for the current object.

- **Quick Access Toolbar** Customize a portion of the toolbar to include commands you regularly use, regardless of which object is currently active.

- **Navigation pane** The customizable Navigation pane replaces the Database window from Access 2003. Display or hide all tables, queries, forms, reports, macros, and modules, or create a custom group that displays only the objects you want to work with at the moment. You can even hide the Navigation pane to make more room on the screen for your database object.

- **View Shortcuts toolbar** This context-sensitive toolbar in the lower-right corner of the program window provides single-click switching among the supported views of the current database object.

- **Tabbed documents** Open multiple database objects and switch between them quickly by clicking tabs on a tab bar.

- **Template library** Quickly locate and download professionally designed templates for common database projects.

- **Improved sorting and filtering** Easily sort all records in a table based on one or more fields, or filter a table or form to display or hide records matching multiple criteria.

- **Layout view** Redesign a form or report while viewing it.

- **Stacked and Tabular layouts** Group controls in a form or report layout so that you can easily manipulate the entire group as one unit.

- **Automatic calendar** The Date/Time data type includes an optional calendar control. Click the calendar, and select the date you want.

- **Rich Text** Memo fields support most common formatting options, including fonts, color, and character formatting. The formatting is stored with the database.

- **Create tab** Quickly create a new table, form, query, report, macro, SharePoint list, or other Access object.

- **Totals function** Add a totals row to a query, and select from a list of formulas to automatically calculate aggregate values for forms and reports.

- **Field List** Drag and drop fields from one or more related or unrelated tables onto your active table.

- **Attachment data type** Attach photos and other files to a database record.

- **Embedded macros** Macros embedded in a form or report offer a higher level of security in database applications.

- **Microsoft Access Help** Easily search end-user and developer help content from within Access.

- **Improved information sharing** Easily import and export data between Access and other Office applications or .xml, .html, and .pdf files; create or link a database with a SharePoint list; or publish your database to a SharePoint library and allow users to update and extract information.

- **Improved report design** Quickly create a professional-looking report, complete with logo, header, and footer; and use Report view, combined with filters, to browse only selected records in the report.

- **Group, Sort, and Total pane** This feature makes it much easier to group and sort data in reports, and add totals from a drop-down list.

- **Enhanced security** Adding password protection to a database causes Access to automatically encrypt the database when it closes, and decrypt it when it opens.

Working in the Access 2013 user interface

The program we work with and depict in images throughout this book is a desktop installation of Access 2013, installed from a DVD as part of the Office 2013 suite of programs. You might have installed Access 2013 as a freestanding program or as part of an Office 365 subscription that allows users to install the desktop programs from the Internet. Regardless of how you installed Access, the program has the same functionality and works the same way.

TIP Office 365 is a cloud-based solution that small, midsize, and enterprise businesses can use to provide a variety of products and services to their employees through a subscription licensing program.

As with all programs in Office 2013, the most common way to start Access is from the Start screen (Windows 8) or the Start menu (Windows 7) displayed when you click at the left end of the Windows Taskbar. When you start Access without opening a database, the program's starting screen appears. From this screen, you can create a new database or open an existing one. Either way, the database is displayed in a program window that contains all the tools you need to create database objects and enter and manipulate data. The Access 2013 interface is designed to closely reflect the way people generally work with a database. If you are not familiar with this interface, which was first introduced with Access 2007, here is a quick description of the program window elements.

Title bar   Ribbon

A new blank table displayed in the Access 2013 program window.

Identifying program window elements

The program window contains the following elements:

- **Title bar** This bar across the top of the program window displays the name of the active database and by default display the path to the folder where it is stored. It also provides tools for managing the program and the program window.

Program icon   Window management buttons

[title bar image with icons] My Database : Database- C:\Users\Joyce\Docum...   TABLE TOOLS   ? — □ ×

Quick Access Toolbar   Microsoft Access Help button

You can use the tools on the title bar to move and size the window, undo or redo changes, save the database, and get help with the program.

At the left end of the title bar is the program icon, which you click to display commands to restore, move, size, minimize, maximize, and close the program window.

To the right of the Access icon is the Quick Access Toolbar. By default, the Quick Access Toolbar displays the Save, Undo, and Redo buttons, but you can customize it to display any command you want.

TIP You might find that you work more efficiently if you organize the commands you use frequently on the Quick Access Toolbar and then display it below the ribbon, directly above the workspace. For information, see "Manipulating the Quick Access Toolbar" in Chapter 13, "Work in Access more efficiently."

At the right end of the title bar are four buttons: a Help button that opens the Access Help window, in which you can use standard techniques to find information; and the familiar Minimize, Maximize/Restore Down, and Close buttons.

SEE ALSO For information about the Access Help system, see the sidebar "Getting help with Access 2013" later in this chapter.

■ **Ribbon** Below the title bar, all the commands for working with an Access database are represented as buttons in this central location so that you can work efficiently with the program.

Tabs

FILE HOME CREATE EXTERNAL DATA DATABASE TOOLS FIELDS TABLE   Joyce Cox

[ribbon image showing groups: Views | Clipboard | Sort & Filter | Records | Find | Text Formatting]

Groups   Dialog box launcher

Each tab of the ribbon contains a specific category of commands.

TIP If your ribbon appears as a row of tabs across the top of the workspace, click the Home tab to temporarily display that tab's buttons so that you can follow along. We tell you how to control the display of the ribbon in a minute. Don't be alarmed if your ribbon looks different from those shown in our screens. You might have installed programs that add their own tabs to the ribbon, or your screen settings might be different. For more information, see "Working with the ribbon" later in this topic.

Across the top of the ribbon is a set of tabs. Clicking a tab displays its associated set of commands.

Commands related to managing Access and Access databases (rather than their content) are gathered together in the Backstage view, which you display by clicking the colored File tab located at the left end of the ribbon. Commands available in the Backstage view are organized on pages, which you display by clicking the page tabs in the colored left pane. You redisplay the database and the ribbon by clicking the Back arrow located above the page tabs.

The Backstage view, where you can manage files and customize the program.

Commands related to working with database content are represented as buttons on the remaining tabs of the ribbon. When an object is selected in a database, one or more tool tabs might appear at the right end of the ribbon to make commands related to that specific object easily accessible. Tool tabs disappear again when their associated object is no longer active or when the current view does not support their use.

TIP Some older commands no longer appear as buttons on the ribbon but are still available in the program. You can make these commands available by adding them to the Quick Access Toolbar. For more information, see "Manipulating the Quick Access Toolbar" in Chapter 13, "Work in Access more efficiently."

On each tab, buttons representing commands are organized into named groups. You can point to any button to display a ScreenTip with the command name and its keyboard shortcut (if it has one).

SEE ALSO For information about controlling the display and content of ScreenTips, see "Changing default program options" in Chapter 13, "Work in Access more efficiently."

Some buttons include an integrated or separate arrow. If a button and its arrow are integrated, clicking the button displays options for refining the action of the button. If the button and its arrow are separate, clicking the button carries out the default action indicated by the button's current icon. You can change the default action by clicking the arrow and then clicking the action you want.

Related but less common commands are not represented as buttons in a group. Instead, they're available in a dialog box or pane, which you display by clicking the dialog box launcher located in the lower-right corner of the group.

To the right of the ribbon group names is the Collapse The Ribbon button. Clicking this button hides the groups of commands but leaves the tab names visible. You can then click any tab name to temporarily display its commands. Clicking anywhere other than the ribbon hides the commands again. When the full ribbon is temporarily visible, you can click the Pin The Ribbon button (the pushpin) to the right of the group names to make the display permanent.

KEYBOARD SHORTCUT Press Ctrl+F1 to minimize or expand the ribbon. For a list of keyboard shortcuts, see "Keyboard shortcuts" at the end of this book.

■ **Navigation pane** On the left side of the program window, the Navigation pane displays lists of database objects. By default, it displays all the objects in the database by type of object, but you can filter the list by clicking the pane's title bar and then clicking the category or group of objects you want to display. You can collapse and expand the groups in the list by clicking the chevrons in the section bars. If the

Navigation pane is in your way, you can click the Shutter Bar Open/Close button in its upper-right corner to minimize it. To redisplay the Navigation pane, click the Shutter Bar Open/Close button again. You can drag the right border of the pane to the left or right to make it wider or narrower.

KEYBOARD SHORTCUT Press F11 to display or hide the Navigation pane.

- **Status bar** Across the bottom of the program window, this bar displays information about the current database and provides access to certain program functions. At the right end of the bar is the View Shortcuts toolbar, which provides convenient buttons for switching the view of the active database object.

View Shortcuts toolbar

Database information   Keyboard information

This status bar tells you the current view and the status of the keyboard.

The goal of all these user interface features is to make working in a database as intuitive as possible. Commands for tasks you perform often are readily available, and even those you might use infrequently are easy to find.

Working with the ribbon

As with all Office 2013 programs, the Access ribbon is dynamic, meaning that as its width changes, its buttons adapt to the available space. As a result, a button might be large or small, it might or might not have a label, or it might even be an entry in a list.

The width of the ribbon depends on the following three factors:

- **Program window width** Maximizing the program window provides the most space for the ribbon.

- **Screen resolution** Screen resolution is the size of your screen display expressed as pixels wide × pixels high. The greater the screen resolution, the greater the amount of information that will fit on one screen. Your screen resolution options are dependent on your graphics adapter and monitor. Common screen resolutions range from 800 × 600 to 2560 × 1600. The greater the number of pixels wide (the first number), the greater the number of buttons that can be shown on the ribbon.

To change your screen resolution:

1 Open the **Screen Resolution** control panel item by using one of the following methods:

   ■ Right-click the Windows desktop, and then click **Screen Resolution**.

   ■ Click a blank area at the top of the Windows 8 **Start** screen, and enter screen resolution. Then in the **Search** pane, click **Settings**, and in the **Settings** results, click **Adjust screen resolution**.

   ■ In Control Panel, open the **Display** control panel item, and then click **Adjust Resolution**. (If Control Panel is set to **Category** view, click **Adjust screen resolution** in the **Appearance and Personalization** category.)

2 On the **Screen Resolution** page, click the **Resolution** arrow, click or drag to select the screen resolution you want, and then click **Apply** or **OK**.

On the Screen Resolution page, you set the resolution by dragging the pointer on the slider.

- **The magnification of your screen display** If you change the screen magnification setting in Windows, text and user interface elements are larger and therefore more legible, but fewer elements fit on the screen. You can set the magnification from 100 to 500 percent.

You can change the screen magnification from the Display control panel item, which you can open from Control Panel or by using one of the following methods:

- Right-click the Windows desktop, click **Personalize**, and then in the lower-left corner of the **Personalization** page, click **Display**.

- Enter display at the top of the Windows 8 **Start** screen, click **Settings**, and then click **Display** in the **Settings** results.

On the Display page, you can choose one of the standard magnification options or change the text size of specific elements.

To change the screen magnification to 125 or 150 percent, click that option on the Display page.

To select another magnification, click the Custom Sizing Options link and then, in the Custom Sizing Options dialog box, click the magnification you want in the drop-down list or drag the ruler to change the magnification even more.

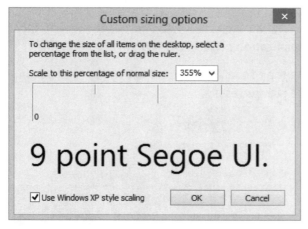

You can set the magnification as high as 500 percent by dragging the ruler in the Custom Sizing Options dialog box.

After you click OK in the Custom Sizing Options dialog box, the custom magnification is shown on the Display page along with any warnings about possible problems with selecting that magnification. Click Apply on the Display page to apply the selected magnification.

Adapting exercise steps

The screen shots shown in this book were captured at a screen resolution of 1024 x 768, at 100-percent magnification. If your settings are different, the ribbon on your screen might not look the same as the one shown in this book. As a result, exercise instructions that involve the ribbon might require a little adaptation.

Our instructions use this format:

- On the **Home** tab, in the **Sort & Filter** group, click the **Ascending** button.

If the command is in a list, our instructions use this format:

- On the **Home** tab, in the **Records** group, click the **More** button and then, in the list, click **Hide Fields**.

If differences between your display settings and ours cause a button to appear differently on your screen than it does in this book, you can easily adapt the steps to locate the command. First click the specified tab, and then locate the specified group. If a group has been collapsed into a group list or under a group button, click the list or button to display the group's commands. If you can't immediately identify the button you want, point to likely candidates to display their names in ScreenTips.

In this book, we provide instructions based on the traditional keyboard and mouse input methods. If you're using Access on a touch-enabled device, you might be giving commands by tapping with your finger or with a stylus. If so, substitute a tapping action any time we instruct you to click a user interface element. Also note that when we tell you to enter information in Access, you can do so by typing on a keyboard, tapping an on-screen keyboard, or even speaking aloud, depending on your computer setup and your personal preferences.

In this exercise, you'll start Access and explore the Backstage view and ribbon.

➡ SET UP You need the GardenCompany01 database located in the Chapter01 practice file folder to complete this exercise, but don't open it yet. Just follow the steps.

1 From the **Start** screen (Windows 8) or the **Start** menu (Windows 7), start **Access 2013**.

2 On the Access starting page, at the bottom of the left pane, click **Open Other Files** to display the **Open** page of the **Backstage** view.

   TIP From the Backstage view, you manage your Access database files, but you don't work with the content of databases. For example, you can create a database, but not a database object. We'll talk about the tasks you can perform in the Backstage view in other chapters of this book.

3 In the left pane of the **Open** page, click **Computer**, and in the right pane, click the **Browse** button. Then in the **Open** dialog box, navigate to the **Chapter01** practice file folder, and double-click **GardenCompany01** to open the database.

4 If a security warning appears, click **Enable Content** in the security warning bar.

   TIP Be sure to read the sidebar "Enabling macros and other active content" later in this chapter to learn about Access security options.

   Let's save the database so that you can explore it without fear of overwriting the original practice file.

5 Click the **File** tab to display the **Backstage** view, and click **Save As**. Then with **Save Database As** selected in the left pane of the **Save As** page and **Access Database** selected in the **Database File Types** area of the right pane, click the **Save As** button.

6　　In the **Save As** dialog box, save the database with a different name, such as MyGardenCompany01.

> **TIP** In this book, we assume you will save files in the practice file folders, but you can save them wherever you want. When we refer to the practice file folders in the instructions, simply substitute the save location you chose.

7　　Click **Enable Content** in the security warning bar.

On the left, the Navigation pane displays a list of all the objects in this database. Spanning the top of the window, the ribbon includes five tabs: File, Home, Create, External Data, and Database Tools. Because no database object is currently open, the Home tab is active by default, but none of its buttons are available.

> **TIP** Databases created in Access 2013 use the file storage format introduced with Access 2007, and their files have the .accdb extension. You can open database files created in earlier versions of Access (which have an .mdb extension) in Access 2013. You can then either work with and save them in the old format or work with and save them in the new format. If you convert them, you can no longer open them in versions prior to Access 2007. For more information about the ACCDB format, search for *accdb* in Access Help.

8　　In the **Navigation** pane title bar, click **All Access Objects**, and then in the **Filter By Group** area of the menu, click **Tables** to list only the tables in the **Navigation** pane.

9　　In the **Navigation** pane, double-click **Categories** to open that table on a tabbed page. Notice that the record navigation bar at the bottom of the page tells you how many records the table contains and which one is active, and enables you to move among records. Notice also that the **Fields** and **Table** tool tabs appear on the ribbon. These tool tabs are displayed only when you are working with a table.

Tool tabs

Filtered Navigation pane   Record navigation bar   Table on tabbed page

Buttons representing commands related to working with database content are organized on the Home tab in six groups: Views, Clipboard, Sort & Filter, Records, Find, and Text Formatting.

TIP By default, Access 2013 displays database objects on tabbed pages. If you want, you can display each object in a separate window instead. In the Access Options dialog box, display the Current Database page, and then in the Application Options area, below Document Window Options, click Overlapping Windows. The window of each object has its own set of Minimize, Restore Down/Maximize, and Close buttons. You can move object windows by dragging their title bars, you can size them by dragging their frames, and you can arrange them by clicking the Switch Windows button in the Window group and selecting an option. (This group is added to the Home tab when you select Overlapping Windows in the Access Options dialog box.)

10 On the **Home** tab, click the **Text Formatting** dialog box launcher to open the **Datasheet Formatting** dialog box.

From the Datasheet Formatting dialog box, you can access settings not available as buttons in the Text Formatting group, such as Gridline Color and Border And Line Styles.

11   Close the **Datasheet Formatting** dialog box.

12   Click the **Create** tab.

Buttons representing commands related to creating database objects are organized on the Create tab in six groups: Templates, Tables, Queries, Forms, Reports, and Macros & Code.

13   Double-click the **Create** tab.

Double-clicking the active tab hides the ribbon's button groups and provides more space for the current database object.

14   Click the **External Data** tab to temporarily display the full ribbon, which drops down over the table.

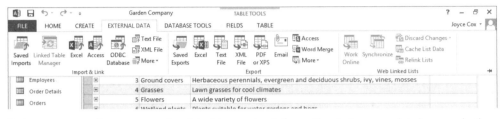

Buttons representing commands related to moving information between a database and other sources are organized on the External Data tab in three groups: Import & Link, Export, and Web Linked Lists.

15   Click anywhere in the open table, and notice that the ribbon disappears again.

16   Double-click the **Database Tools** tab to permanently display the ribbon and activate that tab.

Buttons representing commands related to managing, analyzing, and ensuring data reliability are organized on the Database Tools tab in six groups: Tools, Macro, Relationships, Analyze, Move Data, and Add-Ins.

Before we finish this exercise, let's close first the active database object and then the database. (If you want to close the database and exit Access, click the Close button in the upper-right corner of the program window.)

17   At the right end of the bar where the page tab for the **Categories** table is displayed, click the **Close** button to close the table without closing the database.

18   Display the **Backstage** view, and then click **Close** to close the database without exiting Access.

> **TIP** If you don't close the active database before opening another one, Access prompts you to save your changes and closes the active database for you. You cannot have two databases open simultaneously in a single instance of Access. If you want to have two databases open at the same time, you must start a new instance of Access.

❌ CLEAN UP Retain your version of the GardenCompany01 database for use in later exercises.

Getting help with Access 2013

Whenever you have a question about Access 2013 that is not answered by this book, your next recourse is the Access Help system. This system is a combination of tools and information available from the Office website for reference when you are online, and basic information stored on your computer for reference when you are offline. Online references can include articles, videos, and training tools.

To open the Access Help window and search for information:

1   Near the right end of the title bar, click the **Microsoft Access Help** button to open the **Access Help** window.
    KEYBOARD SHORTCUT Press F1 to display the Access Help window.

    TIP To switch between online and offline reference content, click the arrow to the right of Access Help and then click Access Help From Office.com or Access Help From Your Computer. You can print the information shown in the Help window by clicking the Print button on the toolbar. You can change the font size of the topic by clicking the Use Large Text button on the toolbar to the left of the Search Help box.

2   In the search box, enter your search term, and then click the **Search** button (the magnifying glass) to display a list of related topics.

3   In the results list, click the topic you're interested in to display its information.

4   Jump to related information by clicking any hyperlink identified by blue text.

    TIP When section links appear at the beginning of an article, you can click a link to move directly to that section of the article. You can click the Top Of Page link at the end of an article to return to the beginning.

5   When you finish exploring, close the **Access Help** window by clicking the **Close** button in the upper-right corner.

Understanding database concepts

Simple databases store information in only one table. These simple databases are often called *flat file databases*, or just *flat databases*. More complex database programs, such as Access, store information in multiple related tables, thereby creating what are referred to as *relational databases*. If the information in a relational database is organized correctly, you can treat these multiple tables as a single storage area and pull information electronically from different tables in whatever order meets your needs.

Tables are one of the types of database objects you work with in Access. Other types include forms, queries, reports, macros, and modules. Of these object types, only tables are used to store information. The others are used to enter, manage, manipulate, analyze, retrieve, or display the information stored in tables—in other words, to make the information as accessible and therefore as useful as possible.

In its most basic form, a database is the electronic equivalent of an organized list of information. Typically, this information has a common subject or purpose, such as the list of employees shown in the following table.

ID	First name	Last name	Title	Hire date
1	Karen	Berg	Owner	May 1, 2008
2	Kim	Akers	Head Buyer	June 1, 2008
3	Tom	O'Neill	Assistant	November 2, 2008
4	Naoki	Sato	Sales Manager	August 14, 2009
5	Molly	Dempsey	Gardener	October 17, 2009
6	Nancy	Anderson	Sales Rep	May 1, 2010
7	Michael	Entin	Sales Rep	April 1, 2011
8	Kari	Furse	Buyer	May 3, 2011
9	Chase	Carpenter	Gardener	November 15, 2012

This list is arranged in a table of columns and rows.

- Each column represents a *field*—a specific type of information about an employee: last name, first name, hire date, and so on.
- Each row represents a *record*—all the information about a specific employee.

If a database did nothing more than store information in a table, it would be no more useful than a paper list. But because the database stores information in an electronic format, you can manipulate the information in powerful ways to extend its usefulness.

For example, suppose you want to find someone's phone number. You can look up this information in a phone book, because its information is organized for this purpose. However, if you want to find the phone number of your grandmother's neighbor, a printed phone book won't do you much good, because it isn't organized in a way that makes that information easy to find.

Storing the information published in a phone book in a database, has the following advantages:

- It takes up far less space.
- It costs less to reproduce and distribute.
- If the database is designed correctly, the information can be retrieved in many ways.

The real power of a database isn't in its ability to store information; it is in your ability to quickly retrieve exactly the information you want from the database.

Enabling macros and other active content

Some databases contain macros and other active content that can run code on your computer. In most cases, the code is there to perform a database-related task, but hackers can also use macros to spread a virus to your computer. When you open a database that is not stored in a trusted location or signed by a trusted publisher, Access displays a security warning below the ribbon.

While the security warning is displayed, the active content in the database is disabled.

You can enable macros and other active content in three ways:

- By enabling the macros for use in the current database session.

- By adding the database publisher to the list of trusted publishers. This option is available only if the publisher's digital signature is attached to the database. Access will then automatically enable macro content in any database that is also signed by that publisher.

- By making the location of the database a trusted location, or moving the database to a trusted location. Access automatically enables macro content in any database saved in that location.

To enable macros for the current database session only:

- In the security warning bar, click **Enable Content**.

To add the publisher of a digitally signed database to the Trusted Publishers list:

1 In the security warning bar, click **Some active content has been disabled**.
2 On the **Info** page of the **Backstage** view, click the **Enable Content** button, and then click **Advanced Options**.

3   In the **Microsoft Office Security Options** dialog box, click **Trust all documents from this publisher**, and then click **OK**.

To add the location of a database to the Trusted Locations list:

1   Display the **Backstage** view, and then click **Options**.
2   In the left pane of the **Access Options** dialog box, click **Trust Center**, and then click **Trust Center Settings**.
3   In the left pane of the **Trust Center** dialog box, click **Trusted Locations**.
4   On the **Trusted Locations** page, click **Add new location**.
5   In the **Microsoft Office Trusted Location** dialog box, click **Browse**.
6   In the **Browse** dialog box, navigate to the folder containing the current database, and then click **OK**.
7   In the **Microsoft Office Trusted Location** dialog box, select the **Subfolders of this location are also trusted** check box if appropriate, and then click **OK** in each of the open dialog boxes.

If you prefer, you can change the way Access handles macros in all databases:

1   Display the **Trust Center**, and then in the left pane, click **Macro Settings**.
2   Select the option for the way you want Access to handle macros:

- **Disable all macros without notification** If a database contains macros, Access disables them and doesn't display the security warning to give you the option of enabling them.

- **Disable all macros with notification** Access disables all macros and displays the security warning.

- **Disable all macros except digitally signed macros** Access automatically enables digitally signed macros.

- **Enable all macros** Access enables all macros (not recommended).

3   Click **OK** to close the **Trust Center**, and then click **OK** to close the **Access Options** dialog box.

Exploring tables

Tables are the core database objects. Their purpose is to store information. The purpose of every other database object is to interact in some manner with one or more tables. An Access database can contain thousands of tables, and the number of records each table can contain is limited more by the storage space available than by anything else.

Every Access object has two or more views. For tables, the two most common views are Datasheet view, in which you can display and modify the table's data, and Design view, in which you can display and modify the table's structure. To open a table in Datasheet view, either double-click its name in the Navigation pane, or right-click its name and then click Open. To open a table in Design view, right-click its name and then click Design View. When a table is open in Datasheet view, clicking the View button in the Views group on the Home tab switches to Design view; when it is open in Design view, clicking the button switches to Datasheet view. You can also switch the view by clicking one of the buttons on the View Shortcuts toolbar in the lower-right corner of the program window.

Datasheet view displays the table's data in columns (*fields*) and rows (*records*). The first row contains column headings (*field names*).

Field names

Category I ▾	Category Nam ▾	Description	▾
1	Bulbs	Spring, summer and fall, forced	
2	Cacti	Indoor cactus plants	
3	Ground covers	Herbaceous perennials, evergreen and deciduous shrubs, ivy, vines, mosses	
4	Grasses	Lawn grasses for cool climates	
5	Flowers	A wide variety of flowers	
6	Wetland plants	Plants suitable for water gardens and bogs	
7	Soils/sand	Potting soils, peat moss, mulch, bark	
8	Fertilizers	A variety of fertilizers	
13	Trees	Evergreen and deciduous trees	
14	Herbs	For flavoring and fragrance	
15	Bonsai supplies	Bonsai supplies	
16	Roses	Many types of roses	
17	Rhododendron	Hardy cultivars	
18	Pest control	Non-toxic alternatives	
19	Carnivorous	Meat-eating plants	
20	Tools	Miscellaneous gardening hardware	
21	Berry bushes	Small bush fruits	
22	Shrubs/hedges	Shrubbery suitable for beds, containers, hedges, etc.	
(New)			

Field

Record

In this format, the table is often simply referred to as a datasheet.

If two tables have one or more field names in common, you can embed the datasheet from one table in another. By using an embedded datasheet, called a *subdatasheet*, you can display the information in more than one table at the same time. For example, you might want to embed an Orders datasheet in a Customers table so that the orders each customer has placed are visible in the context of the customer record.

In this exercise, you'll open existing database tables and explore the table structure in two views.

SET UP You need the GardenCompany01 database you worked with in the preceding exercise to complete this exercise. (For practice purposes, you might have saved this database with a different name.) Open the database, ensure that tables are listed in the Navigation pane, and then follow the steps.

1   In the **Navigation** pane, double-click **Products** to open the **Products** table in **Datasheet** view.

2   At the right end of the **Navigation** pane title bar, click the **Shutter Bar Close** button to display more of the table's fields.

Product I ▾	Product Name ▾	Latin Name ▾	Supplier ▾	Category ▾	Quantity P ▴
1	Magic Lily	Lycoris squamigera	The Bulb Basket	Bulbs	One dozen
2	Autumn Crocus	Colchicum	The Bulb Basket	Bulbs	One dozen
3	Compost bin		Garden Hardware Mfg.	Tools	1 - 12 ft cub
4	Cactus sand potting m		Soil and Sand Supplier	Soils/sand	5 lb. bag
5	Weeping Forsythia	Forsythia suspensa	The Shrub Club	Shrubs/hedges	1 ea.
6	Bat box		NoTox Pest Control	Pest control	1 box per ki
7	Electronic insect killer		NoTox Pest Control	Pest control	1 per box
8	Beneficial nematodes	Neoaplectana carpc	NoTox Pest Control	Pest control	1 pt
9	Crown Vetch	Coronilla varia	Cover Up Stuff	Ground covers	3 - 3 inch po
10	English Ivy	Hedera helix	Cover Up Stuff	Ground covers	5 ea. Rooted
11	Austrian Copper	R. foetida bicolor	Rosie's Roses	Roses	Per plant
12	Persian Yellow Rose	R. foetida 'Persiana	Rosie's Roses	Roses	Per plant
13	Indoor Magic potting :		Soil and Sand Supplier	Soils/sand	5 lb. bag
14	GrowGood potting soi		Soil and Sand Supplier	Soils/sand	10 lb. bag
15	Sterilized soil		Soil and Sand Supplier	Soils/sand	5 lb. bag
16	Winterberry	Ilex verticillata	The Shrub Club	Shrubs/hedges	1 ea.
17	Anise	Pimpinella anisum	The Herb House	Herbs	6 - 2" pots
18	Crushed rock		Wholesale Rock & Gra	Soils/sand	Per yard

Record: I◄ ◄ 1 of 189 ► ►I ►☰   No Filter   Search

Each row in this table contains information about a product and each column contains one field from each record. The record navigation bar shows that the selected record is 1 of 189.

TIP To make the graphics in this book readable, from now on we will often work in a program window that is smaller than full screen with the Navigation pane closed. More fields and records might be visible in your tables than those shown in our screen shots.

Let's adjust the width of a couple of columns to accommodate their longest entries.

3   In the row of field names at the top of the table, point to the right border of the
    Product Name column, and when the pointer changes to a double-headed arrow,
    double-click the border.

4   Double-click the right border of the **Category** column to adjust that field's width.
    Notice that the products **Magic Lily** and **Autumn Crocus** are assigned to the **Bulbs**
    category.

    TIP You can also resize a table column by pointing to the border and dragging it to
    the left or right.

    Now let's open a second table.

5   In the **Navigation** pane, click the **Shutter Bar Open** button, and then double-click
    Categories to open the **Categories** table on a new tabbed page in **Datasheet** view.
    Notice that the **Products** table is still open and available if you need it.

    TIP From now on, open the Navigation pane whenever you need to work with a dif-
    ferent object, but feel free to close it if you want to display more of the data.

6   In the **Categories** table, at the left end of the record for the **Bulbs** category, click the
    Expand button (the plus sign) to display a subdatasheet containing all the records
    from the **Products** table that are assigned to the **Bulbs** category.

Subdatasheet

Products	Categories					×
Category I ▾	Category Nam ▾		Description			▾ Cli ▲
⊟ 1	Bulbs	Spring, summer and fall, forced				

Product I ▾	Product Name ▾	Latin Name ▾	Supplier ▾	Quantity Per Unit ▾	Unit Pric ▾
1	Magic Lily	Lycoris squamigera	The Bulb Basket	One dozen	$48.40
2	Autumn Crocus	Colchicum	The Bulb Basket	One dozen	$22.69
69	Anemone	Anemone coronaria	The Bulb Basket	One dozen	$33.88
71	Lily-of-the-Field	Sternbergia lutea	The Bulb Basket	One dozen	$45.98
160	Siberian Iris	Iris Siberica	The Bulb Basket	6 per pkg.	$15.67
161	Daffodil	Ismene calathina	The Bulb Basket	6 per pkg.	$15.67
162	Peony	Paeonia	The Bulb Basket	6 per pkg.	$24.14
163	Lilies	Lilinum Hybrid	The Bulb Basket	6 per pkg.	$12.71
164	Begonias	Begonia	The Bulb Basket	6 per pkg.	$22.93
190	Bulb planter		The Bulb Basket	1 ea.	$8.41
✱ (New)					$0.00

⊞	2	Cacti	Indoor cactus plants	
⊞	3	Ground covers	Herbaceous perennials, evergreen and deciduous shrubs, ivy, vines, mosses	
⊞	4	Grasses	Lawn grasses for cool climates	
⊞	5	Flowers	A wide variety of flowers	
⊞	6	Wetland plants	Plants suitable for water gardens and bogs	

Record: I◄ ◄ 1 of 10 ► ►I ►❑ 🇾 No Filter Search   ◄ |

You can display records from two related tables simultaneously.

TIP Displaying a subdatasheet is only possible if a relationship has been established between two tables. For information about relationships, see "Defining relationships between tables" in Chapter 2, "Create databases and simple tables."

7   To the left of the record for the **Bulbs** category, click the **Collapse** button (the minus sign) to hide the subdatasheet.

8   Click the **Close** button at the right end of the page tab bar (not the **Close** button in the upper-right corner of the program window) to close the **Categories** table.

9   Close the **Products** table, and when Access asks whether you want to save your changes to this table, click **Yes**.

TIP In steps 3 and 4, you changed the look of the table by changing the widths of columns. If you want those changes to be in effect the next time you open the table, you must save them.

Next let's use a table containing order-fulfillment information to practice moving among records.

10   In the **Navigation** pane, double-click the **Orders** table.

	OrderID	CustomerID	AccountRep	OrderDate	ShippedDate	ShippedBy	Freight	Ship
⊞	11079	LANER	Sato	1/5/2012	1/7/2012	Big Things Frei	$18.00	Eric La
⊞	11080	ACKPI	Sato	1/5/2012	1/6/2012	EZ Does It	$13.25	Pilar A
⊞	11081	BROKE	Anderson	1/6/2012	1/7/2012	EZ Does It	$8.95	Kevin
⊞	11082	KHAKA	Anderson	1/6/2012	1/8/2012	Triple P Delive	$5.50	Karan
⊞	11083	KOCRE	Sato	1/8/2012	1/9/2012	Triple P Delive	$28.00	Mary /
⊞	11084	COXBR	Anderson	1/12/2012	1/14/2012	Triple P Delive	$8.50	Arlett
⊞	11085	RAMLU	Entin	1/12/2012	1/13/2012	EZ Does It	$3.00	Luciar
⊞	11086	OVESC	Dempsey	1/12/2012	1/13/2012	Triple P Delive	$6.95	Lani O
⊞	11087	THIRA	Sato	1/12/2012	1/13/2012	Big Things Frei	$20.00	John T
⊞	11088	MILFR	Entin	1/13/2012	1/14/2012	Triple P Delive	$7.95	Geof I
⊞	11089	ESTMO	Anderson	1/14/2012	1/16/2012	EZ Does It	$7.50	Mode
⊞	11090	HOFRO	Entin	1/14/2012	1/16/2012	Big Things Frei	$14.50	Rolan
⊞	11091	HOLMI	Sato	1/15/2012	1/19/2012	EZ Does It	$24.50	Micha
⊞	11092	ASHCH	Entin	1/16/2012	1/19/2012	Triple P Delive	$17.00	Teres
⊞	11093	BENPA	Anderson	1/19/2012	1/21/2012	Big Things Frei	$0.00	Paula
⊞	11094	BANMA	Sato	1/22/2012	1/23/2012	Fast Freddie's I	$4.35	Martir
⊞	11095	GANJO	Entin	1/22/2012	1/24/2012	Big Things Frei	$18.95	Jon Ga
⊞	11096	CORCE	Anderson	1/22/2012	1/23/2012		$14.40	Cecili
⊞	11097	KANJO	Anderson	1/22/2012	1/23/2012	EZ Does It	$30.00	Judy K
⊞	11098	HIGSY	Sato	1/22/2012	1/23/2012		$18.50	Kim H

Record: I◄ ◄ 1 of 87 ► ►I ►□ 🇹 No Filter Search ◄

The record navigation bar at the bottom of the window indicates that this table contains 87 records, and that the active record is number 1 of 87.

11   On the record navigation bar, click the **Next record** button several times to move the selection down the active **OrderID** field.

KEYBOARD SHORTCUT Press the Up Arrow or Down Arrow key to move the selection one record at a time. Press the Page Up or Page Down key to move one screen at a time. Press Ctrl+Home or Ctrl+End to move the selection to the first or last field in the table.

12   Click the record navigation bar, select the current record number, enter **40**, and then press the **Enter** key to move the selection directly to record **40 of 87**.

Finally, let's view the structure of the open table.

13   On the **View Shortcuts** toolbar, click the **Design View** button to display the **Orders** table structure in **Design** view. Notice that the **Design** tool tab now appears on the ribbon.

Datasheet view displays the data stored in the table, whereas Design view displays the underlying table structure.

SEE ALSO For information about table structure, see "Refining table structure" in Chapter 2, "Create databases and simple tables."

⊗ CLEAN UP Close the Orders table. Keep the GardenCompany01 database open for use in later exercises.

Exploring forms

Access tables are dense lists of raw information. Working directly with tables in a database you have created might be quite simple for you, but it might be overwhelming for people who don't know much about databases in general or about this database in particular. To make it easier to enter, display, and print information, you can design forms.

A form acts as a friendly interface for a table. Through a form, you can display and edit the records of the underlying table, or create new records. Most forms provide an interface to only one table. However, by embedding subforms within a main form, you can use one form to interact with multiple tables that are related through one or more common fields.

Forms are essentially collections of controls that either accept information or display information. You can create forms by using a wizard, or you can create them from scratch by manually selecting and placing the controls. Access provides the types of controls that are standard in Windows dialog boxes, such as labels, text boxes, option buttons, and check boxes. With a little ingenuity, you can create forms that look and work much like the dialog boxes in all Windows programs.

As with tables, you can display forms in several views. The following are the three most common views:

- **Form** In this view, you can display and enter data.

- **Layout** In this view, you can work with the elements of the form to refine its appearance and functionality while also displaying the data from the underlying table.

- **Design** In this view, you have more precise control over the appearance, placement, and functionality of form elements, but you cannot display the underlying data.

SEE ALSO For more information about forms, see Chapter 3, "Create simple forms," and Chapter 8, "Create custom forms."

In this exercise, you'll explore forms, subforms, and the available form controls.

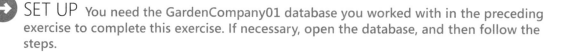 SET UP You need the GardenCompany01 database you worked with in the preceding exercise to complete this exercise. If necessary, open the database, and then follow the steps.

1 In the **Navigation** pane, click the title bar to display the category list, and then in the **Filter By Group** area, click **Forms** to display all the forms that have been saved as part of this database.

2 In the **Navigation** pane, double-click **Products** to open the **Products** form on a tabbed page.

Products					✕
🔯 **Products**					
Product ID	1		Quantity Per Unit	One dozen	
Product Name	Magic Lily		Unit Price	$48.40	
Latin Name	Lycoris squamigera		Units In Stock	40	
Supplier	The Bulb Basket	▾	Units On Order	0	
Category	Bulbs	▾	Reorder Level	10	
			Discontinued	☐	
Record: I◄ ◄ 1 of 189 ► ►I ►❋ 🍢 No Filter Search			◄		►

This form is the interface for the Products table.

3 Click the arrow adjacent to the **Supplier** box to display a list of all the company's suppliers.

This is an example of a list box control.

Now let's open a form that includes a main form and a subform.

4 In the **Navigation** pane, double-click **Categories** to open that form on its own tabbed page. Notice that the main form displays information from the **Categories** table, and the subform, which looks like a datasheet, displays information from the **Products** table for the current record.

Subform

This form is the interface for both the Categories and Products tables.

5   On the main form's record navigation bar, click the **Next Record** button a few times to display the next few records. Notice that the subform changes with each click to display the products in each category.

Next let's display a form containing customer information in various views.

6   In the **Navigation** pane, double-click **Customers** to open that form in **Form** view.

The purpose of this form is to edit or create customer records.

7   On the **Home** tab, in the **Views** group, click the **View** button, which switches between **Form** view and **Layout** view. Notice that three tool tabs (**Design**, **Arrange**, and **Format**) appear on the ribbon.

8   In the **Views** group, click the **View** arrow, and then click **Design View** to display the underlying structure of the form.

In Design view, you can add controls to a form, rearrange controls, format the controls and the form itself, and add pictures and lines to help identify the form and its sections.

9   Switch between **Form** view, **Layout** view, and **Design** view, noticing the similarities and differences.

Finally, let's take a look at the controls available for designing forms.

10 On the **Design** tool tab, in the **Controls** group, do one of the following, depending on the size of your program window:

■ In the lower-right corner of the **Controls** gallery, click the **More** button.

■ Click the **Controls** button.

Either method displays a menu containing the **Controls** gallery.

You can use these controls to assemble custom forms for your database.

SEE ALSO For information about form controls, see "Adding controls" in Chapter 8, "Create custom forms."

11   Click away from the gallery to close it.

12   Close all the open database objects by right-clicking the tab of the **Customers** form and then clicking **Close All**.

❌ CLEAN UP Keep the GardenCompany01 database open for use in later exercises.

Exploring queries

You can locate specific information stored in a table, or in multiple tables, by creating a query that specifies the criteria you want to match. Queries can be quite simple—for example, you might want a list of all products in a specific category that cost less than $10.00. They can also be quite complex—for example, you might want to locate all out-of-state customers who have purchased gloves within the last three months. For the first example, you might be able to sort and filter the data in the Products table fairly quickly to come up with a list. For the second example, sorting and filtering would be very tedious. It would be far simpler to create a query that extracts all records in the Customers table whose billing addresses are not in your state and whose customer IDs map to records that appear in the Orders table within the last three months and whose item IDs map to records classified as gloves in the Products table.

You can create queries by using a Query wizard, and you can also create them from scratch. The most common type is the select query, which extracts matching records from one or more tables. Less common are queries that perform specific types of actions.

Processing a query, commonly referred to as *running a query* or *querying the database*, displays a datasheet containing only the records that match your search criteria. You can use the query results as the basis for further analysis, create other database objects (such as reports) from the results, or export the results in another format, such as an Excel spreadsheet.

If you create a query that you are likely to want to run more than once, you can save it. It then becomes part of the database and appears in the list when you display the Queries group in the Navigation pane. To run the query at any time, you simply double-click it in the Navigation pane. Each time you run the query, Access evaluates the records in the specified table or tables and displays in Datasheet view the current subset of records that match the criteria defined in the query.

To set up a query, you work in Design view. Switching to this view displays the Query Designer, which has two components:

- The top pane displays boxes listing the fields of the tables the query is designed to work with. Each box represents one table. In a query that works with more than one table, lines between the boxes indicate that before the query was created, relationships were established between the tables based on common fields. The relationships enable the query to draw information from the tables.

    SEE ALSO For more information about relationships, see "Defining relationships between tables" in Chapter 2, "Create databases and simple tables."

- The bottom pane displays the design grid, where the query's search criteria are defined. Each column of the grid refers to one field from one of the tables in the top pane. Each row defines a different aspect of the query.

Don't worry if this all sounds a bit complicated at the moment. When you approach queries logically, they soon begin to make perfect sense.

SEE ALSO For more information about queries, see Chapter 7, "Create queries."

In this exercise, you'll explore two existing queries.

 SET UP You need the GardenCompany01 database you worked with in the preceding exercise to complete this exercise. If necessary, open the database, and then follow the steps.

1   In the **Navigation** pane, display the **Queries** group, which includes all the queries that have been saved as part of this database.

2   In the **Navigation** pane, right-click the **Delete Discontinued Products** query, and then click **Object Properties** to display the properties of the query, including a description of its purpose.

Delete Discontinued Products Properties ☒

General

Delete Discontinued Products

Type: Query: Select Query (Local)
Description: Filters records in Products table. Query returns only
                    products that are discontinued. Can be converted to
                    delete query to remove discontinued products.

Created: 6/2/2010 4:59:35 PM
Modified: 6/14/2010 11:30:16 AM
Owner: Admin

Attributes: ☐ Hidden

OK   Cancel   Apply

The icon at the top of the General tab indicates that this is a select query.

3   In the **Delete Discontinued Products Properties** dialog box, click **Cancel**.

Let's run a query.

4   Right-click the **Products By Category** query, and then click **Open** to run the query and display its results in a datasheet. If necessary, close the **Navigation** pane so that you can see all the results.

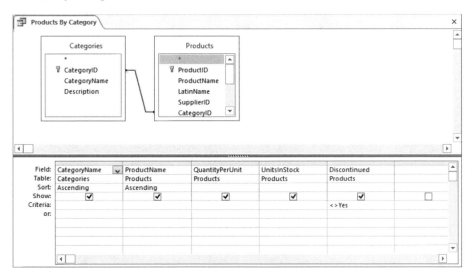

The record navigation bar indicates that 171 records meet the criteria of the Products By Category query.

The Products table contains 189 records. To find out why 18 of the records are missing in the query results, let's look at this query in Design view.

5   On the **View Shortcuts** toolbar, click the **Design View** button to display the query in the Query Designer.

You use the Query Designer to indicate the tables you want to use and the criteria you want to match.

The two boxes in the top pane of the Query Designer list the fields in the Categories and Products tables. The line between the boxes indicates a relationship based on their common CategoryID field. The design grid in the bottom pane defines a query that matches information from both tables. Because <> Yes (not equal to Yes) is entered in the Criteria row for the Discontinued field, this query finds all the records that don't have a value of Yes in that field (in other words, all the records that have not been discontinued) and displays them by category.

As an experiment, let's make a small change to the query design.

6   In the **Criteria** row of the **Discontinued** field, replace <> with =. Then on the **Design** tool tab, in the **Results** group, click the **Run** button to find all the records that have been discontinued.

Category Nam ▾	Product Name ▾	Quantity Per Unit ▾	Units In Stoc ▾	Discontinue ▾
Bonsai supplies	Bonsai mixed garden	1 ea.	0	☑
Bonsai supplies	Bonsai scissors	1 ea.	0	☑
Fertilizers	Guano	5 lb. bag	0	☑
Fertilizers	Muriate of potash	10 lb. bag	0	☑
Grasses	Decorator moss	1 tray	0	☑
Shrubs/hedges	Hedge shears 10"	1 ea.	0	☑
Soils/sand	Buckwheat hulls	5 lb bag	0	☑
Soils/sand	Oyster shells	5 lb bag	0	☑
Soils/sand	Peanut hull meal	5 lb bag	0	☑
Soils/sand	Terrarium soil	5 lb bag	0	☑
Tools	Manure fork	1 ea.	0	☑
Tools	Optional grass catcher	1 ea.	0	☑
Tools	Posthole digger	1 ea.	0	☑
Tools	Push reel lawn mower	1 ea.	0	☑
Tools	Revolving sprinkler	1 ea.	0	☑
Tools	Root waterer	1 ea.	0	☑
Tools	Shade fencing 6'	50' roll	0	☑
Tools	Sharpening kit	1 ea.	0	☑

Record: I◄ ◄ 1 of 18 ► ►I ►□ 🏳x No Filter   Search

The 18 discontinued products account for the difference between the number of records in the Products table and the number of records displayed by the original query.

TIP You can also run a query by switching to Datasheet view.

7   Close the **Products By Category** query. When a message asks whether you want to save your changes to the query, click **No**.

✖ CLEAN UP Keep the GardenCompany01 database open for use in later exercises.

Exploring reports

You can display the information recorded in your tables in nicely formatted, easily accessible reports, either on your computer screen or on paper. A report can include items of information selected from multiple tables and queries, values calculated from information in the database, and formatting elements such as headers, footers, titles, and headings.

You can look at reports in four views:

- **Report view** In this view, you can scroll through the information in the report without being distracted by the page breaks that will be inserted when it is printed.

- **Print Preview** In this view, Access displays your report exactly as it will look when printed.

- **Layout view** This view displays the data in the report (similar to Print Preview) but enables you to edit the layout.

- **Design view** In this view, you can manipulate the design of a report in the same way that you manipulate a form.

SEE ALSO For more information about reports, see Chapter 5, "Create simple reports," and Chapter 9, "Create custom reports."

In this exercise, you'll preview a report as it will appear when printed. You'll also examine another report in Design view.

 SET UP You need the GardenCompany01 database you worked with in the preceding exercise to complete this exercise. If necessary, open the database, and then follow the steps.

1 In the **Navigation** pane, display the **Reports** group, which includes all the reports that have been created and saved as part of this database.

2 In the **Navigation** pane, right-click **Customer Labels**, and then click **Print Preview** to open the **Customer Labels** report in a view that is much like Print Preview in other Office programs.

   TROUBLESHOOTING If Access notifies you that some data may not be displayed because of column widths and spacing, for the purposes of this exercise, simply click OK to continue.

TIP Access provides a wizard that can help you create a mailing label report. You can also create labels like these by using the Customers table as a data source for the Microsoft Word 2013 mail merge tool. For information about mail merge, refer to *Microsoft Word 2013 Step By Step* by Joan Lambert and Joyce Cox (Microsoft Press, 2013)

The report is too small to read easily in Print Preview, so let's adjust the zoom percentage.

3   Move the pointer over the report, where it changes to a magnifying glass. Then with the pointer over the middle label at the top of the report, click the mouse button to change the zoom percentage to **100%**.

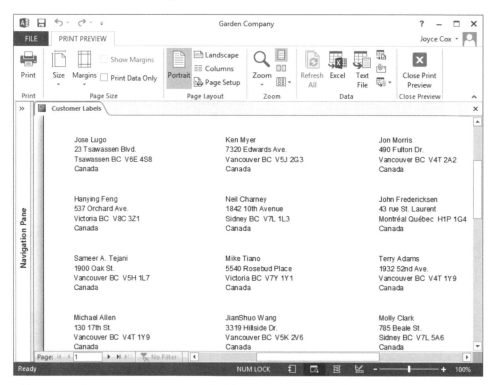

This report prints customer names and addresses in a mailing label format.

TIP Click the Zoom Level button in the lower-right corner to switch back and forth between the current and previous zoom levels. You can also adjust the zoom percentage by clicking the Zoom In or Zoom Out button (the plus or minus sign) at the ends of the Zoom slider or by dragging the Zoom slider. To set a specific zoom percentage, click the Zoom arrow in the Zoom group on the Print Preview tab and then click the percentage you want.

Now let's look at another report.

4   In the **Navigation** pane, right-click the **Sales By Category** report, and then click **Print Preview**. This report generates several pages of information by combining data from the **Categories** table and the **Products** table.

5   Use any method to zoom the page to **100%**.

6   On the page navigation bar in the lower-left corner of the page, click the **Last Page** button to move to the end of the report.

In this report, each category appears on its own page with a list of the products in that category and their prices.

7   Click the **Previous Page** button a few times to view a few more pages of the report.

Let's look at the structure of this report in Design view.

8   On the **View Shortcuts** toolbar, click the **Design View** button. Notice that in this view, the report looks similar to a form.

You create reports by using the same techniques you use to create forms.

❌ CLEAN UP Close the open reports. Keep the GardenCompany01 database open for use in the last exercise.

Previewing and printing database objects

Because Access is a Windows application, it interacts with your printer through standard Windows dialog boxes and drivers. This means that any printer that you can use from other programs can be used from Access, and any special features of that printer, such as color printing or duplex printing, are available in Access.

The commands for printing database objects are available from the Print page of the Backstage view. From this page, you can do the following:

- Print the active object by using the default settings.

- Display the Print dialog box, where you can select the printer you want to use, in addition to adjusting various other settings appropriate to the active object and the current view.

- Display the active object in Print Preview.

In this exercise, you'll explore the printing options for a table and a form.

→ SET UP You need the GardenCompany01 database you worked with in the preceding exercise to complete this exercise. If necessary, open the database, and then follow the steps.

1   In the **Navigation** pane, display the **All Access Objects** group.

2   In the **Tables** group, double-click the **Employees** table to open it in **Datasheet** view.

Access will not print data that is not visible on the screen, so let's first make sure all the columns display all their data.

3   Manually adjust the widths (don't double-click between the columns) of all the columns so that all the values in the fields are visible. (Don't worry about showing the complete column heading; just focus on the values.)

4   Display the **Backstage** view, and in the left pane, click **Print**.

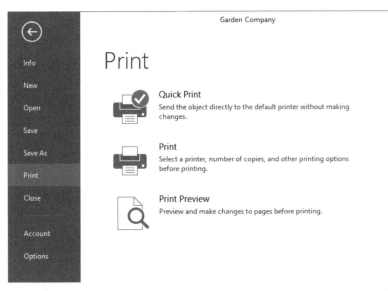

From the Print page of the Backstage view, you can print the current database object with the default print settings, change the settings, and preview the object.

5   On the **Print** page, click **Print Preview** to preview the first page of the **Employees** table.

By default, the Employees table is displayed in Portrait orientation.

TIP This is the only way to preview a table, a query results datasheet, or a form. There is no Print Preview command available when you right-click one of these objects, and there is no Print Preview button on the View Shortcuts toolbar or in the View button list, as there is for reports.

6   On the page navigation bar at the bottom of the window, click the **Next Page** button. Then click the **First Page** button to move back to page **1**.

    With the current settings, this datasheet will print as two short, vertically oriented pages. Let's adjust the settings.

7   On the **Print Preview** tab, in the **Page Layout** group, click the **Landscape** button to switch to that orientation. Then click the **Next Page** button. Notice that the datasheet still occupies two pages, with only one field on the second page.

8   In the **Page Size** group, click the **Margins** button, and then click **Narrow**.

The buttons on the page navigation bar are now gray, indicating that the Employees table fits on one page.

TIP You can set custom margins by clicking the Page Setup button in the Page Layout group and then adjusting the Top, Bottom, Left, and Right settings on the Print Options page of the Page Setup dialog box.

9 In the **Print** group, click the **Print** button to open the **Print** dialog box.

In the Print dialog box, you can select the printer and set print options such as the pages or records to print, and the number of copies.

10   Click **Cancel** to close the **Print** dialog box, and then in the **Close Preview** group, click the **Close Print Preview** button.

Now let's take a look at a report.

11   In the **Navigation** pane, in the **Reports** group, double-click **Alphabetical List of Products**.

12   On the **View Shortcuts** toolbar, click the **Print Preview** button to display the report information as it will be printed.

13   On the **Print Preview** tab, in the **Zoom** group, click the **Two Pages** button to display the first two pages of the report side by side.

You can preview more than one page at a time.

14   On the **View Shortcuts** toolbar, click the **Report View** button to return to that view.

✖ CLEAN UP Close the Alphabetical List Of Products report and the Employees table, saving your changes if you want to. Then close the GardenCompany01 database.

Key points

- The Access user interface provides intuitive access to all the tools you need to create and maintain a database.

- A database is the computer equivalent of an organized list of information.

- Tables are the core database objects. They organize data in columns and rows, called *fields* and *records*.

- In a relational database, tables can be related based on common fields, enabling the retrieval of information from more than one table at the same time.

- The purpose of the other database objects—forms, reports, queries, macros, and modules—is to interact with one or more tables.

- Every database object has two or more views. For example, you view data in a table in Datasheet view and define how the data is structured in Design view.

- If you want to print a database object, be sure the information you need is visible on the screen before you print.

Chapter at a glance

Create

Create databases from templates,
page 54

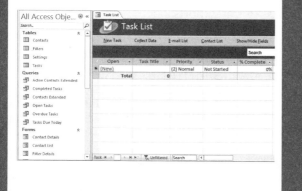

Manipulate

Manipulate table columns and rows,
page 74

Refine

Refine table structure,
page 77

Define

Define relationships between tables,
page 83

Create databases and simple tables

2

IN THIS CHAPTER, YOU WILL LEARN HOW TO

- Create databases from templates.

- Create databases and tables manually.

- Manipulate table columns and rows.

- Refine table structure.

- Define relationships between tables.

Microsoft Access 2013 takes a lot of the difficult and mundane work out of creating and customizing a database by providing database templates. Access also provides templates for common elements that you might want to plug into a database. These *application parts* consist of sets of objects—a table and related forms, queries, or reports—that together provide a complete, functioning part of a database, ready for you to customize. If none of the templates meet your needs, you can create databases manually. However, an empty database is no more useful than an empty document or worksheet. It is only when you fill a database with data (referred to as *populating a database*), that it starts to serve a purpose.

In this chapter, you'll examine web app templates and create a desktop database from a template. You'll also create a table manually. Next, you'll adjust the display of a table to meet your needs. Finally, you'll define relationships between tables. By the end of this chapter, you'll have a desktop database that contains a few tables and you'll understand a bit about how the database tables you will use for the exercises in the remaining chapters of the book were created.

PRACTICE FILES You don't need any practice files to complete the exercises in this chapter.

Creating databases from templates

Access 2013 comes with templates for several databases typically used in business and education, and when you are connected to the Internet, many more are available from the Microsoft Office website. By using predefined templates, you can create a database in far less time than it used to take to design one, because someone has already done the design work for you.

SEE ALSO For information about the basic concepts of database design, see the sidebar "Database design" later in this chapter.

By using templates, you can create two types of database applications:

- **Desktop databases** These databases are stored on your computer or a network server. After using a desktop database template to create the database, you can view and modify it by using Access 2013 on your local computer.

- **Web apps** These database applications are hosted in a Microsoft SharePoint 2013 environment. They are designed to provide an online interface through which people can view and enter data from a web browser. Web apps make it possible for people to access company information from wherever they are and from any computer, whether or not it has Access installed. Several of the templates that come with Access and many of the templates available from the Office website are for web apps. For more information, see the sidebar "Getting started with Access web apps" later in this chapter.

Although using an Access template might not produce exactly the database you want, it can quickly create something you can customize to meet your needs. However, you can customize a database only if you know how to manipulate its basic building blocks: tables, forms, queries, and reports. Due to the complexity of these templates, you probably shouldn't try to modify them until you're comfortable working with database objects in Design view and Layout view. By the time you finish this book, you will know enough to be able to confidently work with the sophisticated pre-packaged database templates that come with Access.

In this exercise, you'll explore the templates that come with Access, and you'll create a desktop database based on the Desktop Task Management template.

→ SET UP You don't need any practice files to complete this exercise. Close any open databases, and then follow the steps.

1   With either the Access starting screen or the **New** page of the **Backstage** view displayed, scroll the page to display the range of available templates. Notice that the icons of desktop database templates are designated by a blank page, and the icons of web app templates are designated by a stylized page with a globe.

The globe distinguishes web app templates from desktop database templates.

2   In the list of templates, click the **Task management** web app template icon.

Clicking a web app template icon displays a description of the template and asks you to name the database and identify the SharePoint site on which it will be stored.

TIP If no template seems to be a good starting point for the database you want to create, you can search for additional templates on the Office website by entering a category in the Search For Online Templates box and then clicking the Start Searching button.

3   To the left and right of the creation window, click the back and forward arrows to scroll through the list of available templates, reading their descriptions. Stop when the creation window for the **Desktop task management** template is displayed.

Unlike other programs that allow you to create a file and then assign a name and storage location, Access requires that you assign a name and storage location before you create a new database file.

4   In the **File Name** box, enter MyTasks.

TIP Naming conventions for Access database files follow those for Windows files. File names cannot contain the following characters: \ / : * ? " < > |. Although you can use spaces between words, because database files are sometimes referenced in programming code, most database developers use words with initial capital letters and no spaces between them.

5   Click the adjacent **Browse** button, and then in the **File New Database** dialog box, navigate to the **Chapter02** practice file folder.

TIP By default, Access creates new databases in your Documents folder. You can change the location when you create each database, or you can change the default folder. To specify a different default folder, open the Access Options dialog box, and then on the General page, in the Creating Databases area, click the Browse button to the right of Default Database Folder. In the Default Database Path dialog box, browse to the folder you want to be the default, and then click OK in each of the open dialog boxes.

6   With **Microsoft Access 2007-2013 Databases** selected in the **Save as type** box, click **OK**.

7   With the path to the specified folder displayed below the **File Name** box in the window, click the **Create** button.

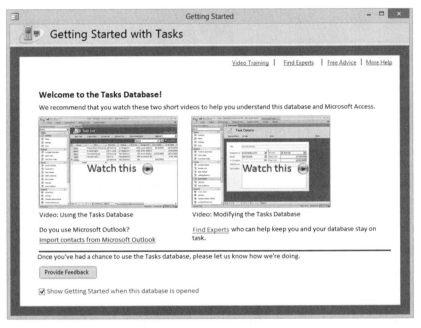

This Getting Started window is a form that provides two videos to help you understand how to use and modify your MyTasks database.

8   If you want, watch the videos to understand how this template works. Then clear the **Show Getting Started when this database is opened** check box, and close the window.

9   Enable the content of the database, and ensure that the **Navigation** pane is open. Then if any of the groups are collapsed, click their chevrons to open them.

By default, the Task List form is displayed in Form view so that you can start adding tasks.

TIP Below the form name is a toolbar that has commands created by embedded macros. A database that has commands like these is called a *database application*. The topic of macros is beyond the scope of this book. For information, search for *macros* in Access Help.

10   Click the field below **Task Title**, enter Monthly Report, and click the field below it to create a record.

11   In the **Navigation** pane, in the **Tables** group, double-click **Tasks** to display the table on which the **Task List** form is based. Notice that the task you just entered in the form is the first record in this table.

12   Right-click the **Tasks** tab, and click **Close All** to close both of the open objects.

Let's use an application part to add a form to this new database.

13   In the **Navigation** pane, click the **All Access Objects** title, and display the **Forms** group. It is now easier to focus on just the seven forms in the database.

14   On the **Create** tab, in the **Templates** group, click the **Application Parts** button to display the **Application Parts** gallery.

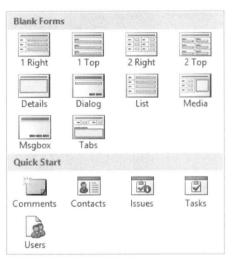

You can add various types of forms and several sets of related tables and other database objects to this or any other database.

TIP These ready-made objects give you a jump start on creating a fully functional database application. But like templates, they involve behind the scenes functionality that you might not know how to manage yet. You can come back and explore application parts more fully when you have a better understanding of them.

15 Point to each thumbnail in turn to display its description, and then in the **Blank Forms** area, click **1 Right**. Notice that when you add this form to the database, Access adds an eighth form called **SingleOneColumnRightLabels** to the **Forms** group in the **Navigation** pane. It also runs a macro that opens the **Task List** form.

16 In the **Navigation** pane, double-click **SingleOneColumnRightLabels** to open the new form.

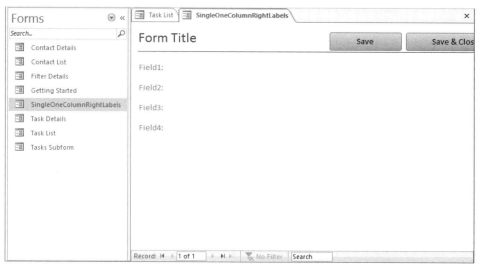

You can customize this form to meet the needs of your own database.

SEE ALSO For information about customizing forms, see Chapter 8, "Create custom forms."

17 On your own, continue exploring the objects that are part of the **MyTasks** database. For each type of object, first filter the **Navigation** pane to display only that group, and then explore its objects.

 CLEAN UP Close the MyTasks database.

Getting started with Access web apps

An Access web app is a database that is designed in Access 2013, stored in Microsoft SQL Server, and hosted on a SharePoint site in such a way that users can connect to the web app through a web browser, even if they don't have Access installed on a local device.

Office 365 plans that include SharePoint (Small Business Premium and Enterprise) are ready to host Access web apps with no extra setup required. Web apps can also be hosted by organizations that set up SharePoint 2013 and SQL Server 2012 on an internal network. To create an Access web app, you must first log in to Office with a SharePoint 2013–enabled account. (This account might not be the same as your Windows account.) Deployment, management, and security of the web app are all controlled within the SharePoint infrastructure.

To create a web app:

1   Start Access, and in the upper-right corner of the program's starting screen, verify that you are logged in to Office with a SharePoint-enabled account. If the account shown is not a SharePoint-enabled account, click **Switch account**, and then click the account you want to use; or click **Add Account** and enter the appropriate credentials.

2   In the right pane of the Access starting screen, click **Custom web app** to create a new blank web app, or click one of the many available ready-made web app templates.

    TIP If you aren't sure which template to choose, enter a keyword in the Search box at the top of the pane, and search online for suggestions.

3   When prompted, enter a name for the web app and the location of the SharePoint site on which it will be hosted. Then click **Create** to download the template and create the application on the designated SharePoint site.

When you create a web app, the Add Tables pane is displayed, giving you four easy ways to add a new table:

- Click an item in the **Suggested searches** list.
- Enter a search term in the **Search** box, and then click an item in the results.
- Add a new blank table.
- Create a table from an existing data source.

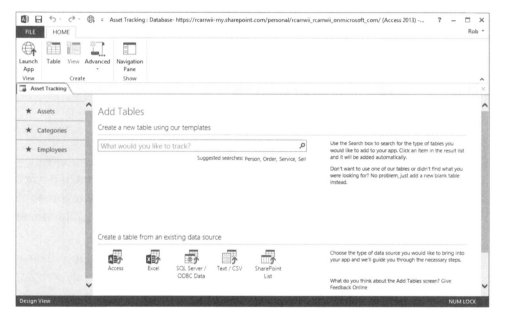

From the initial web app screen, you can add or view existing objects.

The tables you add to the web app are displayed as tiles in the Tile pane on the left side of the page. For each table, Access automatically creates an associated Datasheet form and a List form. Clicking a table shows you an image of the table's form in the right pane. To edit a table's form, display the form in the view you want, and click the Edit button. You can manage the data source and actions of a form's fields, in addition to the formatting of the form itself, in the List and Datasheet form views.

To edit a table, right-click the table's tile, and click Edit Table. You can also open the Navigation pane and edit the tables and forms from there.

In Access web apps, relationships between tables are defined by using the Lookup data type. Start by opening a table in Design view, and then do one of the following:

- To create a relationship, either add a new field or select an existing field, and then set the data type to **Lookup** to start the **Lookup** wizard.

- To manage an existing relationship, select a field that has the **Lookup** data type, and on the **Design** tool tab, click **Modify Lookups** to start the **Lookup** wizard.

The wizard guides you through the process of establishing the relationship. For information about using this wizard, see "Allowing only values in lists" in Chapter 6, "Maintain data integrity."

When you have created the structure for the web app in Access, you can preview it in your web browser by clicking Launch App in the View group on the Home tab.

By default, you can view and edit the data in a table in either List view or Datasheet view.

To make the Access web app available to other users, simply share the web address of the SharePoint site with them. When they launch the web app in their web browser, they can view and manipulate its data by using the buttons on the Action bar (located to the right of the Search box) to add, delete, edit, save, and cancel record edits. Their changes are saved in the centrally stored SQL database.

TIP If you need to make more extensive changes to the database, you can click the Settings button in the upper-right corner of the web app and click Customize In Access to open the database in Access 2013 on your local computer.

Creating databases and tables manually

Suppose you need to store different types of information for different types of people. For example, you might want to maintain information about employees, customers, and suppliers. In addition to the standard information—such as names, addresses, and phone numbers—you might want to track these other kinds of information:

- Employee identification numbers, hire dates, marital status, deductions, and pay rates
- Customer orders and account status
- Supplier contacts, current order status, and discounts

You could start with a template, add fields for all the different items of information to a single Contacts table, and then fill in only the relevant fields for each type of contact. However, cramming all this information into one table would soon get messy. It's better to create a new database based on the Blank Desktop Database template and then manually create separate tables for each type of contact: employee, customer, and supplier.

When you create a new blank database or insert a new table into an existing database, the table is displayed on a tabbed page in Datasheet view with one empty row that is ready to receive data.

TIP When you create a new database, Access displays its name and a path to its storage location in the title bar. For information about how to reduce the clutter caused by the path, see "Controlling which features are available" in Chapter 11, "Make databases user friendly."

Because the active object is a table, Access adds the Table Tools tabs (Fields and Table) to the ribbon so that you can work with the table.

If you close the table at this point, Access discards the table. The simplest way to make the table a permanent part of the database is to create at least one record by entering data.

TIP When you enter data in a new table, Access assigns placeholder field names and creates a basic table structure to hold the data. You can also define the structure of the table without entering data. For information about table structure, see "Refining table structure" later in this chapter. For information about adding new blank fields to a table, see "Specifying the type of data" in Chapter 6, "Maintain data integrity."

Obviously, to create a record, you need to know what information to enter and how.

Every table has an empty row that is ready to receive a new record, as indicated by the asterisk icon in the record selector at the left end of the row. By default, the first field in each new table is an ID field designed to contain an entry that will uniquely identify the record. Also by default, this field is designated as the table's *primary key*. No two records in this table can have the same value in this primary key field.

The asterisk icon indicates that the first record is ready for you to enter data.

Behind the scenes, the data type of this field is set to AutoNumber, so Access will enter a sequential number in this field for you.

In Design view, you can verify that the primary key ID field is assigned the AutoNumber data type.

TIP As you'll discover in a later exercise, the primary key field does not have to be the default AutoNumber data type. If you need to you create your own primary key field, anything meaningful and unique will work. For information about data types, see "Refining table structure" later in this chapter.

The first field you need to be concerned about is the active field labeled *Click To Add*. You enter the first item of information for the new record in this field, and then press the Tab or Enter key to move to the first cell in the field to the right. Access then assigns the value 1 to the ID field, assigns the name Field1 to the second field, and moves the Click To Add label to the third field. The icon in the record selector at the left end of the record changes to two dots and a pencil to indicate that this record has not yet been saved, and the New icon moves to the record selector of the next row.

Table1		
ID ▾	Field1 ▾	Click to Add ▾
ᵖ 1	Sidney	
✱ (New)		

The pencil icon indicates that the data in the first record has not yet been saved.

When creating a new table in Datasheet view, you need to save the first record after enter-ing the first item of data. If you don't, Access increments the ID value for each field you add to that record. For example, if you add seven fields, Access assigns the value 7 to the ID field of the first record. To avoid this problem, you simply click the icon in the record selector after you enter your first value in the first record. This saves the record with the value 1 assigned to the ID field, and subsequent records will be numbered sequentially.

Having entered the first item of data and saved the record, you continue entering items of information in consecutive fields and pressing Tab or Enter. When you finish entering the last item for the first record, you click anywhere in the row below it to tell Access that the record is complete.

After you complete the first record of a new table, you might want to change the default field names to something more meaningful. To rename a field, you simply double-click its field name and then enter the name you want.

At any time while you are entering data in a new table, you can save the table by click-ing the Save button on the Quick Access Toolbar and naming the table. If you try to close the table without explicitly saving it, Access prompts you to save the table. If you click No, Access discards the table and any data you have entered.

After you have saved the table for the first time, Access automatically saves each record when you move away from it. You don't have to worry about losing your changes, but you do have to remember that most data entries can be undone only by editing the record.

Databases almost always contain more than one table. You can create additional empty tables by clicking the Table button in the Tables group on the Create tab. If you need to create a table that is similar in structure to an existing one, simply copy and paste the exist-ing table to create a new one. When you paste the table, Access gives you the option of naming the table and of specifying whether you want the new table to have the existing table's structure or both its structure and its data.

2

For some kinds of tables, Access provides Quick Start fields that you can use to add common sets of fields or kinds of fields to a table. The Quick Start options take the work out of defining these fields and can be very useful when you know exactly what type of field you need.

In this exercise, you'll create a blank database, enter information in the first record of its default table, assign field names, add another record, and save and close the table. Then you'll copy that table to create a second one. Finally, you'll create a new table and experiment with Quick Start fields.

 SET UP You don't need any practice files to complete this exercise. Close any open databases, display the New page of the Backstage view, and then follow the steps.

1   On the **New** page, click the **Blank desktop database** icon.

2   In the creation window, in the **File Name** box, enter MyTables. Then click the **Browse** button, navigate to the **Chapter02** practice file folder, and click **OK**.

> **TIP** Remember, you can't create a blank database without saving it. If you don't provide a file name and location, Access saves the file with the name *Database* followed by a sequential number in the default location (your Documents folder, unless you have changed it).

3   Click the **Create** button to create the blank database in the specified location.

Let's enter data in the first record.

4   With the empty field below **Click to Add** selected in the new blank **Table1** table, enter Scott, and then press the **Tab** key to move to the next field.

5   Notice that the icon in the record selector has changed to a pencil to indicate that this record has not yet been saved. The value **1** appears in the **ID** field, the name of the second column has changed to **Field1**, and the **Click to Add** label has moved to the third column.

6   Click the pencil icon in the record selector to save the record before you move on.

> **TIP** Clicking the record selector is necessary only after you enter the first value in a new table. This action sets the ID field value to 1.

7   Click the cell below **Click to Add**, and enter the following information into the next seven cells. Press **Tab** after each entry.

Bishop
612 E. 2nd
Pocatello
ID
73204
USA
208 555-0161

ID	Field1	Field2	Field3	Field4	Field5	Field6	Field7	Field8	Click to Add
1 Scott	Bishop	612 E. 2nd	Pocatello	ID		73204 USA		208 555-0161	
* (New)						0			

The names of the fields in which you enter data change to Field followed by a sequential number.

TIP Don't be concerned if your screen does not look exactly like ours. In this graphic, we've scrolled the page and adjusted the widths of the columns to display all the fields. For information about adjusting columns, see "Manipulating table columns and rows" later in this chapter.

Before we move to the next record, let's make the field names more useful.

8   Double-click the **ID** field name (not the **ID** value in **Field5**), and then enter **CustomerID** to rename it.

TIP Field names can include spaces, but the spaces can affect how queries have to be constructed, so it is best not to include them.

9   Repeat step 8 for the other fields, changing the field names to the following:

Field1	FirstName	Field4	City	Field7	Country
Field2	LastName	Field5	State	Field8	Phone
Field3	Street	Field6	ZIP		

CustomerID	FirstName	LastName	Street	City	State	ZIP	Country	Phone
1 Scott	Bishop	612 E. 2nd	Pocatello	ID		73204 USA		208 555-0161
* (New)						0		

For readability, capitalize each word of a field name and remove the spaces, or use underscores instead of spaces.

10   Add another record containing the following field values to the table, pressing **Tab** to move from field to field:

FirstName	John	**City**	Montreal	**Country**	Canada
LastName	Yokim	**State**	Quebec	**Phone**	514 555-0167
Street	43 rue St. Laurent	**ZIP**	(press Tab to skip this field)		

Now let's save and close the table.

11   At the right end of the tab bar, click the **Close** button.

12   When Access asks whether you want to save the design of the table, click **Yes** to open the **Save As** dialog box.

You must save the table's design (its structure) before closing it.

TIP Clicking No will delete the new table and its data from the database.

13   In the **Table Name** box, enter **Customers**, and then click **OK** to close the table and add it to the **Tables** group in the **Navigation** pane.

The database now contains one table.

TIP You can rename a table by right-clicking it in the Navigation pane and then clicking Rename. You can delete a table by right-clicking it, clicking Delete, and then confirming the deletion in the message box that appears. (You can also delete a table by selecting it in the Navigation pane and then clicking the Delete button in the Records group on the Home tab, or by pressing the Delete key.)

Let's create a new table with the same structure as Customers.

14   In the **Navigation** pane, click the **Customers** table to select it.

15   On the **Home** tab, in the **Clipboard** group, click the **Copy** button. Then click the **Paste** button to open the **Paste Table As** dialog box.

If you need to create a table that is similar to an existing table, it is sometimes easier to customize a copy than to create it from scratch.

KEYBOARD SHORTCUT Press Ctrl+C to copy data. Press Ctrl+V to paste data. For a list of keyboard shortcuts, see "Keyboard shortcuts" at the end of this book.

16   In the **Table Name** box, enter Employees. In the **Paste Options** area, click **Structure Only** to capture the fields from the **Customers** table but not the customer records. Then click **OK** to create the table and add it to the **Tables** group in the **Navigation** pane.

TIP You can also use the Copy and Paste commands to append the information in the selected table to another existing table. In that case, in the Paste Table As dialog box, enter the name of the destination table in the Table Name box, click Append Data To Existing Table, and then click OK.

17   Double-click **Employees** to open it in **Datasheet** view so that you can view its fields. Then close the table again.

TIP Although you specified that you wanted to copy only the structure of the Customers table, the ZIP field in the Employees table contains 0. This is because Access has automatically assigned this default value to this field. For information about default values, see "Allowing only values in lists" in Chapter 6, "Maintain data integrity."

Now let's create another table and add a couple of Quick Start fields to it.

18   On the **Create** tab, in the **Tables** group, click the **Table** button to create a new table containing an **ID** field and a **Click to Add** field placeholder.

19   With the **Click to Add** field active, on the **Fields** tool tab, in the **Add & Delete** group, click the **More Fields** button to display a menu containing the **Fields** gallery. Then scroll to the bottom of the gallery.

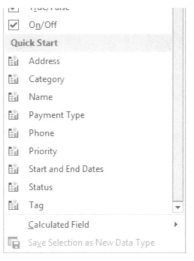

The Quick Start fields are at the bottom of the Fields gallery.

20   In the **Quick Start** area of the gallery, click **Name** to insert ready-made **LastName** and **FirstName** fields.

21   Click the field below **Click to Add**, and then repeat step 19, this time clicking **Address** in the **Quick Start** list to add ready-made **Address**, **City**, **State Province**, **ZIP Postal**, and **Country Region** fields.

TIP Notice that the Address Quick Start option includes a Country Region field. In our practice databases, we use the field name Country. However, you might want to use the more explicit Country Region field name if the tables you create will store international addresses.

22   Close the table, saving it with the name **Shippers** when prompted.

❌ CLEAN UP Keep the MyTables database open for use in later exercises.

Database design

In a well-designed database, each item of data is stored in only one table. If you're capturing the same information in multiple places, that is a sure sign that you need to analyze the data and figure out a way to put the duplicated information in a separate table.

For example, an Orders table should not include information about the customer placing each order, for two significant reasons. First, if the same customer orders more than once, all his or her information has to be repeated for each order, which inflates the size of the Orders table and the database. Second, if the customer moves, his or her address will need to be updated in the record for every order placed.

The way to avoid this type of problem is to put customer information in a Customers table and assign each customer a unique identifier, such as a sequential number or unique string of letters, in the primary key field. Then in the Orders table, you can identify the customer by the unique ID. If you need to know the name and address of the customer who placed a particular order, you can have Access use the unique ID to look up that information in the Customers table.

The process of ensuring that a set of information is stored in only one place is called *normalization*. This process tests a database for compliance with a set of normalization rules that ask questions such as "If I know the information in the primary key field of a record, can I retrieve information from one and only one record?" For example, knowing that a customer's ID is 1002 means you can pull the customer's name and address from the Customers table, whereas knowing that a customer's last name is Jones does not mean that you can pull the customer's name and address from the table, because more than one customer might have the last name Jones.

A detailed discussion of normalization processes is beyond the scope of this book. For more information, see Access Help, or search for *Database design basics* on the Office website.

2

Manipulating table columns and rows

In Chapter 1, "Explore Microsoft Access 2013," we showed you how to quickly adjust the width of table columns to efficiently display their data. In addition to adjusting column width, sometimes you might want to rearrange a table's columns to get a better view of the data. For example, if you want to look up a phone number but the names and phone numbers are several columns apart, you will have to scroll the table to get the information you need. You might want to rearrange or hide a few columns to be able to simultaneously view all the fields you are interested in.

You can manipulate the columns and rows of an Access table without affecting the underlying data in any way. You can size rows and size, hide, move, and freeze columns. You can save your table formatting so that the table will look the same the next time you open it, or you can discard your changes without saving them.

In this exercise, you'll open a table and manipulate its columns and rows.

➡ SET UP You need the MyTables database you worked with in the preceding exercise to complete this exercise. If necessary, open the database. Then follow the steps.

1   In the **Navigation** pane, double-click the **Customers** table to open it in **Datasheet** view.

2   In the field name row, point to the right border of the **Street** column, and when the pointer changes to a double-headed arrow, drag to the right until all of the street addresses are visible.

3   Double-click the right border of any column that seems too wide or too narrow to adjust the column to fit its contents.

   TIP This technique is particularly useful in a large table in which you can't easily determine the length of a field's longest entry.

   Now let's adjust the height of the table's rows.

4   Increase the height of all rows in the table by pointing to the border between any two record selectors and dragging downward.

You cannot adjust the height of just one row.

5   On the **Home** tab, in the **Records** group, click the **More** button, and then click **Row Height** to open the **Row Height** dialog box.

You can set the rows to the precise height you want.

6   In the **Row Height** dialog box, select the **Standard Height** check box, and then click **OK** to reset the height of the rows to the default setting.

Next let's experiment with hiding columns.

7   Click anywhere in the **FirstName** column. Then in the **Records** group, click the **More** button, and click **Hide Fields**.

TIP If you select several columns before clicking Hide Fields, they all disappear. You can select adjacent columns by clicking the field name of the first one, holding down the Shift key, and then clicking the field name of the last one. The two columns and any columns in between are selected.

8   To restore the hidden column, in the **Records** group, click the **More** button, and then click **Unhide Fields** to open the **Unhide Columns** dialog box.

You can select and clear check boxes to control which fields are visible.

TIP If you want to hide several columns that are not adjacent, display the Unhide Columns dialog box and clear their check boxes.

9   In the **Unhide Columns** dialog box, select the **FirstName** check box, and then click **Close**.

Let's freeze the first three columns so that they remain in view as you scroll the table.

10   For the purposes of this exercise, if all of the fields in the table are displayed, adjust the size of the program window until some of the fields are no longer visible.

11   Point to the **CustomerID** field name, and drag through the **FirstName** and **LastName** field names. With these three columns selected, click the **More** button in the **Records** group, and then click **Freeze Fields**.

12   Scroll the page to the right, noticing that the first three columns remain in view as you scroll.

13   When the **Phone** field is adjacent to the **LastName** field, in the **Records** group, click **More,** and then click **Unfreeze All Fields** to restore the fields to their normal condition.

> **TIP** The commands to hide, unhide, freeze, and unfreeze columns are also available from the shortcut menu that appears when you right-click a field name.

Suppose we want to always display the customer's phone number next to his or her name. Let's move the Phone column.

14   Click the **Phone** field name to select that field. Then drag the field to the left, releasing the mouse button when the thick black line appears to the right of the **LastName** field.

15   Close the **Customers** table, clicking **Yes** to save the changes you have made to the column widths and field order. If a message box appears, warning you that this action will clear the Clipboard, click **Yes**.

⊗ CLEAN UP Keep the MyTables database open for use in later exercises.

Refining table structure

Although you can create the structure of a database in Datasheet view, some structural refinements can be carried out only in Design view. When you are familiar with tables, you might even want to create your tables from scratch in Design view, where you have more control over the fields. You can open a new table in Design view by clicking the Table Design button in the Tables group on the Create tab.

When you display an existing table in Design view, the page shows the underlying structure of the table.

The table design page consists of two parts: a field definition grid and a field properties area.

The top part of the table design page consists of the following:

- **Field selector** Identifies the active field with an arrow in the shaded box at the left end of a row. Click any field selector to select the entire field. You can then insert a row above the selected one, delete the row (thereby deleting the field), or drag the row up or down to reposition its field in the table.

  The field selector also identifies the primary key field of the table by displaying the Primary Key icon (a key with a right-pointing arrow).

  TIP If you don't want a table to have a primary key (for example, if none of the fields will contain a unique value for every record), select the field designated as the primary key, and on the Design tool tab, in the Tools group, click the Primary Key button to turn it off. If you want to designate a different field as the primary key, select the new field, and click the Primary Key button to turn it on. (You don't have to remove the primary key from the current field first; it will happen automatically.)

- **Field Name column** Contains the names you specified when you created the table. You can edit the names by using regular text-editing techniques. You can add a new field by entering its name in the first empty cell in this column.

- **Data Type column** Specifies the type of data that the field can contain. By default, the ID field in a new table is assigned the AutoNumber data type, and if you add a new field in Design view, it is assigned the Short Text data type. (If you add a new field in Datasheet view, it is assigned the data type that most closely corresponds with the kind of data you enter in the field.) With the exception of fields with the OLE Object and Attachment data types, you can change the type of any field by clicking its Data Type entry, clicking the arrow that appears, and clicking a new data type in the list.

Data Type
AutoNumber
Short Text
Long Text
Number
Date/Time
Currency
AutoNumber
Yes/No
OLE Object
Hyperlink
Attachment
Calculated
Lookup Wizard...

Clicking an entry in the Data Type column displays a list of the available data types.

SEE ALSO For more information about data types, see "Specifying the type of data" in Chapter 6, "Maintain data integrity."

- **Description column** Contains an optional description of the field.

The Field Properties area in the bottom part of the table design page displays the properties of the field selected in the top part. Different properties are associated with different data types. They determine attributes such as the number of characters allowed in a field, the value inserted if the user doesn't enter anything, and whether an entry is required. Properties can also assess whether an entry is valid and can force the user to select from a list of values rather than entering them manually (with the inherent risk of errors).

All fields, no matter what their data type, can be assigned a Caption property that appears in place of the field name in tables or in other database objects. For example, you might want to use captions to display spaces in the names of fields, such as First Name for the FirstName field.

SEE ALSO For information about using properties to control the accuracy of data entry, see Chapter 6, "Maintain data integrity." For a comprehensive list of data types and properties, search for *data types* on the Office website.

In this exercise, you'll open a table in Design view, add and delete fields, change a data type, set field sizes, and add a caption.

 SET UP You need the MyTables database you worked with in the preceding exercise to complete this exercise. If necessary, open the database. Then follow the steps.

1   In the **Navigation** pane, right-click the **Employees** table, and then click **Design View**.

    This table was created by copying the Customers table. Let's make a few changes to the fields.

2   In the **Field Name** column, select **CustomerID**, enter EmployeeID, and then press the **Tab** key twice.

3   In the **Description** column, enter Unique identifying number.

4   Click the **Country** field's selector, and then on the **Design** tool tab, in the **Tools** group, click the **Delete Rows** button.

5   In the empty row below the **Phone** field, click the **Field Name** cell, and enter Birthdate. Then click the **Data Type** cell, which indicates that the default **Short Text** data type is assigned to the new field.

6   Click the arrow at the right end of the **Data Type** cell, and in the list, click **Date/Time**.

7   Repeat steps 5 and 6 to add another **Date/Time** field named DateHired.

8   Select the **ZIP** field name, change it to PostalCode, and then change its data type to **Short Text**.

The Field Properties area shows the properties you can set for the Short Text data type.

TIP If you use only five-digit ZIP codes, the Number data type is fine. But by setting it to Short Text, you can enter ZIP+4 codes or the letter-number postal codes used in Canada and some other countries.

Now let's change some of the properties for the PostalCode field.

9   In the box to the right of **Field Size**, double-click **255**, and enter **10** to limit the entries in this field to 10 characters.

10   Change the **Field Size** property of the following fields as shown:

FirstName	50	City	50	Phone	30
LastName	50	State	20		

TIP Sometimes changing the field properties of a table that already contains data can produce unanticipated results. If you make a change to a field property that might cause data to be lost (for example, if you make the Field Size property smaller than one of the field's existing values), Access warns you of this problem when you attempt to save the table. For more information, see Chapter 6, "Maintain data integrity."

11   Click the **State** field. Then in the **Field Properties** area, click the **Caption** box, and enter State or Region.

Field Name	Data Type	Description (Optional)
EmployeeID	AutoNumber	Unique identifying number
FirstName	Short Text	
LastName	Short Text	
Street	Short Text	
City	Short Text	
State	Short Text	
PostalCode	Short Text	
Phone	Short Text	
Birthdate	Date/Time	
DateHired	Date/Time	

Field Properties

General | Lookup

Field Size	20
Format	
Input Mask	
Caption	State or Region
Default Value	
Validation Rule	
Validation Text	
Required	No
Allow Zero Length	Yes
Indexed	No
Unicode Compression	Yes
IME Mode	No Control
IME Sentence Mode	None
Text Align	General

The label for the field when used on a view. If you don't enter a caption, the field name is used as the label. Press F1 for help on captions.

You have changed the Field Size and Caption properties of the State field.

12   Notice that in the top part of the design page, the entry in the **Field Name** column remains **State**. Then switch to **Datasheet** view.

13   When Access tells you that you must save the table before leaving **Design** view, click **Yes** to save the table.

14   If necessary, widen the **State** field, and notice that in this view, the field name is replaced by the **State or Region** caption property.

While the table is displayed in Datasheet view, let's add another field.

15   Click the **LastName** field name. Then on the **Fields** tool tab, in the **Add & Delete** group, click the **Short Text** button to add a new **Field1** that has the specified data type.

TIP You can also click the Click To Add label to the right of the last field in the field name row, and then in the list that appears, click the data type you want.

16   With **Field1** selected, enter Title, and then press the **Enter** key.

17   Click the **Title** field name. Then on the **Fields** tool tab, in the **Properties** group, click **255** in the **Field Size** box to select it, enter **50**, and press the **Enter** key.

18   Enter the following information in the first record, pressing the **Tab** key after each entry:

FirstName   Karen

LastName   Berg

Title   Owner

The Employees table is now ready for you to enter more employee records.

19   Close the **Employees** table, clicking **Yes** to save changes to the layout when prompted.

❌ CLEAN UP Keep the MyTables database open for use in the last exercise.

Defining relationships between tables

In Access, a relationship is an association that links the primary key field in one table to a field that contains the same information in another table. The field in the other table is called the *foreign key*. For example, if customer accounts are assigned to specific sales employees, you can establish a relationship by linking the primary key EmployeeID field in the Employees table with the foreign key EmployeeID field in the Customers table. Each customer account is assigned to only one employee, but each employee can manage many customer accounts, so this type of relationship—the most common—is known as a *one-to-many relationship*.

Similarly, if every order is associated with a customer, you can establish a relationship by linking the primary key CustomerID field in the Customers table and foreign key CustomerID field in the Orders table. Each order is placed by only one customer, but each customer can place many orders. So again, this is a one-to-many relationship.

Less common relationships include:

- **One-to-one** In this type of relationship, each record in one table can have one and only one related record in the other table. This type of relationship isn't commonly used because it is easier to put all the fields in one table. However, you might use two related tables instead of one to break up a table with many fields, or to track information that applies to only some of the records in the first table.

- **Many-to-many** This type of relationship is really two one-to-many relationships tied together through a third table. You might find this relationship in a database that contains Products, Orders, and Order Details tables. The Products table has one record for each product, and each product has a unique ProductID. The Orders table has one record for each order placed, and each record in it has a unique OrderID. However, the Orders table doesn't specify which products were included in each order; that information is in the Order Details table—the table in the middle that ties the other two tables together. Products and Orders each have a one-to-many relationship with Order Details. Products and Orders therefore have a many-to-many relationship with each other. In plain language, this means that every product can appear in many orders, and every order can include many products.

The most common way of creating a relationship between two tables is to add the tables to the Relationships page displayed when you click the Relationships button in the Relationships group on the Database Tools tab. You then drag a field in one table to the common field in the other table and complete the relationship definition in the Edit Relationships dialog box. In this dialog box, you are given the opportunity to impose a restriction called *referential integrity* on the data, which means that an entry will not be allowed in one table unless it already exists in the other table.

After you have created a relationship, you can delete it by deleting the line connecting the tables on the Relationships page. You can clear all the boxes from the page by clicking the Clear Layout button in the Tools group on the Design tool tab.

TIP The coverage of relationships in this topic is deliberately simple. However, relationships are what make relational databases tick, and Access provides a number of fairly complex mechanisms to ensure the integrity of the data on either end of the relationship. Some of these mechanisms are covered in Chapter 6, "Maintain data integrity." For a good overview, search for *Guide to table relationships* in Access Help.

TIP Access web apps don't use the Relationships page to create and manage relationships. Instead, they use fields set to the Lookup data type. For information about this data type, see "Allowing only values in other tables" in Chapter 6, "Maintain data integrity."

In this exercise, you'll create relationships between one table and two other tables. Then you'll test the referential integrity of one of the relationships.

 SET UP You need the MyTables database you worked with in the preceding exercise to complete this exercise. If necessary, open the database. Then follow the steps.

1   On the **Create** tab, in the **Tables** group, click the **Table** button to create a new table. Before we add fields to this table, let's save it.

2   On the **Quick Access Toolbar**, click the **Save** button, name the table Orders, and click **OK**.

3   To the right of **Click to Add**, click the arrow, and in the data type list, click **Number**. Repeat this step to create a second field that has the **Number** data type.

4   Rename **Field1** as CustomerID and **Field2** as EmployeeID.

Each order in the Orders table will be placed by one customer and will be handled by one employee. Let's create relationships between the Orders table and the Customers and Employees tables so that we don't create records for orders from customers who don't exist or that seem to have been handled by employees who don't exist.

5   Close the **Orders** table.

TIP You cannot create a relationship for an open table.

6   On the **Database Tools** tab, in the **Relationships** group, click the **Relationships** button to open the **Show Table** dialog box.

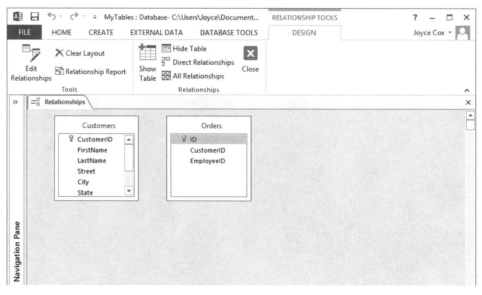

You select the tables for which you want to create relationships from the Tables page of the Show Table dialog box.

TROUBLESHOOTING If the dialog box doesn't open automatically, click the Show Table button in the Relationships group on the Design tool tab.

7 To indicate that you want to create a relationship for the selected **Customers** table, click **Add**. Then double-click **Orders**, and click **Close**. Then on the **Relationships** page, notice that the **CustomerID** field appears in the field lists of both tables.

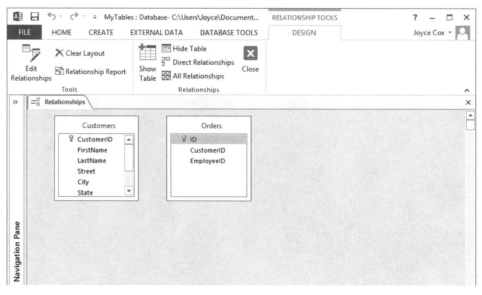

The two boxes list all the fields in their respective tables.

8   In the **Customers** field list, click **CustomerID**, and drag it down and over **CustomerID** in the **Orders** field list. Release the mouse button to open the **Edit Relationships** dialog box.

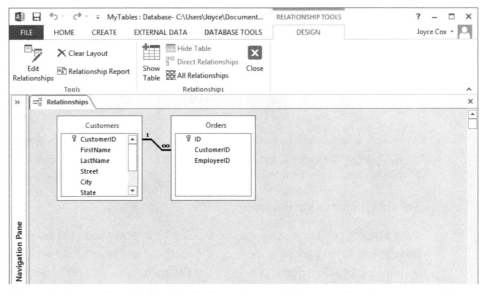

At the bottom of the dialog box, Access indicates that this will be a one-to-many relationship.

9   Select the **Enforce Referential Integrity** check box, and then click **Create**. Notice on the **Relationships** page that a line now connects the two field lists, linking the primary key in the **Customers** table and the foreign key in the **Orders** table.

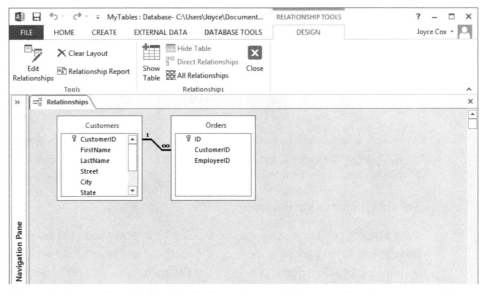

The symbols at each end of the line indicate that each Customer ID value appears only once in the Customers table but can appear many times in the Orders table.

Let's add the Employees table to the Relationships page so that we can create a relationship that links that table to the Orders table.

10   On the **Design** tool tab, in the **Relationships** group, click the **Show Table** button. Then in the **Show Table** dialog box, double-click the **Employees** table, and click **Close**.

> **TIP** You can also add tables by dragging them from the Tables group of the Navigation pane to the Relationships page.

11   If necessary, drag the title bars of the three field lists to arrange them so that they are side by side and equidistant.

12   In the **Employees** field list, click the **EmployeeID** field, and drag it down and over the **EmployeeID** field in the **Orders** field list. Then in the **Edit Relationships** dialog box, select the **Enforce Referential Integrity** check box, and click **Create**.

13   After Access draws the relationship line between the primary key and the foreign key, close the **Relationships** page, clicking **Yes** to save its layout.

Now let's test the relationships.

14   Open the **Orders** table. Then in the **CustomerID** field of the first record, change the **0** value to **11**, and click below the record to complete it. Access displays a message box telling you that you cannot add the new record to the table.

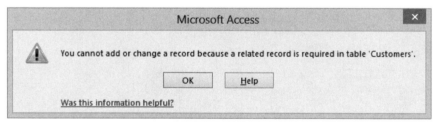

The value in the CustomerID field in the Orders table must match a value in the primary key CustomerID field in the Customer table.

15   Click **OK**. Then change the value to **1**.

16   In the **EmployeeID** field, change the **0** value to **1**, and then click below the record to complete it. Access accepts the record because there is a record with the value **1** in the primary key **CustomerID** field of the **Customers** table and a record with the value **1** in the primary key **EmployeeID** field of the **Employees** table.

❌ CLEAN UP Close the Orders table, and then close the My Tables database.

Key points

- Access 2013 includes templates to help you create web apps and desktop databases, and application parts to help you add related tables and other database objects.

- Rather than storing all information in one table, create different tables for each type of information, such as customers, orders, and suppliers.

- In Datasheet view, you can create a simple table structure by entering data and naming fields. You can also set the data type and certain properties.

- Manipulating or hiding columns and rows has no effect on the underlying data.

- In Design view, you can modify the structure of any table, whether you created it manually or as part of a template.

- Data types and properties determine what data can be entered in a field, and how the data will look on the screen. Caution: changing some properties might affect the data.

- By creating a relationship between the primary key field of one table and the foreign key field of another, you can combine information from both tables.

2

Chapter at a glance

Create

Create forms by using the Form tool,
page 92

Format

Format forms,
page 98

Arrange

Arrange the layout of forms,
page 107

Create simple forms

3

IN THIS CHAPTER, YOU WILL LEARN HOW TO

- Create forms by using the Form tool.

- Format forms.

- Arrange the layout of forms.

A database that contains the day-to-day records of an active company is useful only if it is kept current and if the information stored in it can be found quickly. Entering, editing, and retrieving information from tables in Datasheet view is fairly easy for someone who is familiar with Access. But for occasional users or people who are not familiar with Access, these tasks might be tedious and inefficient and leave far too much room for error, especially if details of complex transactions have to be entered into several related tables. The solution to this problem is to create and use forms.

A form is an organized and formatted view of some or all of the fields from one or more tables. Forms work interactively with the tables in a database. You use controls in the form to enter new information, to edit or remove existing information, or to locate information. The controls you will use most frequently in an Access form are as follows:

- **Text box controls** You can view or enter information in these controls. Think of a text box control as a little window through which you can insert data into the corresponding field of the related table or view information that is already in that field.

- **Label controls** You can tell what type of information you are looking at in the corresponding text box control, or what you are expected to enter in the text box control by using these controls.

TIP An Access form can also include a variety of other controls that transform the form into something very much like a Windows dialog box or wizard page. For information, see "Allowing only values in lists" in Chapter 6, "Maintain data integrity."

In this chapter, you'll discover how easy it is to create forms to view and enter information. You'll also modify forms to suit your needs by changing their appearance and the arrangement of their controls.

Creating forms by using the Form tool

Before you begin creating a form for a desktop database, you need to know the following:

- Which table the form should be based on
- How the form will be used

After making these decisions, you can create a form in the following ways:

- Click the table you want in the **Navigation** pane, and then click the **Form** button in the **Forms** group on the **Create** tab. This method creates a simple form that uses all the fields in the table.

- Use a wizard. This method enables you to choose which of the table's fields you want to use in the form.

  SEE ALSO For information about using wizards to create forms, see "Modifying forms created by using a wizard" in Chapter 8, "Create custom forms."

- Switch to **Layout** view, where you can create the form manually while viewing the underlying data, or switch to **Design** view, where you have more control over form elements.

  SEE ALSO For information about manipulating forms in Layout view, see the other two topics in this chapter. For information about manually creating forms in Design view, see "Adding controls" in Chapter 8, "Create custom forms."

  TIP When you create an Access web app, you can view the data in tables in List view, which includes a mechanism for adding, deleting, and editing records in a pane that is much like a form.

You will usually want to start the process of creating forms that are based on tables by using the Form tool or a wizard—not because the manual process is especially difficult, but because it is simply more efficient to have the tool or a wizard create the basic form for you and then refine that form manually.

In this exercise, you'll use the Form tool to create a form based on a table. You will then enter a couple of records by using the new form and refresh the table to reflect the new entries.

SET UP You need the GardenCompany03 database located in the Chapter03 practice file folder to complete this exercise. The practice file for this exercise contains tables that look similar to those in the practice file for Chapter 1. However, to simplify the steps, we have removed the relationships between the tables. Be sure to use the practice database for this chapter rather than continuing on with the database from an earlier chapter. Open the database, and if you want, save your own version to avoid overwriting the original. Then follow the steps.

3

1 With **All Access Objects** displayed in the **Navigation** pane, in the **Tables** group, double-click **Customers** to open the **Customers** table in **Datasheet** view.

CustomerID	FirstName	LastName	Address	City	Region	PostalCode	Count
ACKPI	Pilar	Ackerman	8808 Backbay S	Bellevue	WA	88004	USA
ADATE	Terry	Adams	1932 52nd Ave.	Vancouver	BC	V4T 1Y9	Canada
ALLMI	Michael	Allen	130 17th St.	Vancouver	BC	V4T 1Y9	Canada
BANMA	Martin	Bankov	78 Riverside Dr	Woodinville	WA	88072	USA
BENPA	Paula	Bento	6778 Cypress P	Oak Harbor	WA	88277	USA
BERKA	Karen	Berg	PO Box 69	Yakima	WA	88902	USA
BOSRA	Randall	Boseman	55 Grizzly Peak	Butte	MT	49707	USA
BRETE	Ted	Bremer	311 87th Pl.	Beaverton	OR	87008	USA
BROKE	Kevin F.	Browne	666 Fords Land	Seattle	WA	88121	USA
CAMDA	David	Campbell	22 Market St.	San Francisco	CA	84112	USA
CANCH	Chris	Cannon	89 W. Hilltop D	Palo Alto	CA	84306	USA
CHANE	Neil	Charney	1842 10th Aven	Sidney	BC	V7L 1L3	Canada
CLAMO	Molly	Clark	785 Beale St.	Sidney	BC	V7L 5A6	Canada
COLPA	Pat	Coleman	876 Western A	Seattle	WA	88119	USA
CORCE	Cecilia	Cornejo	778 Ancient Rd	Bellevue	WA	88007	USA
COXBR	Brian	Cox	14 S. Elm Dr.	Moscow	ID	73844	USA
CULSC	Scott	Culp	14 E. University	Seattle	WA	88115	USA
DANMI	Mike	Danseglio	55 Newton	Seattle	WA	88102	USA

Record: 14 ◀ 1 of 108 ▶ ▶I ▶□ No Filter Search

The record navigation bar shows that there are 108 records in this table.

TIP The CustomerID field contains a unique identifier for each customer and is the table's primary key field. In this case, the unique identifier is not an autogenerated number, but the first three letters of the customer's last name combined with the first two letters of his or her first name. For more information about this type of primary key, see "Allowing only values in other tables" in Chapter 6, "Maintain data integrity."

2 On the **Create** tab, in the **Forms** group, click the **Form** button to create a simple form based on the active table and display the form in **Layout** view.

TIP You don't have to open a table to create a form based on it. You can simply click the table in the Navigation pane to select it and then click the Form button in the Forms group on the Create tab. But it is sometimes useful to have the table open behind the form so that you can verify the form contents against the table contents.

The form displays the first record in the Customers table in Layout view. (We have closed the Navigation pane to show more of the form.)

The Form tool has configured all the field names in the table as label controls and all the fields as text box controls. In the header at the top of the form, the name of the table appears as a title, and the form icon appears to the left of the title as a placeholder for a logo. Because the form is displayed in Layout view, the Design, Arrange, and Format tool tabs appear on the ribbon so that you can modify selected controls.

3   Move the mouse pointer over the form, and click any label or text box control to select it for manipulation.

We won't make any changes to the form right now. Instead let's experiment with how the form looks and behaves in Form view.

4   Switch to **Form** view. Then move the mouse pointer over the form, and click the **City** label.

CustomerID	ACKPI
FirstName	Pilar
LastName	Ackerman
Address	8808 Backbay St.
City	Bellevue
Region	WA
PostalCode	88004
Country	USA
PhoneNumber	(425) 555-0194

In Form view, the tool tabs are no longer displayed, and clicking a label selects the entry in the adjacent text box, ready for editing.

5   In the record navigation bar at the bottom of the form, click the **Next record** button to display the second record in the table.

6   Use the record navigation bar to display a few more records.

TIP You can easily compare the information shown in the form to that in the table by alternately clicking the Customers table tab and the Customers form tab to switch back and forth between their pages.

Now let's use the form to enter a couple of new records in the table.

7   At the right end of the record navigation bar, click the **New (blank) record** button to display a blank **Customers** form.

The record navigation bar shows that this will be record number 109.

8   Click the **CustomerID** label to position the cursor in the text box to the right.

9   Enter **ASHCH**, noticing that the icon that indicates a record is receiving data (two dots and a pencil) appears at the top of the bar to the left. Then press the **Tab** key, which moves the cursor to the next text box.

10   Enter the following information, pressing **Tab** after each entry except the last one to move to the next text box.

FirstName	Chris
LastName	Ashton
Address	89 Cedar Way
City	Redmond
Region	WA
PostalCode	88052
Country	USA
PhoneNumber	(425) 555-0191

11   When you finish entering the phone number (the last field value in the record), press the **Enter** key to complete the record and display another blank form. Notice that the record navigation bar shows that this will be record number 110 in the table.

12 Enter the following information, pressing **Tab** after each entry except the last one to move from text box to text box.

CustomerID   BASSH

FirstName   Shai

LastName   Bassli

Address   407 Sunny Way

City   Kirkland

Region   WA

PostalCode   88053

Country   USA

PhoneNumber   (425) 555-0187

13 When you finish entering the phone number, press **Enter**. Then in the record navigation bar, click the **Previous record** button to cancel the new record and display the record you just created.

The information you entered for record number 110.

Let's verify that the two records you entered in the form also appear in the table.

14 Click the **Customers** table tab, and on the record navigation bar, click the **Last record** button. Notice that the two records you entered in the form do not appear at the bottom of the table, and the record navigator bar indicates that there are only 108 records in the table.

15   On the **Home** tab, in the **Records** group, click the **Refresh All** button to synchronize the table and the form data input.

First new record

CustomerID	FirstName	LastName	Address	City	Region	PostalCode	Count
ACKPI	Pilar	Ackerman	8808 Backbay S	Bellevue	WA	88004	USA
ADATE	Terry	Adams	1932 52nd Ave.	Vancouver	BC	V4T 1Y9	Canada
ALLMI	Michael	Allen	130 17th St.	Vancouver	BC	V4T 1Y9	Canada
ASHCH	Chris	Ashton	89 Cedar Way	Redmond	WA	88052	USA
BANMA	Martin	Bankov	78 Riverside Dr	Woodinville	WA	88072	USA
BASSH	Shai	Bassli	407 Sunny Way	Kirkland	WA	88053	USA
BENPA	Paula	Bento	6778 Cypress P	Oak Harbor	WA	88277	USA
BERKA	Karen	Berg	PO Box 69	Yakima	WA	88902	USA
BOSRA	Randall	Boseman	55 Grizzly Peak	Butte	MT	49707	USA
BRETE	Ted	Bremer	311 87th Pl.	Beaverton	OR	87008	USA
BROKE	Kevin F.	Browne	666 Fords Land	Seattle	WA	88121	USA
CAMDA	David	Campbell	22 Market St.	San Francisco	CA	84112	USA
CANCH	Chris	Cannon	89 W. Hilltop D	Palo Alto	CA	84306	USA
CHANE	Neil	Charney	1842 10th Aven	Sidney	BC	V7L 1L3	Canada
CLAMO	Molly	Clark	785 Beale St.	Sidney	BC	V7L 5A6	Canada
COLPA	Pat	Coleman	876 Western A	Seattle	WA	88119	USA
CORCE	Cecilia	Cornejo	778 Ancient Rd	Bellevue	WA	88007	USA
COXBR	Brian	Cox	14 S. Elm Dr.	Moscow	ID	73844	USA

Record: ◄ ◄ 1 of 110 ► ► ►* No Filter Search

Second new record

The two new records have been added to the Customers table and appear in alphabetical order based on their CustomerID field values.

16   Close the **Customers** table.

17   On the **Quick Access Toolbar**, click the **Save** button. Then in the **Save As** dialog box, click **OK** to accept **Customers** as the form name and add the form to the **Forms** group in the **Navigation** pane.

❌ CLEAN UP Close the form. Keep the GardenCompany03 database open for use in later exercises.

Formatting forms

When you create a form by using the Form tool, as you did in the previous exercise, the form includes every field in the table on which it is based. Each field is represented on the form by a text box control and its associated label control. The form is linked, or *bound*, to the table, and each text box is bound to its corresponding field. The table is called the *record source*, and the field is called the *control source*.

Forms and their controls have properties that determine how they behave and look. A form inherits some of its properties from the table on which it is based. For example, each text box name on the form reflects the corresponding field name in the source table. The text box label also reflects the field name, unless the field has been assigned a Caption property, in which case it reflects the caption. The width of each text box is determined by the Field Size property in the table.

Even though a form is bound to its table, the properties of the form are not bound to the table's properties. After you have created the form, you can change the properties of the form's fields independently of those in the table. You might want to change these properties to improve the form's appearance—for example, you can change the font, font size, alignment, fill color, and border.

One of the quickest ways to change the look of a form is to change the theme applied to the database. A theme is a combination of colors and fonts that controls the look of certain objects. In the case of a form, it controls the color and text of the header at the top of the form and the text of the labels and text boxes. By default, the Office theme is applied to all databases based on the Blank Desktop Database template and their objects, but you can easily change the theme by clicking the Themes button in the Themes group on the Design tool tab, and then making a selection from the Themes gallery. While the gallery is displayed, you can point to a theme to display a live preview of how the active database object will look with that theme's colors and fonts applied.

If you like the colors of one theme and the fonts of another, you can mix and match theme elements. First apply the theme that most closely resembles the look you want, and then in the Themes group, change the colors by clicking the Colors button or the fonts by clicking the Fonts button.

TIP If you create a combination of colors and fonts that you would like to be able to use with other databases, you can save the combination as a new theme by clicking Save Current Theme at the bottom of the menu containing the Themes gallery.

If you like most of the formatting of a theme but you want to fine-tune some form elements, you can do so by changing properties in Layout view. In this view, you can view the records from the table to which the form is bound, so when you make formatting adjustments, you can assess the impact on the data. (Changes to the data can be made only in Form view.) You might also want to add your organization's logo or a small graphic that represents the form's contents.

In this exercise, you'll first apply a theme to a form and add a logo to the form's title. Then you'll change the form properties that control its colors and text attributes.

→ SET UP You need the GardenCompany03 database you worked with in the preceding exercise and the Logo graphic located in the Chapter03 practice file folder to complete this exercise. If necessary, open the database. Then follow the steps.

1 In the **Navigation** pane, in the **Forms** group, right-click **Customers**, and then click **Layout View**.

2 On the **Design** tool tab, in the **Themes** group, click the **Themes** button to display a menu containing the **Themes** gallery.

Each thumbnail represents a theme. By default, the Office theme is applied to this database.

3 Point to each thumbnail in turn, pausing until its name appears in a ScreenTip.

4 Click the **Wisp** thumbnail to apply that theme.

Now let's replace the form icon to the left of the title in the form header with a logo.

5 On the **Design** tab, in the **Header/Footer** group, click the **Logo** button.

6   In the **Insert Picture** dialog box, navigate to the **Chapter03** practice file folder, and double-click the **Logo** picture.

You have inserted a custom logo in the form header.

Next let's experiment with properties.

7   On the **Customers** form, click the **CustomerID** label control (not its text box) to select it for manipulation.

8   On the **Format** tool tab, in the **Font** group, click the **Font Size** arrow, and then in the list, click **8** to make the label text significantly smaller.

9   Click the **CustomerID** text box control (not its label), and then on the **Design** tool tab, in the **Tools** group, click the **Property Sheet** button to open the **Property Sheet** pane.

KEYBOARD SHORTCUT Press Alt+Enter to open and close the Property Sheet pane. For a list of keyboard shortcuts, see "Keyboard shortcuts" at the end of this book.

Property Sheet ▾ ✕

Selection type: Text Box

CustomerID ▾

| Format | Data | Event | Other | All |

Name	CustomerID
Control Source	CustomerID
Format	
Decimal Places	Auto
Visible	Yes
Text Format	Plain Text
Datasheet Caption	
Show Date Picker	For dates
Width	6.8229"
Height	0.2493"
Top	0.25"
Left	1.3542"
Back Style	Normal
Back Color	Background 1
Border Style	Solid
Border Width	Hairline
Border Color	Background 1, D
Special Effect	Flat
Scroll Bars	None
Font Name	Century Gothic (l
Font Size	11
Text Align	Left
Font Weight	Normal
Font Underline	No
Font Italic	No
Fore Color	Text 1, Lighter 25
Line Spacing	0"
Is Hyperlink	No
Display As Hyperlink	If Hyperlink

The properties of the CustomerID text box control are organized on four pages: Format, Data, Event, and Other. As its name suggests, the All page displays all the properties on one page.

TIP Don't change the properties on the Data page until you know more about controls and their sources.

10   Notice that the **Property Sheet** pane displays the properties for the object whose name appears in the text box at the top of the pane, and that above the box, the type of object is identified.

11   In the **Property Sheet** pane, click the **Format** tab

Property Sheet ▾ ✕

Selection type: Text Box

CustomerID ⌄

Format	Data	Event	Other	All

Format	⌄
Decimal Places	Auto
Visible	Yes
Show Date Picker	For dates
Width	6.8229"
Height	0.2493"
Top	0.25"
Left	1.3542"
Back Style	Normal
Back Color	Background 1
Border Style	Solid
Border Width	Hairline
Border Color	Background 1, D
Special Effect	Flat
Scroll Bars	None
Font Name	Century Gothic (I
Font Size	11
Text Align	Left
Font Weight	Normal
Font Underline	No
Font Italic	No
Fore Color	Text 1, Lighter 25
Line Spacing	0"
Is Hyperlink	No
Display As Hyperlink	If Hyperlink
Hyperlink Target	
Gridline Style Top	Transparent
Gridline Style Bottom	Transparent
Gridline Style Left	Transparent

The Format page of the Property Sheet pane displays all the commands available in the Font group on the Format tab of the ribbon (plus a few more).

12 On the **Format** page, click **Font Size**, click the arrow to the right of the adjacent property, and in the list, click **8**.

13 Set the **Font Weight** property to **Bold**.

TIP If the Property Sheet pane obscures your view of the controls on the form, change its width (or the width of any pane) by dragging its left border to the left or right. To change the width of the Property Sheet columns, drag the right border of the first column to the left or right. You can undock the Property Sheet pane from the edge of the window and move it elsewhere by dragging its title bar. Double-click the title bar to dock it again.

Let's use the Property Sheet pane to display the properties of a different control and then change its properties.

14 At the right end of the box at the top of the **Property Sheet** pane, click the arrow, and then in the object list, click **Label3** to select the **FirstName** label.

15 Repeat step 12 to change the font size of the **FirstName** label to **8** points.

These different ways of selecting a control and changing its properties provide some flexibility and convenience, but using this technique to make changes to several controls in a form is tedious. Let's use a faster method.

16 In the upper-left corner of the dotted frame surrounding all the controls on the form, click the **Select All** button (the four headed arrow) to surround all the controls with thick orange borders to indicate that they are selected.

17 In the **Property Sheet** pane, notice that the selection type is **Multiple selection**, and the box below is blank. Only the settings that are the same for all the selected controls are displayed. Because the changes you made in the previous steps are not shared by all the selected controls, the **Font Size** and **Font Weight** settings are now blank.

18 Repeat steps 12 and 13 to set the **Font Size** and **Font Weight** properties of the selected controls to **8** and **Bold**.

You have applied character formatting to all the label and text box controls in the form.

Although it's not apparent, the background of the labels is transparent. Let's change this property and then apply a theme color and effect.

19   With the controls still selected, set the **Back Style** property to **Normal**.

20   Click the **Back Color** property, and then click the **Ellipsis** button at the right end of the property to display a menu containing two color palettes.

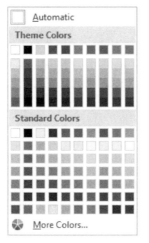

The colors in the Theme Colors palette reflect the color scheme that is part of the Wisp theme.

TIP The Ellipsis button has different names and serves different purposes for different properties.

21   In the top row of the **Theme Colors** palette, click the third swatch (**Light Green, Background 2**) to change the background of all the controls to light green.

TIP If the palettes on the Back Color menu don't include a color you want to use, click More Colors at the bottom of the menu, select a color on the Standard or Custom page of the Colors dialog box, and then click OK to set the color and add it to the Recent Colors palette at the bottom of the menu.

22   Set the **Special Effect** property to **Shadowed**, and the **Border Color** property to the eighth swatch in the first row of the **Theme Colors** palette (**Olive Green, Accent 4**).

23   Close the **Property Sheet** pane, and in the form, click away from the selected controls to release the selection and display the results.

Applying a color and shadow effect to the labels and text boxes makes them stand out.

The label controls reflect the field names assigned to the table fields they are bound to. Let's assign captions to some of the label controls so that their names include spaces.

24   In the form, click the **FirstName** label control. Then open the **Property Sheet** pane, click the **Caption** property, change **FirstName** to First Name, and press **Enter**.

25   Repeat step 24 to change **LastName** to Last Name and **PhoneNumber** to Phone.

TIP Changing the Caption property of the form does not affect the Caption property of the bound field in the table.

26   On the **Quick Access Toolbar**, click the **Save** button to save the design of the **Customers** form. Then close the form, which also closes the **Property Sheet** pane.

✖ CLEAN UP Keep the GardenCompany03 database open for use in the last exercise.

Arranging the layout of forms

Forms generated with the Form tool are functional, not fancy. By default, they are arranged in the Stacked layout, which arranges all the label controls in a single column on the left and all their corresponding text box controls in a single column to their right. All the boxes of each type are the same size, and in the boxes, the text is left-aligned.

If it suits the needs of your data better to display records in a tabular layout much like that of a table in Datasheet view, click Tabular in the Table group on the Arrange tool tab.

SEE ALSO For more information about layouts, see the sidebar "Layouts" in Chapter 9, "Create custom reports."

If the default layout doesn't suit your needs or preferences, you can customize it. Most of the rearranging you are likely to want to do can be accomplished in Layout view, where you can view the impact on the underlying data. If you want to make more extensive changes to the layout of a database, you can switch to Design view.

SEE ALSO For information about customizing forms in Design view, see Chapter 8, "Create custom forms."

In Layout view, you can do the following to improve the form's layout and make it attractive and easy to use:

- Add and delete a variety of controls.
- Change the size of controls.
- Move controls.
- Change text alignment.
- Change the margins of controls.

TIP The order in which you make changes can have an impact on the results. If the results aren't what you expect, click the Undo button on the Quick Access Toolbar to reverse your previous action, or click the Undo arrow, and click an action in the list to reverse more than one action.

In this exercise, you'll align, size, and rearrange the label and text box controls in a form.

SET UP You need the GardenCompany03 database you worked with in the preceding exercise to complete this exercise. If necessary, open the database. Then follow the steps.

1 In the **Navigation** pane, in the **Forms** group, right-click **Customers**, click **Layout View**.

   TIP If the Property Sheet pane was open when you last closed the form, it is displayed with the form.

2 Click the **CustomerID** label control (not its text box), and on the **Arrange** tool tab, in the **Rows & Columns** group, click the **Select Column** button.

   TIP You can also point above the selected control, and when the pointer changes to a single downward-pointing arrow, click to select the column of controls.

3 With all the label controls selected, on the **Format** page of the **Property Sheet** pane, set the **Text Align** property to **Right** to right-align all the labels in their controls.

You can efficiently adjust the alignment of multiple selected controls by changing the Text Align property in the Property Sheet pane.

The Property Sheet pane indicates that the Width property of the label controls is 1.0611". Let's make them narrower.

TIP Throughout this book, we refer to measurements in inches. If your computer is set to display measurements in centimeters, substitute the equivalent metric measurement. As long as you are entering the default units, you don't have to specify the unit type.

4 Point to the right border of the **CustomerID** label, and when the pointer changes to a two-headed horizontal arrow, drag to the left until **CustomerID** just fits in its box.

5 In the **Property Sheet** pane, adjust the **Width** property to **0.85"**, and press **Enter**.

TIP It is often easier to adjust the size of controls visually and then fine-tune them in the Property Sheet pane than it is to guess what property settings might work.

6 Select the **CustomerID** text box (not its label), change its **Width** property to **1.5"**, and press **Enter**. Notice that when you size one control in a **Stacked** layout, all the controls in the same column are adjusted, not just the selected control.

In a Stacked layout, all the controls in each column are the same width.

The controls are the same width but have different heights and interior margins. Let's fix that next.

7   Above the upper-left corner of the dotted border that surrounds all the controls, click the **Select All** button to select all the controls within the border. Then in the **Property Sheet** pane, set the **Height** property to $0.25''$, and press **Enter**.

8   On the **Arrange** tool tab, in the **Position** group, click the **Control Margins** button, and then click **Narrow**.

You can control not only the size of the controls but also the distance from the control's border to its text.

Now let's rearrange some controls.

9   Click the **Phone** label (not its text box), and on the **Arrange** tool tab, in the **Rows & Columns** group, click the **Select Row** button.

TIP You can also point to the left of the selected control, and when the pointer changes to a single right-pointing arrow, click to select the row of controls.

10   Point anywhere in the selection, and drag upward, releasing the mouse button when the insertion line sits below the **Last Name** label or text box.

11   Click the **Last Name** label, and then press the **Delete** key.

12   Click the **LastName** text box, point to the **A** in *Ackerman*, and drag the four-headed arrow pointer up and to the right until the pointer sits slightly to the right of the **FirstName** text box. When the insertion bar appears, release the mouse button.

> **TIP** The control snaps to an invisible grid that helps maintain consistent spacing on the form.

13   Repeat step 11 to delete the **Region** and **PostalCode** labels.

14   Repeat step 12 to move the **Region** and **PostalCode** text boxes to the right of the **City** text box.

15   Select the **City** controls row and move it down one grid space. Then do the same for the **Address** controls row.

Now that the controls are arranged, let's remove the Stacked layout from the form so that we can make more extensive layout adjustments.

16   In the upper-left corner of the dotted layout border, click the **Select All** button. Then right-click the selection, click **Layout**, and click **Remove Layout**.

With the Stacked layout removed, let's adjust the widths of individual controls.

17   Select the **Region** text box, and on the **Format** page of the **Property** Sheet pane, adjust the **Width** property to .5".

18   Select the **PostalCode** text box. Then adjust the **Width** property to **.5"** and the **Left** property to **3.25"**.

19   Click the **First Name** label, and change the label's **Caption** property to Name. Then repeat the process to change the **City** label's caption to City/State/ZIP.

20   Close the **Property Sheet** pane, and release the selection by clicking a blank area.

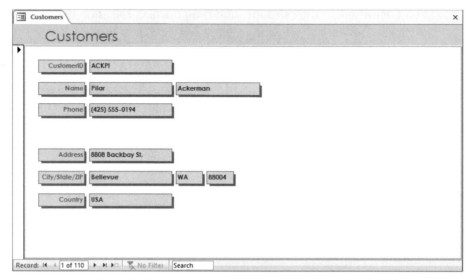

In Layout view, this kind of arrangement can be achieved only if you remove the default layout, which constrains sizing and positioning of individual controls.

TIP If you rearrange controls or add new controls to a form and then find that pressing Tab jumps around erratically instead of sequentially from one control to the next, you can change the tab order. When working in Layout view, click the Other tab in the Property Sheet pane, and set the Tab Index property for each control in the tab order you want. When working in Design view, click the Tab Order button in the Tools group on the Design tool tab to display the Tab Order dialog box, where you can drag fields into the correct order. For more information about working with forms in Design view, see Chapter 8, "Create custom forms."

21 Close the **Customers** form, clicking **Yes** when prompted to save its layout.

❌ CLEAN UP Close the GardenCompany03 database.

Key points

- The quickest way to create a form that includes all the fields from one table is by using the Form tool. You can then use the form to view and enter records.

- A form that is based on a table is bound to that table. The table is called the *record source*.

- By default, the form displays one text box control and its associated label control for each field in the table.

- Each text box control is bound to its field, which is called the *control source*.

- Each control has several properties that you can change in Layout view or Design view to improve the look and layout of the form

3

Chapter at a glance

Sort

Sort information in tables,
page 116

Filter

Filter information in tables,
page 121

Filter

Filter information by using forms,
page 125

Locate

Locate information that matches multiple
criteria, page 129

Display data

4

IN THIS CHAPTER, YOU WILL LEARN HOW TO

- Sort information in tables.

- Filter information in tables.

- Filter information by using forms.

- Locate information that matches multiple criteria.

A database is a repository for information. It might contain only a few records or thousands of records, stored in one table or multiple tables. No matter how much information a database contains, it is useful only if you can locate the information you need when you need it. In a small database, you can find information simply by scrolling through a table until you find what you are looking for. But as a database grows in size and complexity, locating and analyzing information becomes more difficult.

Microsoft Access 2013 provides a variety of tools you can use to organize the display of information stored in a database. For example, you can organize all the records in a table by quickly sorting it based on any field or combination of fields. You can also filter the table so that information containing a combination of characters is displayed or excluded from the display.

In this chapter, you'll first sort information in a table based on one and two columns. Then you'll explore ways to filter tables and forms to display only the records that meet specific criteria.

PRACTICE FILES To complete the exercises in this chapter, you need the practice file contained in the Chapter04 practice file folder. For more information, see "Download the practice files" in this book's Introduction.

Sorting information in tables

You can sort the information stored in a table based on the values in one or more fields, in either ascending or descending order. For example, you could sort customer information alphabetically by last name and then by first name. This would result in the order found in telephone books.

Last name	First name
Smith	Brian
Smith	Denise
Smith	Jeff
Taylor	Daniel
Taylor	Maurice

Sorting a table groups all entries of one type together, which can be useful. For example, to qualify for a discount on postage, you might want to group customer records by postal code before printing mailing labels.

Access can sort by more than one field, but it always sorts sequentially from left to right. You can sort by the first field, and if the second field you want to sort by is immediately to the right of the first, you can then add the next field to the sort. If you want to sort by more than one field in one operation, the fields must be adjacent, and they must be arranged in the order in which you want to sort them.

SEE ALSO For information about moving fields, see "Manipulating table columns and rows" in Chapter 2, "Create databases and simple tables."

TIP You can sort records while viewing them in a form. Click the field on which you want to base the sort, and then click the Sort command you want. You can't sort by multiple fields at the same time in Form view, but you can sort by one field and then the next to achieve the same results.

In this exercise, you'll sort records first by one field, and then by multiple fields.

 SET UP You need the GardenCompany04 database located in the Chapter04 practice file folder to complete this exercise. Be sure to use the practice database for this chapter rather than continuing on with the database from an earlier chapter. Open the database, and if you want, save your own version to avoid overwriting the original. Then follow the steps.

1   With **All Access Objects** displayed in the **Navigation** pane, in the **Tables** group, double-click **Customers** to open the **Customers** table in **Datasheet** view.

2   Click the arrow to the right of the **Region** field name to display a menu of sorting and filtering options.

The list at the bottom of the menu includes check boxes for every unique value in the field.

3   Click **Sort A to Z** to rearrange the records in ascending alphabetical order by region.

CustomerID ▾	FirstName ▾	LastName ▾	Address ▾	City ▾	Region ▾	PostalCode ▾	Cou ▲
⊞ LUGJO	Jose	Lugo	23 Tsawassen E	Tsawassen	BC	V6E 4S8	Canad
⊞ CHANE	Neil	Charney	1842 10th Aven	Sidney	BC	V7L 1L3	Canad
⊞ TIAMI	Mike	Tiano	5540 Rosebud I	Victoria	BC	V7Y 1Y1	Canad
⊞ CLAMO	Molly	Clark	785 Beale St.	Sidney	BC	V7L 5A6	Canad
⊞ WANJI	JianShuo	Wang	3319 Hillside D	Vancouver	BC	V5K 2V6	Canad
⊞ TEJSA	Sameer A.	Tejani	1900 Oak St.	Vancouver	BC	V5H 1L7	Canad
⊞ MORJO	Jon	Morris	490 Fulton Dr.	Vancouver	BC	V4T 2A2	Canad
⊞ MYEKE	Ken	Myer	7320 Edwards A	Vancouver	BC	V5J 2G3	Canad
⊞ ALLMI	Michael	Allen	130 17th St.	Vancouver	BC	V4T 1Y9	Canad
⊞ FENHA	Hanying	Feng	537 Orchard Av	Victoria	BC	V8C 3Z1	Canad
⊞ ADATE	Terry	Adams	1932 52nd Ave.	Vancouver	BC	V4T 1Y9	Canad
⊞ FLOKA	Kathie	Flood	8887 Western A	Glendale	CA	81203	USA
⊞ SIMDA	David	Simpson	45 Park St.	San Jose	CA	85123	USA
⊞ MITSC	Scott	Mitchell	47 Eucalyptus D	Escondido	CA	82029	USA
⊞ SANPA	Patrick	Sands	98 N. Hyde St.	San Francisco	CA	84140	USA
⊞ SEIJO	Joachim	Seidler	9308 Dartridge	San Francisco	CA	84167	USA
⊞ POLCA	Carole	Poland	10 Pepper Dr.	San Jose	CA	85111	USA
⊞ CAMDA	David	Campbell	22 Market St.	San Francisco	CA	84112	USA

Record: I◄ ◄ 1 of 110 ► ►I ►□   ▧ No Filter   Search

The upward-pointing arrow at the right end of the Region field name indicates that the table is sorted in ascending order on this field.

Suppose we want to display the records for customers living in Washington (WA) at the top of the list. Let's reverse the sort order by using a different method.

4 On the **Home** tab, in the **Sort & Filter** group, click the **Descending** button.

In both sorts, the region was sorted alphabetically, but the City field was left in a seemingly random order. Let's sort the City field and then the Region field to display the records arranged by city within each region..

5 Click the arrow to the right of the **City** field name, and then click **Sort A to Z** to sort the records alphabetically by city.

6 To finish the process, right-click anywhere in the **Region** column, and then click **Sort A to Z**.

CustomerID	FirstName	LastName	Address	City	Region	PostalCode	Cou
⊞ CHANE	Neil	Charney	1842 10th Aven	Sidney	BC	V7L 1L3	Canad
⊞ CLAMO	Molly	Clark	785 Beale St.	Sidney	BC	V7L 5A6	Canad
⊞ LUGJO	Jose	Lugo	23 Tsawassen E	Tsawassen	BC	V6E 4S8	Canad
⊞ MYEKE	Ken	Myer	7320 Edwards A	Vancouver	BC	V5J 2G3	Canad
⊞ TEJSA	Sameer A.	Tejani	1900 Oak St.	Vancouver	BC	V5H 1L7	Canad
⊞ MORJO	Jon	Morris	490 Fulton Dr.	Vancouver	BC	V4T 2A2	Canad
⊞ WANJI	JianShuo	Wang	3319 Hillside D	Vancouver	BC	V5K 2V6	Canad
⊞ ALLMI	Michael	Allen	130 17th St.	Vancouver	BC	V4T 1Y9	Canad
⊞ ADATE	Terry	Adams	1932 52nd Ave.	Vancouver	BC	V4T 1Y9	Canad
⊞ TIAMI	Mike	Tiano	5540 Rosebud I	Victoria	BC	V7Y 1Y1	Canad
⊞ FENHA	Hanying	Feng	537 Orchard Av	Victoria	BC	V8C 3Z1	Canad
⊞ DOYPA	Patricia	Doyle	1630 Hillcrest V	Carmel Valley	CA	83924	USA
⊞ MITSC	Scott	Mitchell	47 Eucalyptus D	Escondido	CA	82029	USA
⊞ FLOKA	Kathie	Flood	8887 Western A	Glendale	CA	81203	USA
⊞ MILBE	Ben	Miller	23 High Pass Dr	Granada Hills	CA	81344	USA
⊞ MATJO	Joseph	Matthews	96 Jefferson Lo	Loma Linda	CA	82350	USA
⊞ CANCH	Chris	Cannon	89 W. Hilltop D	Palo Alto	CA	84306	USA
⊞ CAMDA	David	Campbell	22 Market St.	San Francisco	CA	84112	USA

Record: I◀ ◀ 1 of 110 ▶ ▶I ▶⊞ No Filter Search

Both the City and Region field names have upward-pointing arrows, indicating that the records have been sorted on both fields.

Now let's sort both fields at the same time. First we have to revert to the previously saved sort order.

7 On the **Home** tab, in the **Sort & Filter** group, click the **Remove Sort** button to clear the sort from both fields.

8   Click the **City** field name, hold down the **Shift** key, and click the **Region** field name. Then in the **Sort & Filter** group, click the **Ascending** button. Notice that because the **City** field is to the left of the **Region** field, this sort does not achieve the result you want.

Customers							✕
CustomerID ▾	FirstName ▾	LastName ▾	Address ▾	City ▾	Region ▾	PostalCode ▾	Cou ▲
⊞ YOURO	Rob	Young	231 N. Ukiah Rc	Aloha	OR	87006	USA
⊞ MARSA	Sandra I.	Martinez	780 West Blvd.	Arlington	WA	88223	USA
⊞ KHAKA	Karan	Khanna	401 Rodeo Dr.	Auburn	WA	88001	USA
⊞ BRETE	Ted	Bremer	311 87th Pl.	Beaverton	OR	87008	USA
⊞ HOEHE	Helge	Hoeing	431 Freemont S	Bellevue	WA	88005	USA
⊞ ACKPI	Pilar	Ackerman	8808 Backbay S	Bellevue	WA	88004	USA
⊞ NISCH	Chad	Niswonger	3300 Colorado	Bellevue	WA	88005	USA
⊞ TRASH	Shirleen H.	Travers	46 E. Orange St	Bellevue	WA	88004	USA
⊞ CORCE	Cecilia	Cornejo	778 Ancient Rd	Bellevue	WA	88007	USA
⊞ HOLMI	Michael	Holm	4220 Main St.	Bellevue	WA	88006	USA
⊞ JACLO	Lola	Jacobsen	998 Kirk Rd.	Bellingham	WA	88227	USA
⊞ LUMRI	Richard	Lum	187 Suffolk Ln.	Boise	ID	73704	USA
⊞ LANER	Eric	Lang	991 S. Mississip	Bothell	WA	88011	USA
⊞ ESTMO	Modesto	Estrada	511 Lincoln Ave	Burns	OR	87710	USA
⊞ BOSRA	Randall	Boseman	55 Grizzly Peak	Butte	MT	49707	USA
⊞ DOYPA	Patricia	Doyle	1630 Hillcrest V	Carmel Valley	CA	83924	USA
⊞ HONQI	Qin	Hong	234 Samuel Pl.	Carnation	WA	88014	USA
⊞ ZIMKA	Karin	Zimprich	472 Lexington /	Carnation	WA	88014	USA

Record: I◄ ◄ 1 of 110 ► ►I ►❋ ❋ No Filter | Search

The City sort is overriding the Region sort.

9   Remove the sort, and then click away from the **City** and **Region** fields to clear the selection.

10   Click the **Region** field name, and drag the field name to the left of the **City** field name, releasing the mouse button when a heavy black line appears between the **Address** and **City** field names.

11   With the **Region** field selected, hold down the **Shift** key, and click the **City** field name to include that field in the selection.

12   In the **Sort & Filter** group, click the **Ascending** button to arrange the records with the regions in ascending order and the cities in ascending order within each region.

13   Experiment with various ways of sorting the records to display different results. Then close the **Customers** table, clicking **No** when prompted to save the table layout.

✖ CLEAN UP Keep the GardenCompany04 database open for use in later exercises.

How Access sorts

The concept of sorting seems quite intuitive, but sometimes the way Access sorts numbers might seem puzzling. In Access, numbers can be treated as either text or numerals. Because of the spaces, hyphens, and punctuation typically used in street addresses, postal codes, and phone numbers, the data type of these fields is usually Short Text, and the numbers are sorted the same way as all other text. In contrast, numbers in a field assigned the Number or Currency data type are sorted as numerals.

When Access sorts text, it sorts first on the first character in the selected field in every record, then on the next character, then on the next, and so on—until it runs out of characters. When Access sorts numbers, it treats the contents of each field as a single value, and sorts the records based on that value. This tactic can result in seemingly strange sort orders. For example, sorting the list in the first column of the following table as text produces the list in the second column. Sorting the same list as numerals produces the list in the third column.

Original	Sort as text	Sort as numerals
1	1	1
1234	11	3
23	12	4
3	1234	11
11	22	12
22	23	22
12	3	23
4	4	1234

If a field with the Short Text data type contains numbers, you can sort the field numerically by padding the numbers with leading zeros so that all entries are the same length. For example, 001, 011, and 101 are sorted correctly even if the numbers are defined as text.

Filtering information in tables

Sorting the information in a table organizes it in a logical manner, but you still have the entire table to deal with. For locating only the records containing (or not containing) specific information, filtering is more effective than sorting. For example, you could quickly create a filter to locate only customers who live in Seattle, only items that were purchased on January 13, or only orders that were not shipped by standard mail.

When you filter a table, Access doesn't remove the records that don't match the filter; it simply hides them. To filter information by multiple criteria, you can apply additional filters to the results of the first one.

The Filter commands are available in the Sort & Filter group on the Home tab, on the menu displayed when you click the arrow at the right end of a field name, and on the shortcut menu displayed when you right-click anywhere in a field's column. However, not all Filter commands are available in all of these places.

4

TIP You can filter records while displaying them in a form by using the same commands as you do to filter records in a table.

In this exercise, you'll filter records by using a single criterion and then by using multiple criteria.

SET UP You need the GardenCompany04 database you worked with in the preceding exercise to complete this exercise. If necessary, open the database. Then follow the steps.

1 In the **Navigation** pane, in the **Tables** group, double-click **Customers** to open the **Customers** table in **Datasheet** view.

2 In the **City** field, click any instance of **Vancouver**.

3 On the **Home** tab, in the **Sort & Filter** group, click the **Selection** button, and then in the list, click **Equals "Vancouver"**. Notice that a small filter icon shaped like a funnel appears at the right end of the **City** field name to indicate that the table is filtered by that field. The record navigation bar at the bottom of the table changes to **1 of 6** because only six records have the value **Vancouver** in the **City** field. Also on the record navigation bar, the filter status changes to **Filtered**.

Only the six records for customers who live in Vancouver are displayed in the table.

TIP In the list displayed when you click the arrow to the right of a field name (or the Filter button in the Sort & Filter group) are check boxes for all the unique entries in the active field. Clearing the Select All check box clears all the boxes, and you can then select the check boxes of any values you want to be displayed in the filtered table.

In the Sort & Filter group on the Home tab, the Toggle Filter button is now active. This button is dynamic; it is called Apply Filter and is inactive when no filter is applied, and it is called Remove Filter and is active when a filter is applied. Let's use this button to quickly turn off the applied filter.

4   In the **Sort & Filter** group, click the **Remove Filter** button to toggle off the filter and display all the records.

   TIP If you click the Toggle Filter button again, the current filter will be reapplied.

   Now let's display a list of all customers with postal codes starting with 880.

5   Click the arrow to the right of the **PostalCode** field name, and point to **Text Filters** to display a list of criteria.

You start specifying filtering criteria for the text you want to find by selecting an option from the Text Filters list.

TIP The sort and filter options displayed when you click the arrow to the right of a field name (or when you click the Filter button in the Sort & Filter group) are determined by the data type of the field. The PostalCode field is assigned the Short Text data type to allow for ZIP+4 codes. If you display the sort and filter list for a field that is assigned the Number data type, the sort and filter list includes Number Filters instead of Text Filters, and different options are available.

6   In the list, click **Begins With** to open the **Custom Filter** dialog box.

The name of the text box is customized with the field name and the filter you chose.

7   In the **PostalCode begins with** box, enter 880. Then click **OK** to filter the table and display only the records that match your criteria.

Customers								×
CustomerID ▼	FirstName ▼	LastName ▼	Address ▼	City ▼	Region ▼	PostalCode ▼	Cou ▲
⊞ KHAKA	Karan	Khanna	401 Rodeo Dr.	Auburn	WA	88001	USA
⊞ ACKPI	Pilar	Ackerman	8808 Backbay S	Bellevue	WA	88004	USA
⊞ TRASH	Shirleen H.	Travers	46 E. Orange St	Bellevue	WA	88004	USA
⊞ HOEHE	Helge	Hoeing	431 Freemont !	Bellevue	WA	88005	USA
⊞ NISCH	Chad	Niswonger	3300 Colorado	Bellevue	WA	88005	USA
⊞ HOLMI	Michael	Holm	4220 Main St.	Bellevue	WA	88006	USA
⊞ CORCE	Cecilia	Cornejo	778 Ancient Rd	Bellevue	WA	88007	USA
⊞ LANER	Eric	Lang	991 S. Mississip	Bothell	WA	88011	USA
⊞ HONQI	Qin	Hong	234 Samuel Pl.	Carnation	WA	88014	USA
⊞ ZIMKA	Karin	Zimprich	472 Lexington /	Carnation	WA	88014	USA
⊞ JIAST	Stephen Yuan	Jiang	7316 Taylor Lar	Duvall	WA	88019	USA
⊞ KELBO	Bob	Kelly	6 Cranbrook Hc	Duvall	WA	88019	USA
⊞ ZWIMI	Michael	Zwilling	76 Kings Way	Fall City	WA	88024	USA
⊞ KLISE	Sergey	Klimov	333 Baseline A'	Kenmore	WA	88028	USA
⊞ KIMSH	Shane	Kim	33 Hilo Loop SV	Kirkland	WA	88032	USA
⊞ REITS	Tsvi	Reiter	98 Bitter Creek	Kirkland	WA	88032	USA
⊞ HOUPE	Peter	Houston	11 Skyline Blvd	Kirkland	WA	88033	USA
⊞ MEYCH	Chris	Meyer	722 DaVinci Blv	Kirkland	WA	88033	USA

Record: I◄ ◄ 1 of 30 ► ►I ►* ▼ Filtered Search

Only the 30 records for customers who live in postal codes starting with 880 are displayed in the table.

8   In the **Sort & Filter** group, click the **Remove Filter** button to turn off the filter and display all the records.

Now let's display only the records of the customers who live outside of the United States.

9   In the **Country** field, right-click any instance of **USA**, and then click **Does Not Equal "USA"** to display the records of all the customers from countries other than the United States (in this case, only Canada).

TIP If the text you want to base this filter on is buried in a large table, you can quickly locate it by clicking the Find button in the Find group on the Home tab, entering the term you want in the Find What box in the Find And Replace dialog box, and clicking Find Next. Then right-click the found text to apply the filter.

10   Turn off the filter, and close the **Customers** table, clicking **No** when prompted to save your changes.

Finally, let's filter a different table to create a list of orders placed with a selected employee on or after a specified date.

11   Open the **Orders** table in **Datasheet** view.

12   In the **EmployeeID** field, right-click **Entin, Michael**, and then click **Equals "Entin, Michael"**.

13   With 19 records displayed in the filtered table, right-click **2/1/2012** in the **OrderDate** field, and then click **On or After 2/1/2012** to find the six records that meet this criterion.

> **TIP** To display a list of the available options for date filters, right-click any cell in the OrderDate field, and then point to Date Filters.

14   Close the **Orders** table, clicking **No** when prompted to save the table layout.

 CLEAN UP Keep the GardenCompany04 database open for use in later exercises.

Filtering information by using forms

When you want to filter a table based on the information in several fields, the quickest method is to use the Filter By Form command, which is available from the Advanced Filter Options list in the Sort & Filter group on the Home tab. If you choose this command when a table is active, Access displays a filter form that resembles a datasheet. Each of the cells in the form has an associated list of all the unique values in that field in the underlying table.

CustomerID	FirstName	LastName	Address	City	Region	PostalCode	Country

Aloha
Arlington
Auburn
Beaverton
Bellevue
Bellingham
Boise
Bothell
Burns
Butte
Carmel Valle
Carnation
Clinton
Duvall
Elgin
Escondido

Look for Or

In the filter form for a table, clicking the cell below a field name displays an arrow that you can use to display a list of that field's unique values.

For each field, you can select a value from the list or enter a value. When you have finished defining the filter values, click the Apply Filter button to display only the records that contain the specified values.

Using Filter By Form on a table that has only a few fields, such as the one shown in the preceding graphic, is easy. But using it on a table that has a few dozen fields can be cumbersome, and it is often simpler to find information in the form version of the table. Using Filter By Form on a form replaces the form with its Filter By Form version, which has a blank box for each field.

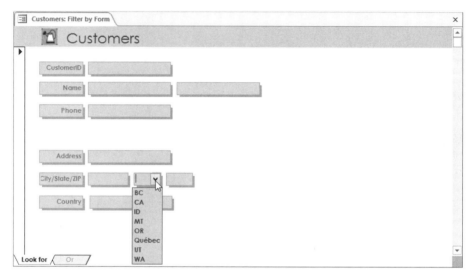

In the filter form for a form, clicking a text box displays an arrow that you can use to display a list of that field's unique values.

In any field, you can select filtering criteria from the field's associated list of unique values, or you can enter the criteria you want. If you know only part of the value you are looking for, you can use the asterisk wildcard character to represent the character or string of characters you don't know. For example, to filter out all the records with *Philip*, *Philips*, *Phillip*, or *Phillips* in the LastName field, you can enter *Phil**. Access then converts your entry to *Like "Phil*"*, which is the correct format, called the *syntax*, for this type of criterion.

SEE ALSO For information about wildcards, see the sidebar "Wildcards" following this topic.

If you want to enter alternative criteria to those you entered on the Look For page of the filter form, use the Or page. Clicking the Or tab at the bottom of the form displays another form with blank fields so that you can enter alternatives for the same fields.

When you display the Or page, a second Or tab appears so that you can include a third criterion for the same field if you want.

After you have applied the filter, you can click the buttons on the record navigation bar at the bottom of the filter form to move among the matched records in the usual way.

In this exercise, you'll filter a form by using the Filter By Form command.

SET UP You need the GardenCompany04 database you worked with in the preceding exercise to complete this exercise. If necessary, open the database. Then follow the steps.

1 In the **Navigation** pane, in the **Forms** group, double-click **Customers** to open the **Customers** form in **Form** view.

2 On the **Home** tab, in the **Sort & Filter** group, click the **Advanced Filter Options** button, and then in the list, click **Filter By Form** to replace the form with its filter version.

3 Click the second text box to the right of the **Name** label (the box that normally displays the customer's last name), enter s*, and then press the **Enter** key to replace the entry with its correct syntax, **Like "s*"**.

4 In the **Sort & Filter** group, click the **Apply Filter** button to toggle the filter on and display the first record that has a **LastName** value starting with **S**.

The record navigation bar shows that six records match the filter criterion.

Now let's add a second criterion that filters out only the records that have a Region value of CA.

5   Click the **Advanced Filter Options** button and then click **Filter By Form** to redisplay the filter form, which still contains the current filter criterion.

>   **TIP** No matter what method you use to enter filter criteria, the criteria are saved as a form property and are available until they are replaced by other criteria.

6   Click the second box to the right of the **City/State/ZIP** label (the box that normally displays the state or region), click the arrow that appears, and then in the list, click **CA**.

Only records matching both of the criteria will be displayed.

7   Click the **Apply Filter** button to display the first of three records that have both a **Region** value of **CA** *and* **LastName** values starting with **S**.

Next let's enter alternative filtering criteria.

8   Switch back to the filter form, and at the bottom of the form page, click the **Or** tab.

9   Enter s* in the second **Name** box, and click **WA** in the list for the second **City/State/ZIP** box.

10 Click the **Apply Filter** button to find and display records that have either a **Region** value of **CA** *and* **LastName** values starting with **S**, *or* a **Region** value of **WA** *and* **LastName** values starting with **S**.

11   Use the record navigation bar to view the six records in the filtered **Customers** form.

12   Click the **Remove Filter** button to turn off the filter. Then close the form.

❌ CLEAN UP Keep the GardenCompany04 database open for use in the last exercise.

Wildcards

If you want to filter a table to display records containing certain information but you aren't sure of all the characters, or if you want your filter to match variations of a base set of characters, include wildcard characters in your filter criteria. The most common wildcards are the following:

- ***** The asterisk represents any number of characters. For example, filtering the LastName field on *Co** returns records containing *Colman* and *Conroy*.

- **?** The question mark represents any single alphabetic character. For example, filtering the FirstName field on *Er??* returns records containing *Eric* and *Erma*.

- **#** The number sign represents any single numeric character. For example, filtering the ID field on *1##* returns any ID from *100* through *199*.

TIP Access supports several other wildcards. For more information, search for *wildcards* in Access Help.

When searching for information in a Short Text or Long Text field, you can also use the Contains text filter to locate records containing words or character strings.

Locating information that matches multiple criteria

As long as your filter criteria are fairly simple, filtering is a quick and easy way to narrow down the amount of information displayed in a table or to locate information that matches what you are looking for. But suppose you need to locate something more complex, such as all the orders shipped to Midwestern states between specific dates by either of two shippers. When you need to search a single table for records that meet multiple criteria, or when the criteria involve complex expressions, use the Advanced Filter/Sort command, available from the Advanced Filter Options list.

Choosing the Advanced Filter/Sort command displays the Query Designer, which you use to enter filtering criteria. As you'll discover, filters with multiple criteria are actually simple queries.

SEE ALSO For information about queries, see Chapter 7, "Create queries."

In this exercise, you'll filter a table to display the data for customers located in two states. Then you'll experiment with the Query Designer to better understand its filtering capabilities.

 SET UP You need the GardenCompany04 database you worked with in the preceding exercise to complete this exercise. If necessary, open the database. Then follow the steps.

1   In the **Navigation** pane, in the **Tables** group, double-click **Customers** to open the **Customers** table in **Datasheet** view.

2   On the **Home** tab, in the **Sort & Filter** group, click the **Advanced Filter Options** button, and then in the list, click **Advanced Filter/Sort** to display the **Query Designer** with the **Customers** field list in the top pane and a design grid in the bottom pane.

Clicking the Advanced Filter/Sort button displays the Query Designer.

3   In the **Customers** field list, double-click **LastName** to copy it to the **Field** row of the first column in the design grid.

4   In the **Criteria** row of the **LastName** field, enter s*, and then press **Enter**. Notice that because you have used the * wildcard, the criterion changes to **Like "s*"**.

Suppose we want this query to filter the table to display the records for only those customers with last names beginning with the letter *S* who live in California or Washington. Let's add the second criterion.

5   If necessary, scroll the field list box or enlarge it by dragging its bottom border downward. Then in the **Customers** field list, double-click **Region** to copy it to the **Field** row of the next available column in the design grid.

6   In the **Criteria** row of the **Region** field, enter ca or wa, and then press **Enter**. Notice that this entry changes to **"ca" Or "wa"**.

TIP If you want to find the records for customers who live in California or Oregon, you cannot enter *ca or or*, because Access treats *or* as a reserved word. You must enter *ca or "or"* in the Criteria row. Anytime you want to enter a criterion that will be interpreted as an instruction rather than a string of characters, enclose the characters in quotation marks to achieve the results you want.

Field:	LastName	Region			
Sort:					
Criteria:	Like "s*"	"ca" Or "wa"			
or:					

You have entered two criteria involving two fields in the design grid.

7   In the **Sort & Filter** group, click the **Apply Filter** button to display only the records that match the criteria.

	CustomerID	FirstName	LastName	Address	City	Region	PostalCode	Countr
⊞	SAMPR	Prasanna	Samarawickran	17331 Fairhave	Seattle	WA	88136	USA
⊞	SANPA	Patrick	Sands	98 N. Hyde St.	San Francisco	CA	84140	USA
⊞	SEIJO	Joachim	Seidler	9308 Dartridge	San Francisco	CA	84167	USA
⊞	SIMDA	David	Simpson	45 Park St.	San Jose	CA	85123	USA
⊞	SMIJE	Jeff	Smith	17 Wilken Rd.	La Conner	WA	88257	USA
⊞	SMISA	Samantha	Smith	74 S. Western E	Seattle	WA	88188	USA

Record: 14 ‹ 1 of 6 › ►I ►☰ ▼ Filtered Search

Six customers with last names beginning with S live in either California or Washington.

Now let's filter the table to display only the records for customers with last names beginning with the letter *S* or *B* who live in California or Washington.

8   Click the **CustomersFilter1** tab to switch to the filter page.

9   In the **or** row of the **LastName** field, enter **b***, and then press **Enter**.

Field:	LastName	Region				▲
Sort:						
Criteria:	Like "s*"	"ca" Or "wa"				
or:	Like "b*"					▼
	◄ ☐					►

You have entered two criteria involving two fields in the design grid.

10   In the **Sort & Filter** group, click the **Apply Filter** button to apply the filter to the **Customers** table. Then notice that the result includes records for all customers with last names that begin with **S** or **B**, but some of the **B** names live in **Montana** and **Oregon**.

11   Click the **CustomersFilter1** tab to switch to the filter page, and look carefully at the design grid.

The filter first works with the two criteria in the Criteria row and searches for customers with names beginning with *S* who live in California or Washington. Then it works with the criteria in the Or row and searches for customers with names beginning with *B*, regardless of where they live. To get the results we want, we need to repeat the criterion from the Region field in the Or row.

12   In the **or** row of the **Region** field, enter **ca or wa**, and then press **Enter**.

13   Apply the filter, which now correctly displays only the records for customers with last names beginning with **S** or **B** who are located in **California** or **Washington**.

14   Close the **Customers** table, clicking **Yes** when prompted to save changes to the design of the table.

❌ CLEAN UP Close the GardenCompany04 database.

Saving filters as queries

If a filter takes more than a few minutes to set up and you are likely to want to use it again, you might want to save it as a query. Then you can run the query to display the filtered results at any time.

To save a filter as a query:

1. On the **Home** tab, in the **Sort & Filter** group, click the **Advanced Filter Options** button and then click **Advanced Filter/Sort**.

2. In the **Sort & Filter** group, click the **Advanced Filter Options** button again, and then click **Save As Query**.

SEE ALSO For information about queries, see Chapter 7, "Create queries."

Key points

- You can sort a table in either ascending or descending order, based on the values in any field or field combination.

- You can filter a table so that information containing a combination of characters is displayed or excluded from the display.

- To further refine a search, apply another filter to the results of the previous one.

- The Filter By Form command filters a table or form based on the information in several fields.

- To search a single table for records that meet multiple criteria, use the Advanced Filter/Sort command.

Chapter at a glance

Create

Create reports by using a wizard,
page 136

Modify

Modify report design,
page 142

Preview

Preview and print reports,
page 150

Create simple reports

5

IN THIS CHAPTER, YOU WILL LEARN HOW TO

- Create reports by using a wizard.

- Modify report design.

- Preview and print reports.

Like forms, reports give people easy access to the information stored in a database. However, there are several differences between forms and reports, including the following:

- Forms are used to view, enter, and edit information. Reports are used only to view information.

- Forms are usually displayed on the screen. Reports can be previewed on the screen, but they are usually printed.

- Forms generally provide a detailed look at records, and they are usually for people who actually work with the database. Reports are often used to group and summarize data, and they are often for people who don't work with the database but who use the information stored in the database for other business tasks.

Reports usually present summaries of larger bodies of information. For example, your database might hold detailed information about thousands of orders. If you want to edit those orders or enter new ones, you can do so directly in the table or through a form. If you want to summarize those orders to illustrate the rate of growth of the company's sales, you generate a report.

Like a book report or an annual report of an organization's activities, a report created in Microsoft Access 2013 is typically used to summarize and organize information to express a particular point of view to a specific audience. When you are designing a report, it is important to consider the point you are trying to make, the intended audience, and the level of information they will need.

In this chapter, you'll create a report by using a wizard. After modifying the layout and content of the report, you'll preview how it will look when printed.

Creating reports by using a wizard

You can divide the content of an Access report into two general categories: information derived from records in one or more tables, and everything else. The *everything else* category includes the title, page headers and footers, introductory and explanatory text, and any logos and other graphics.

Just as you can create a form that includes all the fields in a table by using the Form tool, you can create a report that includes all the fields by using the Report tool, which is located in the Reports group on the Create tab. But such a report is merely a prettier version of the table, and it does not summarize the data in any meaningful way. You are more likely to want to create a report based on only some of the fields in the table, and that is a job for the Report wizard.

TIP In addition to basing a report on a table, you can base it on the datasheet created when you run a query. For information about queries, see Chapter 7, "Create queries."

The Report wizard leads you through a series of questions and then creates a report based on your answers. So the first step in creating a report is to consider the end result you want and what information you need to include in the report to achieve that result. After you provide that information, the wizard creates a simple report layout and adds a text box control and its associated label control for each field you specify.

For example, you might want to use a Products table as the basis for a report that groups products by category. When you give the grouping instruction to the wizard, it first sorts the table based on the category, and then sorts the products in each category. In the space at the top of each group (called the *group header*), the wizard inserts the name of the category.

In this exercise, you'll use the Report wizard to create a simple report that displays an alphabetical list of products.

SET UP You need the GardenCompany05 database located in the Chapter05 practice file folder to complete this exercise. Be sure to use the practice database for this chapter rather than continuing on with the database from an earlier chapter. Open the database, and if you want, save your own version to avoid overwriting the original. Then follow the steps.

1 With **All Access Objects** displayed in the **Navigation** pane, in the **Tables** group, click (don't double-click) **Categories**.

2 On the **Create** tab, in the **Reports** group, click the **Report** button to create a report based on all the fields in the **Categories** table and display it in **Layout** view.

Category ID	Category Name	Description
1	Bulbs	Spring, summer and fall, forced
2	Cacti	Indoor cactus plants
3	Ground covers	Herbaceous perennials, evergreen and deciduous shrubs, ivy, vines, mosses
4	Grasses	Lawn grasses for cool climates
5	Flowers	A wide variety of flowers
6	Wetland plants	Plants suitable for water gardens and bogs
7	Soils/sand	Potting soils, peat moss, mulch, bark
8	Fertilizers	A variety of fertilizers

By using the Report tool, you can create a report that contains all the fields in the table.

3 This is not the report we want, so close the **Categories** report, clicking **No** when prompted to save it.

4 On the **Create** tab, in the **Reports** group, click the **Report Wizard** button to start the wizard.

Because the Categories table was still selected in the Navigation pane, that table is specified in the wizard's Tables/Queries box and its fields are listed in the Available Fields box. Let's tell the wizard that we want to base this report on the Products table instead.

5   Display the **Tables/Queries** list, and then click **Table: Products** to list that table's fields in the **Available Fields** box.

On the first page of the Report wizard, you can specify the table you want to work with.

6   In the **Available Fields** list, double-click **ProductName**, **QuantityPerUnit**, and **UnitsInStock** to move them to the **Selected Fields** box.

TIP Fields appear in a report in the order in which they appear in the Selected Fields list. You can save yourself the effort of rearranging the fields in the report by entering them in the desired order in the wizard.

7   At the bottom of the page, click **Next**.

The wizard asks whether you want to group the records. When you group by a field, the report inserts a group header at the top of each group of records that have the same value in that field. Let's specify that we want the products grouped by the first letter of their names.

8   In the field list on the left, double-click **ProductName** to move that field into the group header area of the box on the right.

9   In the lower-left corner of the page, click **Grouping Options** to open the **Grouping Intervals** dialog box.

Grouping Intervals

What grouping intervals do you want for group-level fields?

Group-level fields:	Grouping intervals:
ProductName	Normal ⌄

OK

Cancel

You can refine the grouping specification in the Grouping Intervals dialog box.

10   In the **Grouping intervals** list, click **1st Letter**, and then click **OK**.

Report Wizard

Do you want to add any grouping levels?

ProductName by 1st Letter

ProductName, QuantityPerUnit, UnitsInStock

ProductName
QuantityPerUnit
UnitsInStock

>
<

Priority

Grouping Options ...   Cancel   < Back   Next >   Finish

The types of grouping intervals available vary depending on the data type of the field by which you are grouping records.

11   Click **Next** to move to a page on which you can sort and summarize the grouped records.

You can sort by up to four fields, each in ascending or descending order.

TIP For any field that contains numeric information, you can click Summary Options near the bottom of the wizard page to display the Summary Options dialog box, in which you can instruct Access to insert a group footer in the report and to display the sum, average, minimum, or maximum value for the field. The only numeric field in this report is UnitsInStock, and it is not appropriate to summarize that field.

12   Click the arrow to the right of the **1** box to display a list of fields, and click **ProductName**. Then click **Next**.

The wizard asks which of three layouts and which orientation you want for this report. Let's set this report up in outline format.

13   In the **Layout** area, click each option in turn to display a preview in the report thumbnail to the left.

14   When you have finished exploring, click **Outline**.

The preview on the left shows the effect of the options on the right.

15 With **Portrait** selected in the **Orientation** area and the **Adjust the field width so all fields fit on a page** check box selected, click **Next**.

By default, the report will have the same title as the table on which it is based.

Let's give this report a title that easily conveys its content.

16   In the title box, enter Alphabetical List of Products, and then with **Preview the report** selected, click **Finish** to create the report and display it in **Print Preview**.

You can use the scroll bar and page navigation bar to preview the report.

17   Page through the nine-page report, noticing how it is arranged. Then close it.

✖ CLEAN UP Keep the GardenCompany05 database open for use in later exercises.

Modifying report design

You can use the Report wizard to get a quick start on a report, but you will frequently want to modify the report to obtain the result you need. As with forms, the report consists of text box controls that are bound to the corresponding fields in the underlying table and their associated labels. You can add labels, text boxes, images, and other controls, and you can format them, either by using commands on the ribbon or by setting their properties in the Property Sheet pane.

TIP For reports, the Property Sheet pane works the same way as it does for forms. For information, see "Formatting forms" in Chapter 3, "Create simple forms."

You can adjust the layout and content of reports in either Layout view or Design view. For simple adjustments, it is easier to work in Layout view so that you can view the layout with live data, making the process more intuitive.

SEE ALSO For information about creating and modifying reports in Design view, see Chapter 9, "Create custom reports."

TIP Automatic error checking identifies common errors in forms and reports and gives you a chance to fix them. For example, Access informs you if a report is wider than the page it will be printed on. Error checking is turned on by default. If you want to turn it off, display the Backstage view, and click Options to open the Access Options dialog box. In the left pane, click Object Designers, clear the error-checking check boxes at the bottom of the page, and then click OK.

5

In this exercise, you'll modify the layout of a report. You'll then apply a theme, change some of the colors, and dress up the text by using character formatting. You will also apply a simple rule that formats values differently if they meet a specific criterion.

→ SET UP **You need the GardenCompany05 database you worked with in the preceding exercise to complete this exercise. If necessary, open the database. Then follow the steps.**

1 In the **Navigation** pane, in the **Reports** group, open the **Alphabetical List of Products** report in **Print Preview**.

2 With the program window maximized, point to the previewed report page. Notice that the pointer changes to a magnifying glass with a plus sign in it, indicating that you can magnify the page

   TIP You can also zoom in and out by dragging the Zoom slider at the right end of the status bar. The current zoom level appears to the right of the slider.

Alphabetical List of Products		
ProductName by 1st A		
Product Name	Quantity Per Unit	Units In Stock
Ambrosia	6 - 2" pots	16
American Pitcher Plant	1 ea.	4
Anacharis	1 ea.	2
Anemone	One dozen	26
Animal repellent	1 qt.	3
Animal trap	1 ea.	2
Anise	6 - 2" pots	20
Austrian Copper	Per plant	7
Austrian Pine	One gal container	10
Autumn Crocus	One dozen	37
ProductName by 1st B		
Product Name	Quantity Per Unit	Units In Stock
Baby's Breath	1 ea.	23
Bat box	1 box per kit	12
Beautybush	1 ea.	2
Beebalm	1 ea.	14
Begonias	6 per pkg.	12
Beneficial nematodes	1 pt.	4
Blackberries	8 starts per pkg	18
Bladderwort	1 ea.	6
Bladderwort	One 3" starter	5
Blood meal	3 lbs.	14
Bone meal	5 lbs.	12
Bonsai mixed garden	1 ea.	0

Sunday, November 18, 2012   Page 1 of 9

In Print Preview, the magnifying glass pointer indicates that you can zoom in on the page.

3   Click the previewed page once to zoom in.

Notice that the report has the following design problems:

- Extraneous text

- Spacey arrangement

- Uninviting formatting

Let's fix these problems.

4   Switch to **Layout** view, and if the **Field List** pane opens, close it. Then on the **Design** tool tab, in the **Grouping & Totals** group, click the **Hide Details** button. Notice that the controls that are bound to fields in the **Products** table are now hidden so that you can concentrate on the group header controls.

5   Below the title, click **ProductName by 1s**, and press the **Delete** key to remove that
    label from all the group headers.

6   Click the control containing **A**, and drag it to the left edge of the header. Notice that
    when you release the mouse button, all the corresponding controls move to the
    corresponding location in their own group headers.

    KEYBOARD SHORTCUT Press the Arrow keys to move the selected control in small
    increments. When the shadow box is positioned where you want it, click away from
    the control. For a list of keyboard shortcuts, see "Keyboard shortcuts" at the end of
    this book.

7   Point to the right border of the selected **A** control, and when the pointer changes to
    a double-headed arrow, drag to the left until the control is just big enough to hold
    its contents. Notice that this action changes the size of all the corresponding controls.

It is easier to work with the controls in the group header when the report details are hidden.

Let's consolidate the controls in the group header so that they require less room.

8   With the **A** control still selected, hold down the **Ctrl** key, and in turn, click the
    Product Name, **Quantity Per Unit**, and **Units In Stock** label controls to add them to
    the selection.

9   On the **Design** tab, in the **Tools** group, click the **Property Sheet** button to open the
    Property Sheet pane.

Property Sheet				▼ ✕

Selection type: Multiple selection

Format	Data	Event	Other	All

Visible	Yes
Width	
Height	
Top	
Left	
Back Style	
Back Color	Background 1
Border Style	Transparent
Border Width	Hairline
Border Color	
Special Effect	Flat
Font Name	Century Gothic (E
Font Size	11
Text Align	
Font Weight	Normal
Font Underline	No
Font Italic	No
Fore Color	
Line Spacing	0"
Hyperlink Target	
Gridline Style Top	Transparent
Gridline Style Bottom	
Gridline Style Left	Transparent
Gridline Style Right	Transparent
Gridline Width Top	1 pt
Gridline Width Bottom	1 pt
Gridline Width Left	1 pt
Gridline Width Right	1 pt
Top Margin	0"

Because more than one control is selected, the Selection Type in the Property Sheet pane is Multiple Selection.

10 On the **Format** page of the **Property Sheet** pane, in the **Top** property box, enter **0.25"** and press the **Enter** key to align the controls a quarter inch from the top of the group header. Then close the **Property Sheet** pane.

11 To view how the group header looks with its data, in the **Grouping & Totals** group, click the **Hide Details** button to turn it off.

The numbers in the Units In Stock column are right-aligned. Let's center them.

12 Click the first text box control in the **Units In Stock** column, and on the **Format** tool tab, in the **Font** group, click the **Center** button.

Now let's add some color and format the text.

13   On the **Design** tool tab, in the **Themes** group, click the **Themes** button, and in the gallery, click the **Whisp** thumbnail.

    TIP Although nothing much appears to change, the report has taken on the color scheme and font scheme assigned to the selected theme.

14   Inside the shaded area of the report header, but away from the title, click a blank area. On the **Format** tool tab, in the **Control Formatting** group, click the **Shape Fill** button. Then in the **Theme Colors** palette, click the third swatch in the third column row (**Light Green, Background 2, Darker 25%**).

    By default, alternate group headers are a different color, which confuses rather than clarifies the report structure. Let's turn off this alternate row color.

15   Click outside the dotted border to the left of the first group header. In the **Background** group, click the **Alternate Row Color** arrow, and in the menu, below the palettes, click **No Color**.

16   In the **Control Formatting** group, click the **Shape Fill** button, and in the **Theme Colors** palette, click a light orange color. (We chose the third swatch in the sixth column: **Orange, Accent 2, Lighter 60%**.)

    TIP The entire group header is shaded except the alphabet controls (A, B, C, and so on) that you moved earlier. If you want them to be shaded, select one of them and repeat step 16 to apply the light orange fill.

17   Click outside the dotted border to the left of the first row of data in the report, and remove the alternate row color of the data rows. Then click the white space above the report header to verify that only the backgrounds of the report header and group headers are now colored.

    TIP In Layout view, the only places you can click that don't select at least one object are above the first object and below the last object.

Removing the alternate row color makes the structure of this report more obvious.

Next let's format the text in the controls. It is usually most efficient to change the character formatting of all the controls and then adjust the ones you want to be different.

18   Click any control, and then on the **Format** tool tab, in the **Selection** group, click the **Select All** button.

KEYBOARD SHORTCUT Press Ctrl+A to select all the controls.

19   In the **Font** group, click the **Font Size** arrow, and then click **9**.

20   Click the report's title control, and then use the commands in the **Font** group to make the text **24** points, **Bold**, and dark green. (We chose the fifth swatch in the ninth column, **Olive Green, Accent 5, Darker 25%**.)

21   Select the controls in the group header, and make them bold and dark green.

22   Scroll the report, noticing that a few of the values in the **Units In Stock** column are **0**.

Let's make zero values bold and red so that they stand out in the report and alert buyers that it is time to order more of these products.

23   Click any control in the **Units In Stock** column. Then in the **Control Formatting** group, click the **Conditional Formatting** button to open the **Conditional Formatting Rules Manager**.

24   Click **New Rule** to open the **New Formatting Rule** dialog box.

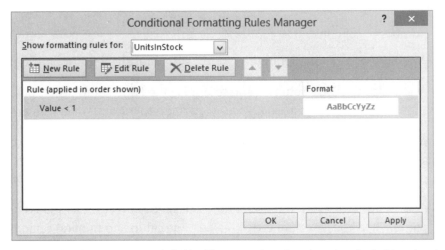

You can create rules that compare the current field value to a specific value or to other values in the same field.

25   With **Check values in the current record or use an expression** selected as the rule type, in the **Format only cells where the** area, click the arrow for the second box, and click **less than**. Then in the third box, enter **1**.

26   In the **Preview** area, click the **Bold** button, and change the **Font color** setting to red. Then click **OK**.

This rule for the Units In Stock field will cause values less than 1 to be bold and red.

27   Click **OK**. Then switch to **Report** view, and scroll down the report.

28   Close the report, clicking **Yes** to save your changes to its design.

❌ CLEAN UP Keep the GardenCompany05 database open for use in the last exercise.

Previewing and printing reports

Using Print Preview to preview Access reports is very similar to using this view in other Microsoft Office 2013 programs. If you preview your reports carefully, you won't have any major surprises when you print them.

When previewing reports, you will want to pay special attention to how the pages break. In a grouped report, you can control whether group headings are allowed to appear at the bottom of a page with no data and whether groups are allowed to break across pages.

You can make changes to the setup of your report pages from the Page Setup tool tab in Layout view or from the tab displayed when you switch to Print Preview. For example, you can specify the following:

- Paper size

- Margins

- Orientation

- Number of columns

- Whether Access should print the report's structural elements or only its data

You can also click the Page Setup button to display the Page Setup dialog box, in which you can change all these settings in one place, in addition to making other refinements.

When you are ready to print, click the Print button on the Print Preview tab to display the Print dialog box. You can also display the Print page of the Backstage view and then print one copy of the report with the default print settings by clicking the Quick Print button.

In this exercise, you'll preview a report, and you'll specify that groups should not break across pages. Then you'll explore the available page setup and printing options.

SET UP You need the GardenCompany05 database you worked with in the preceding exercise to complete this exercise. If necessary, open the database. Then follow the steps.

1 In the **Navigation** pane, right-click the **Alphabetical List of Products** report, and then click **Print Preview.**

2 On the page navigation bar at the bottom of the window, click the **Next Page** button repeatedly to view the six pages of this report.

The group at the top of this page is a continuation of one that started on the previous page.

Several of the groups start on one page and continue on the next page. For readability, let's fix this layout problem.

3 Switch to **Layout** view, and then on the **Design** tool tab, in the **Grouping & Totals** group, click the **Group & Sort** button to open the **Group, Sort, and Total** pane.

4   In the **Group, Sort, and Total** pane, in the **Group on** bar, click **More** to display additional layout options.

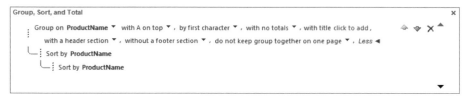

In the Group On area, you can verify the current grouping settings.

5   Click the **do not keep group together on one page** arrow, and in the list, click **keep whole group together on one page**. Then close the **Group, Sort, and Total** pane by clicking the **Group & Sort** button again.

6   Switch to **Print Preview**, and page through the report, noticing that groups are no longer broken across pages.

Let's make the top, left, and right margins wider.

7   On the **Print Preview** tab, in the **Page Layout** group, click the **Page Setup** button to open the **Page Setup** dialog box.

You can set margins on the Print Options page of the Page Setup dialog box.

8   Click the **Page** tab, and verify that the paper size is **Letter**.

9   Return to the **Print Options** page, and change the **Top**, **Left**, and **Right** margins to **0.75**. Then click **OK**.

10 Scroll through the report to examine the results.

Although all the data in the report fits on the page, the page number in the footer is set too far to the right. Let's move the page number control so that it no longer produces extra pages.

11 Switch to **Layout** view, scroll down to the bottom of the report, and then scroll to the right until the page number appears.

12 Click the page number control, and move and resize it so that it aligns approximately with the **Units In Stock** column heading. Then click below the report footer to release the selection.

Alphabetical List of Products			
Tree & shrub fertilizer spikes	12 per pkg.	16	
Tree fertilizer	1 gal.	6	
Tree pruners	1 ea.	8	
V Product Name	Quantity Per Unit	Units In Stock	
Venus Flytrap	1 ea.	8	
W Product Name	Quantity Per Unit	Units In Stock	
Water Milfoil	1 ea.	5	
Water Snowflakes	1 ea.	5	
Watering can 3-gal	1 ea.	15	
Weed whacker	1 ea.	5	
Weeping Forsythia	1 ea.	3	
Wheelbarrow	1 ea.	12	
White Poplar	Per 6-18" sappling	8	
Winterberry	1 ea.	4	
Sunday, November 18, 2012		Page 1 of 1	

By adjusting the position of the page number, you can eliminate the extra pages in the report.

13   Switch to **Print Preview**, and page through the report, which now fits neatly on seven pages.

14   If you want, print the report by using the same techniques you would use to print any database object.

15   Close the report, clicking **Yes** to save your changes.

❌ CLEAN UP   Close the GardenCompany05 database.

Key points

- When designing a report, consider the point you are trying to make, the intended audience, and the level of detail needed.

- You can create a report that displays only some of the fields in a table by using the Report wizard. The report can be sorted and grouped to summarize the data in a meaningful way.

- In Layout view, you can refine a report by manipulating its controls and setting its properties. You can also format the controls to structure and highlight data.

- In Print Preview, you can preview how the report will look when printed and make adjustments before you print.

Relational database techniques

Chapter at a glance

Specify

Specify the type of data,
page 158

Restrict

Restrict the format of data,
page 165

Validate

Validate the data,
page 173

Allow

Allow only values in lists,
page 183

Maintain data integrity 6

IN THIS CHAPTER, YOU WILL LEARN HOW TO

- Specify the type of data.

- Set the field size.

- Restrict the format of data.

- Validate the data.

- Allow only values in lists.

- Allow only values in other tables.

Depending on how organized you are, you might compare a database to a file cabinet into which you toss items such as bills, receipts, statements, and a variety of other paperwork for later retrieval. The cabinet does not restrict what items you can place in it (unless they are simply too big to physically fit) or impose any order on the items. It is up to you to decide what you store there and to organize it so that you can find it the next time you need it.

When you create a database by using Microsoft Access 2013, you can set properties that restrict what data can be entered and you can impose a structure on the data to help you keep the database organized and useful. For example, you can prevent employees from entering text in a Price field, and you can require a simple "yes" or "no" answer in a Signature Required field.

In this chapter, you'll restrict the type, amount, and format of data allowed in a field. You'll create validation rules that accept only data that meets specific criteria. You'll also use lookup lists and lookup fields to limit the possible values allowed in a field.

PRACTICE FILES To complete the exercises in this chapter, you need the practice file contained in the Chapter06 practice file folder. For more information, see "Download the practice files" in this book's Introduction.

Specifying the type of data

You learned in Chapter 2, "Create databases and simple tables," that a field's data type restricts entries in that field to a specific type of data. For example, if the data type is set to Number and you try to enter text, Access refuses the entry and displays a warning.

When setting the data type of a field in a table in Design view, you can choose from the following types:

- **Short Text** Use for text fields that require up to 255 alphanumeric characters.

- **Long Text** Use for text fields that require up to 65,535 alphanumeric characters.

   TIP When adding fields in Datasheet view, you can assign the Rich Text data type to fields that require up to 65,535 alphanumeric characters with character formatting. This is actually the Long Text data type with the Text Format property set to Rich Text instead of Plain Text.

- **Number** Use for numeric values. The size of the entry is controlled by the Field Size property.

   SEE ALSO For information about the possible settings for Number fields, see "Setting the field size" later in this chapter.

- **Date/Time** Use for dates in the years from 100 through 9999. Dates and times can be expressed in a variety of formats.

- **Currency** Use for decimal values with up to 15 digits to the left of the decimal point and up to 4 digits to the right.

- **AutoNumber** Use when you want Access to assign a unique number to each new record. If you delete a record, its AutoNumber value is not reused, and remaining records are not updated.

- **Yes/No** Use for fields that can have only two possible mutually exclusive values, such as True or False.

   TIP In the database world, the Yes/No data type is more commonly called *Boolean*, in honor of George Boole, an early mathematician and logistician.

- **OLE Object** Use to hold a graphic or object such as a Microsoft Excel worksheet or Microsoft Word document.

- **Hyperlink** Use to hold a clickable path to a folder on your hard disk, a network location, or a website.

- **Attachment** Use to attach a file to a record in the same way that you might attach a file to an email message.

  TIP The Attachment data type can be assigned to a field only when the field is first created. You can't assign the Attachment type to an existing field, nor can you change an Attachment field to another data type. For information about the Attachment data type, search for *Attach files and graphics to the records in your database* in Access Help.

- **Calculated** Use to hold the results of a calculation based on other fields in the same table.

  TIP The last option in the list displayed when you click the Data Type arrow in Design view is Lookup Wizard. For information about using this wizard, see "Allowing only values in lists" later in this chapter.

You can also click the More Fields button in the Add & Delete group on the Fields tool tab to display a menu containing a list of data types with predefined properties that produce fields with common data type refinements.

In this exercise, you'll use various methods to add fields of the most common data types to a table. Then you'll enter data to test the data type restrictions.

SET UP You need the GardenCompany06 database located in the Chapter06 practice file folder to complete this exercise. Be sure to use the practice database for this chapter rather than continuing on with the database from an earlier chapter. Open the database, and if you want, save your own version to avoid overwriting the original. Then follow the steps.

1   On the **Create** tab, in the **Tables** group, click the **Table** button to start a new blank table with an **ID** field that has been assigned the **AutoNumber** data type.

    Let's add five fields with specific data types.

2   On the **Fields** tool tab, in the **Add & Delete** group, click the **Short Text** button. Then change the selected field name to fShortText.

    TIP If you use the name of a data type as the name of a field, Access warns you that the name might cause problems. We will identify all the fields in this table by their data type, preceded by the letter *f*.

3   Display the **Click to Add** list, click **Currency**, and then change the field name to fMoney.

4   In the **Add & Delete** group, click the **More Fields** button to display a menu containing a list of data types, some with refinements.

Clicking an option in the list sets the data type and any predefined property settings.

TIP At the bottom of the data types list is a group of Quick Start options that provide ready-made fields for common business tables. Clicking some Quick Start options, such as Address, inserts more than one field with the appropriate properties already set.

5   In the **Number** area of the list, click **Standard**. Then change the field name to fNumber.

6 Display the **More Fields** menu, click **Medium Date** in the **Date and Time** area of the list, and change the field name to **fDate**. Then display the menu again, click **Check Box** in the **Yes/No** area, and name the field **fBoolean**.

ID	fShortText	fMoney	fNumber	fDate	fBoolean	Click to Add
✱ (New)		$0.00	0.00		☐	

Clicking the check box in the fBoolean field will indicate a Yes or True entry.

7 Save the table with the name **FieldTest**.

KEYBOARD SHORTCUT Press Ctrl+S to display the Save As dialog box. For a list of keyboard shortcuts, see "Keyboard shortcuts" at the end of this book.

8 Switch to **Design** view.

9 In turn, click each entry in the **Field Name** column at the top of the design page, noticing the setting in the **Data Type** column and the property settings in the **Field Properties** area. In particular, notice that the **Default Value** property of the **fMoney** and **fNumber** fields is set to **0**.

Now let's examine how the data type restricts what you can enter in a field.

10 Switch back to **Datasheet** view. Then in the **fShortText** field of the first record, enter **This entry is 32 characters long** (don't add ending punctuation).

11 In the **fMoney** field, replace **$0.00** with the word **currency**, and then press the **Tab** key.

ID	fShortText	fMoney	fNumber	fDate	fBoolean	Click to Add
1 This entry ! ▾		currency	0.00		☐	
✱ (New)						

The value you entered does not match the Currency data type in this column.

Enter new value.

Convert the data in this column to the Text data type.

Help with data types and formats.

When you press Tab, Access blocks the entry, explaining that it is the wrong data type and providing options for fixing the error.

12 In the list, click **Enter new value**. Then enter −45.3456, and press **Tab**.

TIP Access stores the number the way you entered it but displays ($45.35), the default format for negative currency numbers. Your currency symbol might be different—for example, it might be the pound, peso, or euro symbol—because Access uses your computer's region and language settings to determine the display format for date, time, currency, and other numbers. If you want the symbol to remain the same no matter what the region and language settings, you can create a custom format to ensure that currency values always display a specific symbol. For information about custom formats, see the sidebar "Creating custom formats" later in this chapter.

13   In the **fNumber** field, enter Five hundred, and then press **Tab**.

14   When Access displays a message that it cannot accept this type of entry in this field, click **Enter new value** in the list of options, enter 500, and press **Tab**.

15   In the **fDate** cell, enter 123456, and press **Tab**.

16   When Access blocks the entry, click the **Calendar** button to the right of the field, and click **Today** to insert today's date. Then press **Tab**.

TIP All Date/Time fields come with an associated interactive calendar. Using the Calendar button to insert a date works well if the date you want is close to the current date. (You can click the arrows at either end of the title bar to display the previous or next month.) However, for distant dates such as birthdates, it is easier to ignore the Calendar button and enter the date. Access accepts almost any entry that can be recognized as a date and displays it in the format you specified when you created the field. If you enter a month and day but no year in a Date/Time field, Access assumes the date is in the current year. If you enter a month, day, and two-digit year from 00 through 29, Access assumes the year is 2000 through 2029. If you enter a two-digit year that is greater than 29, Access assumes you mean 1930 through 1999.

17   In the **fBoolean** field, try to enter abc and 123. Then click several times anywhere in the field to toggle the check box between the selected and cleared states, finishing with the field in the selected state.

ID	fShortText	fMoney	fNumber	fDate	fBoolean	Click to Add
1	This entry is 32	($45.35)	500.00	26-Nov-12	✔	
(New)		$0.00	0.00		☐	

The table, after entering the correct type of data in each field.

TIP Fields that have been assigned the Yes/No data type won't accept anything you enter; you can only switch between two predefined values. The stored value of a Yes/No field is always either 1 (Yes) or 0 (No). On the General page of the Field Properties area in Design view, you can set the Format property of the field to interpret the stored value as True/False, Yes/No, or On/Off. On the Lookup page, you can set the field to display as a check box, text box, or combo box. (In a combo box, you can select from a list or enter an entry.)

18   Press **Tab** to complete the record.

❌ CLEAN UP **Close the FieldTest table. Keep the GardenCompany06 database open for use in later exercises.**

Setting the field size

In Chapter 2, "Create databases and simple tables," you changed the Field Size property of several Short Text fields. You entered the new sizes by making adjustments to the Field Size setting in the Properties group on the Fields tool tab and to the Field Size property in the Field Properties area in Design view. As you saw, changing the size of a Short Text field is a simple matter of estimating the largest number of characters that will be entered in the field, up to 255.

Like the Short Text data type, the AutoNumber and Number data types have an associated Field Size property that restricts the number of digits that can be entered in the field. Of the two, the Field Size property of the Number data type is the most complex. You can set Number fields to any of the sizes shown in the following table.

Size	Description
Byte	Whole numbers from 0 to 255
Integer	Whole numbers from −32,768 to 32,767
Long Integer	Whole numbers from −2,147,483,648 to 2,147,483,647 (the default)
Single	Numeric floating point values from -3.4×10 to the 38th to $+3.4 \times 10$ to the 38th
Double	Numeric floating point values from -1.797×10 to the 38th to $+1.797 \times 10$ to the 38th
Replication ID	Randomly generated numbers that are 16 bytes long
Decimal	Numbers from $-9.999... \times 10$ to the 27th to $+9.999... \times 10$ to the 27th

The Field Size property of AutoNumber fields can be set to either Long Integer (the default) or Replication ID.

By setting the Field Size property to the setting that allows the largest valid entry, you prevent the entry of invalid values. Access rejects any value that is below or above the size limits of the field when you try to move out of the field.

SEE ALSO For more information about field sizes, search for *Introduction to data types and field properties* on the Office.com website.

In this exercise, you'll change the Field Size property for two fields to examine the impact on data already in the table and on new data that you enter.

SET UP You need the GardenCompany06 database you worked with in the preceding exercise to complete this exercise. If necessary, open the database. Then display the FieldTest table in Datasheet view, and follow the steps.

1 Review the field values in the only record in the **FieldTest** table, and then switch to **Design** view.

2 Click anywhere in the **fShortText** row, and then in the **Field Properties** area, change the **Field Size** property from **255** to **18** to restrict the number of characters to that maximum.

3 Click anywhere in the **fNumber** row, click anywhere in the **Field Size** property, click the arrow that appears, and then in the list, click **Byte** to restrict the number of characters to the range 0 through 255 (inclusive).

4 Switch to **Datasheet** view, and click **Yes** when prompted to save the table. Access displays a warning that some data might be lost.

The table contains data that doesn't fit the new property settings.

5   Click **Yes** to acknowledge the risk, and click **Yes** again to accept the deletion of the contents of one field.

Now let's examine the impact of the field size changes on the fields.

6   Double-click the right border of the **fShortText** field to widen the column to fit its entry.

FieldTest							✕
ID ▾	fShortText ▾	fMoney ▾	fNumber ▾	fDate ▾	fBoolean ▾	Click to Add ▾	
1	This entry is 32 c	($45.35)		26-Nov-12	☑		
* (New)		$0.00	0.00		☐		

The fShortText value has been truncated, and the fNumber value has been deleted.

You entered 32 characters in the fShortText field. It can now hold only 18, so 14 characters have been permanently deleted. You entered 500 in the fNumber field. It can now hold only whole numbers from 0 through 255, so the value has been permanently deleted.

7   In the **fNumber** field, enter 2.5, and press **Tab**. Notice that Access rounds the value to the nearest whole number.

TIP Because you chose Standard when setting the data type for this field in the previous exercise, the whole number is displayed as 2.00.

✖ CLEAN UP Close the FieldTest table, saving your changes. Keep the Garden-Company06 database open for use in later exercises.

Restricting the format of data

Two properties control the appearance of information in database tables: the Format property and the Input Mask property. Both properties affect how information is displayed after it has been entered in a table, but the Input Mask property also serves an important function during data entry. As its name implies, when you use an input mask, anyone entering new records knows the format required for the field and how long the entry should be.

SEE ALSO For information about the Format property, see the sidebar "Creating custom formats" later in this chapter.

You can use the Input Mask property to control how data is entered in Short Text, Number, Date/Time, and Currency fields. For Short Text and Date/Time fields, an Input Mask wizard is available to help you apply several common, predefined masks. For Number and Currency fields, you have to know how to create a mask from scratch.

The Input Mask property has three sections, separated by semicolons. For example, the following mask is for a phone number:

!\(000") "000\-0000;1;#

The first section contains characters that are used as placeholders for the information to be entered, in addition to characters such as parentheses and hyphens. Together, all these characters control the appearance of the entry. The following table explains the purpose of the most common input mask characters.

Character	Description
0	Required digit (0 through 9).
9	Optional digit or space.
#	Optional digit or space; blank positions are converted to spaces; plus and minus signs are allowed.
L	Required letter (A through Z).
?	Optional letter (A through Z).
A	Required letter or digit.
a	Optional letter or digit.
&	Required character (any kind) or a space.
C	Optional character (any kind) or a space.
<	All characters that follow are converted to lowercase.
>	All characters that follow are converted to uppercase.
!	Characters entered into the mask fill it from left to right. You can include the exclamation point anywhere in the input mask.
\	Character that follows is displayed as a literal character.
"any text"	Characters enclosed in double quotation marks are treated as literal characters.

Any characters not included in this list are displayed the way you enter them and are known as *literal characters*. If you want to use one of the special characters in this list as a literal character, precede it with the \ (backslash) character.

The second and third sections of the input mask are optional. Including a 1 in the second section (or leaving it blank) tells Access to store only the characters entered; including a

0 tells Access to store both the characters entered and the literal characters. Entering a character in the third section causes Access to display that character as the placeholder for each of the characters to be entered; leaving it blank causes Access to display an underscore as the placeholder.

The input mask *!\(000") "000\-0000;1;#* creates this display in a field in either a table or a form:

(###) ###-####

In this example, the 0s in the first part of the mask restrict the entry to 10 digits—no more and no less. The database user does not enter the literal characters—the parentheses, space, and hyphen. The 1 in the second part tells Access to store only the 10 digits, not the literal characters. The # sign in the third part tells Access to use that character as the placeholder for the required 10 digits.

TIP An input mask can contain text in addition to placeholders for the data to be entered. For example, if you enter *The number is* in front of the phone number input mask, the default entry for the field is *The number is (###) ###-####*. The numbers you enter replace the # placeholders, not the text. The Field Size property does not apply to the literal characters in the mask, so if this property is set to 15, the entry will not be truncated even though the number of displayed characters (including spaces) is 28.

In this exercise, you'll use the Input Mask wizard to apply a predefined input mask for a phone number to a Short Text field. Then you'll modify the input mask to display the phone number in a slightly different way. Finally, in another field you'll create a custom mask that displays a text entry with an initial capital letter, no matter how it is actually entered.

→ SET UP You need the GardenCompany06 database you worked with in the preceding exercise to complete this exercise. If necessary, open the database. Then display the FieldTest table in Design view, and follow the steps.

1 Click the row selector for the **fShortText** field, and on the **Design** tool tab, in the **Tools** group, click the **Insert Rows** button.

2 Add a new field named **fPhone** that is assigned the **Short Text** data type. Then save the table.

   Now let's use the Input Mask wizard to create an input mask that shows the format expected for a phone number.

3 With the **fPhone** field still selected, in the **Field Properties** area, click anywhere in the **Input Mask** property.

4   Click the **Ellipsis** button to the right of the property to open the **Input Mask** wizard.

You can click the Try It box to display how the mask will look and then
enter a number to test how the mask behaves.

5   With **Phone Number** selected in the **Input Mask** column, click **Next**.

You can change the structure of the input mask and the placeholder character
that will indicate what to enter.

The barely visible exclamation point at the left end of the mask causes Access to fill the mask from left to right with whatever characters are entered. The parentheses and hyphen are characters that Access will insert in the specified places. The nines represent optional digits, and the zeros represent required digits. By using this combination, you can enter a phone number either with or without an area code.

TIP Because Access fills the mask from left to right, you need to press the Right Arrow key to move the insertion point past the first three placeholders to enter a phone number without an area code.

6   Change **999** to **000** to require an area code. Then display the **Placeholder character** list, click **#**, and click **Next**.

Input Mask Wizard

How do you want to store the data?

○ With the symbols in the mask, like this:

   (264) 316-8517

◉ Without the symbols in the mask, like this:

   4442315281

| Cancel | < Back | Next > | Finish |

If you store the symbols, they will always be included when the data is displayed in tables, forms, and reports. However, they take up space, meaning that your database will be larger.

7   Accept the default selection—to store the data without the symbols—by clicking **Finish**. (Clicking Next simply displays a page announcing that the wizard has all the information it needs to create the mask.)

General	Lookup	
Field Size	255	
Format		
Input Mask	!\(000") "000\-0000;;#	...
Caption		
Default Value		
Validation Rule		
Validation Text		
Required	No	
Allow Zero Length	Yes	
Indexed	No	
Unicode Compression	Yes	
IME Mode	No Control	
IME Sentence Mode	None	
Text Align	General	

The edited mask is inserted into the Input Mask property.

8   Press **Enter** to accept **!\(000")** "**000\-0000;;#** as the mask. Double quotation marks ensure that the closing parenthesis and following space are treated as literal characters. Two semicolons separate the mask into its three sections. Because you told Access to store data without the symbols, nothing is displayed in the second section of the mask.

Now let's test this input mask.

9   Save the table, and then switch to **Datasheet** view.

10   Click the **ID** field in the first record, and press the **Tab** key to move to the **fPhone** field. Then enter a series of 8 digits, and press **Tab**. Access displays a message that the entry is not in the correct format.

Garden Company	✕

    ⓘ   The value you entered isn't appropriate for the input mask '!\(000") "000\-0000;;#' specified for this field.

       [OK]   [Help]

    Was this information helpful?

The input mask requires 10, and only 10, digits.

11   Click **OK** to acknowledge the message. Then enter a series of 11 digits, and press **Tab**. Notice that Access formats the first 10 digits as a phone number and ignores the additional digit.

Now let's create an input mask that controls the case of text entries.

12   Switch to **Design** view, and click anywhere in the **fShortText** field.

13   In the **Field Properties** area, click the **Input Mask** property, enter the following, and then press **Enter**:

>L<????????????????? (16 question marks)

General	Lookup	
Field Size		18
Format		
Input Mask		>L<?????????????????
Caption		
Default Value		
Validation Rule		
Validation Text		
Required		No
Allow Zero Length		Yes
Indexed		No
Unicode Compression		Yes
IME Mode		No Control
IME Sentence Mode		None
Text Align		General

The Field Size setting must be greater than the maximum number of characters allowed by the input mask.

The greater than symbol (>) forces all following text to be uppercase. The *L* requires a letter. The less than symbol (<) forces all following text to be lowercase. Each question mark allows any letter or no letter. The total number of characters (17) is one fewer than the maximum number allowed in the field by this field's Field Size property (18).

TIP When you press Enter, the Property Update Options button appears. Clicking this button displays a list of options. In this case, the only options are to apply the input mask everywhere fShortText is used (which is called *propagating the field property*) and to display Access Help to find out more about this task. This button disappears when you edit any other property or move to a different field, so you can ignore it.

Let's test this input mask.

14   Save the table, and then switch to **Datasheet** view.

15   Delete the current entry in the **fShortText** field, enter smith, and press **Tab**.

16   Replace the entry with SMITH, and then with McDonald. Notice that regardless of how you enter the name, only its first letter is capitalized.

TIP You can create custom input masks and have the Input Mask wizard store them for future use. On the wizard's first page, click Edit List, and in the record navigation bar of the Customize Input Mask Wizard dialog box, click the New Record button. Then enter the information for the custom mask, and click Close.

❌ CLEAN UP Close the FieldTest table. Keep the GardenCompany06 database open for use in later exercises.

6

Creating custom formats

For all data types except AutoNumber, an arrow appears at the right end of the Format box when you click it. For some data types, clicking the arrow displays predefined Format property options. For example, clicking the arrow after selecting the Format box for a field assigned the Yes/No data type displays a list that includes the True/False, Yes/No, and On/Off formatting options, with their default values. Clicking the arrow after selecting the Format box for a field assigned the Date/Time data type displays a list of predefined date and time formats. However, a field assigned the Short Text data type has no default predefined formats.

You can construct custom Format properties to control the display of fields assigned the Short Text data type in much the same way you construct input masks. The following table describes the characters that are available.

Character	Description
@	Required character (can be blank).
&	Optional character.
!	Characters entered into the placeholder string fill it from left to right. You can include the exclamation point anywhere in the string.
<	All characters that follow are converted to lowercase.
>	All characters that follow are converted to uppercase.
*	Character that follows becomes a fill character.
\	Character that follows is displayed as a literal character.
"any text"	Characters enclosed in double quotation marks are treated as literal characters.
[color]	Applies a color to all characters in a section of the format. Can be black, blue, cyan, magenta, red, yellow, or white.

TIP Blank spaces; plus (+), minus (-), and financial symbols ($, £, ¥); and parentheses are recognized as literal characters without double quotation marks and can be placed anywhere in the format. Other common math symbols, such as slash (\ or /) and the asterisk (*), must be surrounded with double quotation marks.

To build a custom format:

1 With the table open in **Design** view, select the field you want to apply the custom format to.

2 In the **Field Properties** area, in the **Format** box, enter the format.

3 Switch to **Datasheet** view, saving the table.

Any existing data will be displayed according to the format. New data you enter will conform to the format when you leave the field. As an example, consider the following format:

> @".com";"no link"[red]

This format specifies two customizations separated by a semicolon. The part before the semicolon specifies what Access should do if characters are entered—in this case, append *.com*; and the part after the semicolon specifies what Access should do if the field is empty—in this case, display *no link* in red.

6

Validating the data

A validation rule precisely defines the information that will be accepted in one or several fields in a record. You might use a validation rule in a field containing the date an employee was hired to prevent a date in the future from being entered. Or if you deliver orders to only certain local areas, you might use a validation rule on the postal code field to refuse entries from other areas. You can create validation rules for all data types except AutoNumber, OLE Object, and Attachment.

In a table, you might want to create validation rules for individual fields or for entire records:

- **Field validation** At this level, Access uses the validation rule to test an entry when you attempt to leave the field.

- **Record validation** At this level, Access uses the rule to test the contents of more than one field when you attempt to leave the record.

If a field or record doesn't satisfy the rule, Access rejects the entry and displays a message explaining why.

TIP If you create a form by using one of the commands in the Form group on the Create tab, the form's controls inherit any validation rules set for the corresponding fields in the table on which the form is based. To prevent errors likely to be introduced by inexperienced users of the form, you can add more restrictive rules to the form's controls, in the same way you set rules for table fields. For information, search on *validation* in Access Help.

You create a validation rule by building an expression. In Access jargon, the term *expression* is synonymous with *formula*. It is a combination of operators, constants, functions, and identifiers that evaluates to a single value. Access builds a formula in the format $a=b+c$, where a is the result and $=b+c$ is the expression.

TIP In addition to using expressions as validation rules, you can use them to assign properties to tables or forms, to determine values in fields or reports, to define a set of conditions that a record must meet to be included in the result of a query, and so on. For information about queries, see Chapter 7, "Create queries."

The expression you use in a validation rule combines multiple criteria to define a set of conditions that a value in a field must meet in order to be a valid entry for that field. Multiple criteria are combined using logical, comparison, and arithmetic operators. Different types of expressions use different operators. The following are the most common operators:

- **Logical operators**
    - **And** Selects records that meet all the specified criteria
    - **Or** Selects records that meet at least one of the criteria
    - **Not** Selects records that don't match the criteria
- **Comparison operators**
    - **<** Less than
    - **>** Greater than
    - **=** Equal to

You can combine these basic operators to form the following:

- **<=** Less than or equal to

- **>=** Greater than or equal to

- **<>** Not equal to

The Like operator is sometimes grouped with the comparison operators and is used to test whether or not text matches a pattern.

- **Arithmetic operators**

    - **+** Add

    - **-** Subtract

    - ***** Multiply

    - **/** Divide

    A related operator, & (a text form of +) is used to concatenate (combine) two text strings.

You can enter validation rules in the Validation Rule property box by hand, or you can use a tool called the *Expression Builder* to create them. The Expression Builder isn't a wizard; it doesn't lead you through the process of building an expression. It provides a hierarchical list of common elements that you might want to include in an expression, and an expression box to build the expression in. To open the Expression Builder dialog box, click the Validation button in the Field Validation group on the Fields tool tab, and then click either Field Validation Rule or Validation Rule. In the dialog box, either select functions, operators, and other elements from the list to copy them into the expression box, or enter the expression directly in the expression box.

To explain a validation rule to users, you can create a message that appears if someone tries to enter an invalid value. A well-crafted message tells users what data is expected and what format it should be entered in. For example, the message *Please enter a whole number between 1 and 99* is more useful than *Invalid entry.*

Simple validation rules

The Field Validation group on the Fields tool tab includes two commands that provide simple validation tests for fields without requiring you to build an expression:

- **Required** By default, the Required property is set to No. Selecting the Required check box in the Field Validation group sets this property to Yes, meaning that every record must have an entry in this field; it cannot be blank. (A blank field is called a *Null field*.)

- **Unique** By default, the Indexed property of all fields except AutoNumber fields is set to No. This property has two Yes options:

  - **Yes (Duplicates OK)** This option is set if you select the Indexed check box in the Field Validation group.

  - **Yes (No Duplicates)** This option is set if you select the Unique check box. (It is set by default for AutoNumber fields.)

  In both Yes cases, Access creates an index of the data in the field and its location, similar to the index in a book. The index speeds up data searching, because Access can look up the location of the data in the index instead of searching the actual database.

In terms of validation, selecting the Required check box causes Access to verify that there is an entry in the field before it accepts the record. Selecting the Unique check box causes Access to verify that no other record has the same value in the field before it accepts the field entry.

TIP For Short Text, Long Text, and Hyperlink fields, the Required property can be refined by the Allow Zero Length property. When this property is set to Yes (the default), you can enter an empty string (two quotation marks with nothing between them) and the field will not be considered blank. In other words, a required field can be empty but not Null. The differentiation between Null and empty might seem silly, but it becomes important if someone uses programming code to work with the database, because some commands produce different results for Null fields than they do for empty fields.

In this exercise, you'll create and test a field validation rule and a record validation rule in a table.

 SET UP You need the GardenCompany06 database you worked with in the preceding exercise to complete this exercise. If necessary, open the database. Then display the FieldTest table in Database view, and follow the steps.

1   Point at the left end of the **fPhone** field, and when the pointer changes to a thick cross, click to select the contents of the field. Then replace the current entry with 6785550101, allowing the mask to format the entry for you.

2   With the **fPhone** field still selected, on the **Fields** tool tab, in the **Field Validation** group, click the **Validation** button to display a list of options.

> **Field Validation Rule**
> Create an expression that restricts the values that can be entered in the field.
>
> **Field Validation Message**
> Set the error message for the Field Validation Rule.
>
> **Validation Rule**
> Create an expression that restricts the values that can be entered into a record. For example, [StartDate] < [EndDate].
>
> **Validation Message**
> Set the error message for the Record Validation Rule.

The top set of options is for validating the field and the bottom set is for validating the entire record.

3   Click **Field Validation Rule** to open the **Expression Builder** dialog box.

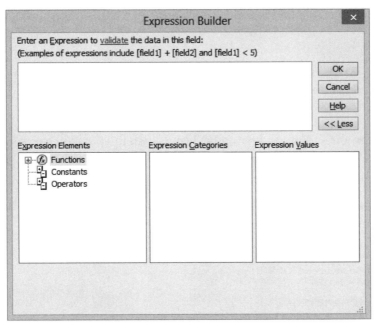

You build an expression in the box at the top of the dialog box by selecting elements, categories, and values from the boxes at the bottom.

Let's specify that only phone numbers in the 206 or 425 area codes can be accepted in the fPhone field.

4   In the **Expression Elements** list, click **Operators**; in the **Expression Categories** list, click **Comparison**; and in the **Expression Values** list, double-click **Like** to transfer that operator to the expression box.

5   With the cursor positioned to the right of the space following the word **Like** in the expression box, enter **"206*"** (including the quotation marks and the asterisk), and then press the **Spacebar**.

TROUBLESHOOTING Be sure to include the asterisk after 206. The fPhone field contains the phone number in addition to the area code, so you need the wildcard to allow the additional characters. For information about wildcards, see the sidebar "Wildcards" in Chapter 4, "Display data."

6   In the **Expression Categories** list, click **Logical**, and in the **Expression Values** list, double-click **Or**.

7   In the **Expression Categories** list, click **Comparison**, and in the **Expression Values** list, double-click **Like**.

> **TIP** The Expression Builder inserts <<Expr>> before the Like operator as a placeholder for any other expressions you might add. You can ignore this for now.

8   With the cursor positioned to the right of the space following the second **Like** in the expression box, enter *"425*"* (including the quotation marks and the asterisk).

9   Click **<<Expr>>**, and press the **Delete** key. Then delete the extra space before the second **Like**.

If you want to enter an expression directly in the expression box, you can click Less to hide the hierarchical boxes.

10   Click **OK** to close the **Expression Builder** dialog box.

11   When Access warns that existing data violates the new validation rule, click **Yes** to close the message box and keep the rule. Notice that the **fPhone** field is now active so that you can change the phone number to one that is in either of the required area codes.

12   Enter **4255550101**.

Let's add an error message that will appear if someone attempts to enter a phone number with an invalid area code.

13   On the **Fields** tool tab, in the **Field Validation** group, click the **Validation** button, and then click **Field Validation Message** to open the **Enter Validation Message** dialog box.

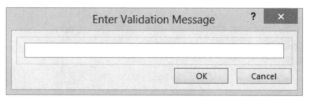

You can enter a guiding message here.

14   In the box, enter **Area code must be 206 or 425**, and then click **OK**.

15   Save the table, and then switch to **Design** view. Notice that, in the **Field Properties** area, the **Validation Rule** property and **Validation Text** property are set to the new rule and message.

General	Lookup	
Field Size	255
Format	
Input Mask	!\(000") "000\-0000;;#
Caption	
Default Value	
Validation Rule	Like "206*" Or Like "425*"
Validation Text	Area code must be 206 or 425
Required	No
Allow Zero Length	Yes
Indexed	No
Unicode Compression	Yes
IME Mode	No Control
IME Sentence Mode	None
Text Align	General

If you prefer, you can enter the rule and message directly in their boxes in the Field Properties area.

TROUBLESHOOTING If the message does not appear in the Validation Text property, verify that you did not press Tab after entering the new phone number and then inadvertently assign the message to the adjacent fShortText field.

Let's test this field validation rule.

16   Switch to **Datasheet** view. Then click anywhere in the **fPhone** entry, and press the **Home** key to place the cursor at the beginning of the field.

17   Enter 3605550109, and then press **Tab**, which displays a warning.

Access warns that the area code must be either 206 or 425.

TIP The Was This Information Helpful? link appears only if you have enrolled in the Microsoft Customer Experience Improvement Program. Clicking the link displays a dialog box in which you can give your opinion about the usefulness of warnings generated by the Access program. Because this warning was generated by a validation rule that you have created, you can ignore the link.

18   Click **OK** to close the alert box, enter a new phone number with one of the allowed area codes, and press **Tab**.

Now let's create a record validation rule that compares one date with another to verify that it is later.

19   Click the **Click to Add** field. Then create a **Date/Time** field that has the **Medium Date** format, name the field fDate2, and click the field below it.

20   On the **Fields** tool tab, in the **Field Validation** group, click the **Validation** button. Then click **Validation Rule**. Notice that the **Expression Builder** dialog box opens with the **FieldTest** table selected in the **Expression Elements** list and its fields displayed in the **Expression Categories** list.

21   In the **Expression Categories** list, double-click **fDate2** to insert it into the expression box. Then double-click **fDate**.

The field names are enclosed in square brackets to indicate that those field values will be used when this expression is evaluated.

22   In the expression box, click **<<Expr>>**. Then in the **Expression Elements** list, click **Operators**; in the **Expression Categories** list, click **Comparison**; and in the **Expression Values** list, double-click **>** to replace <<Expr>> with the greater than sign.

23   Click **OK** to close the **Expression Builder** dialog box, and then click **Yes** to keep the new rule.

24   Create a record validation message that says fDate2 must be later than fDate, and then save the table.

Let's test this record validation rule.

25   Replace the entry in the **fDate** field with 11/22/22.

26   Click the **fDate2** field, click the **Calendar** button, and click **Today**. Then click in the record below it, which displays a warning box containing the record validation text.

You cannot leave the record until you resolve this data error.

27   Click **OK**, change the value in **fDate2** to 12/22/22, and then click in the record below it.

❌ CLEAN UP Close the FieldTest table. Keep the GardenCompany06 database open for use in later exercises.

Allowing only values in lists

It is interesting how many different ways people can come up with to enter the same items of information in a database. Asked to enter the name of their home state, for example, residents of the state of Washington will enter *Washington*, *Wash*, or *WA*, plus various typographical errors and misspellings.

Minor inconsistencies in the way data is entered might not be really important to someone who later reads the information and makes decisions. For example, *Arizona* and *AZ* refer to the same state. But a computer is very literal, and if you tell it to create a list so that you can send catalogs to everyone living in *AZ*, the computer won't include anyone whose state is listed in the database as *Arizona*.

You can limit the options for entering information in a database in several ways:

- If one entry is more likely than any other, you can set the Default Value property of the field to that entry. Users can then press Tab to skip over that field, leaving the default entry intact. Even if users enter something else, the format of the default entry might guide them when choosing their entry's format.

- For only two options, you can use a Yes/No field represented by a check box. A selected check box indicates one choice, and a cleared check box indicates the other choice.

- For a short list of choices that won't change often, you can use a combo box. Clicking the arrow at the right end of the combo box displays the list of choices, which you provide as a lookup list. Depending on the properties associated with the combo box, database users might be able to enter something else or they might be able to add entries to the lookup list displayed in the future. Although you can create a lookup list by hand, it is a lot easier to use the Lookup wizard.

TIP Access comes with three Quick Start lookup lists that are commonly used in businesses: Payment Type, Priority, and Status. You can efficiently add one of these ready-made lookup lists to a table by clicking the More Fields button in the Add & Delete group on the Fields tool tab, and then clicking the field you want.

In this exercise, you'll use the Lookup wizard to create a list of states and provinces from which users can choose.

 SET UP You need the GardenCompany06 database you worked with in the preceding exercise to complete this exercise. If necessary, open the database. Then display the FieldTest table in Datasheet view, and follow the steps.

1   At the right end of the first record in the table, click the **Click to Add** field. On the **Fields** tool tab, in the **Add & Delete** group, click the **More Fields** button, and then in the **Basic Types** area, click **Lookup & Relationship** to start the **Lookup** wizard.

Lookup Wizard

This wizard creates a lookup field, which displays a list of values you can choose from. How do you want your lookup field to get its values?

⊙ I want the lookup field to get the values from another table or query.

○ I will type in the values that I want.

| Cancel | < Back | Next > | Finish |

You can specify that the values in the list already exist in another table or that you will enter them manually.

TIP If a field has only a few possible entries that won't change, typing the list directly in the wizard is easier. If a field has a lot of potential entries, or if the entries will change often, you can link them to a table. (You might have to create a table expressly for this purpose.) For information about creating lookup fields based on another table, see "Allowing only values in other tables" later in this chapter.

2 Click **I will type in the values that I want**, and then click **Next**.

3 Leave the number of columns set to **1**, and click in the first cell in the **Col1** column.

4 Enter the following state and province abbreviations, pressing **Tab** (not Enter) after each one to move to a new row.

BC
CA
ID
MT
OR
WA

5 Click **Next**.

You assign a name to the new field on this page.

SEE ALSO For information about creating fields that can hold multiple values, see the sidebar "Multivalued fields" later in this chapter.

6   Enter **fLookup** as the name of the field, and select the **Limit To List** check box. Then click **Finish**.

7   Save the table, and switch to **Design** view.

8   Click anywhere in the **fLookup** field, and then in the **Field Properties** area, click the **Lookup** tab to display the properties that control the lookup list.

General	Lookup	
Display Control	Combo Box	
Row Source Type	Value List	
Row Source	"BC";"CA";"ID";"MT";"OR";"WA"	
Bound Column	1	
Column Count	1	
Column Heads	No	
Column Widths	1"	
List Rows	16	
List Width	1"	
Limit To List	Yes	
Allow Multiple Values	No	
Allow Value List Edits	Yes	
List Items Edit Form		
Show Only Row Source V	No	

The list you entered is stored in the Row Source property.

Let's set a default value for the fLookup field.

9   In the **Field Properties** area, click the **General** tab. Then click anywhere in the **Default Value** property, enter **WA**, and press **Enter**.

Now let's test how the lookup list works.

10   Switch to **Datasheet** view, clicking **Yes** to save your changes to the table. Notice that **WA** appears in the **fLookup** field of the new record.

11   Click in the **fLookup** field of the first record, and then click the arrow at the right end of the field to display the list of possible entries.

The list reflects the entries you entered on the wizard's second page.

TIP Clicking the button that appears below the options list opens the Edit List Items dialog box. If you don't want users to be able to edit the list, you can disable this property, as we do later in this exercise.

12 Click **MT** to enter the abbreviation for Montana in the field.

13 With **MT** selected, enter b.

14 After Access completes the entry by displaying **C**, click the record below it, and watch as Access converts **bC** to **BC**.

15 Select **BC**, enter Utah, and press **Tab**. When Access tells you that the entry isn't in the list and asks whether you want to edit the list, click **Yes** to open the **Edit List Items** dialog box. Notice that **Utah** has been added to the bottom of the lookup list.

16 Click **Cancel**, and then click **BC** in the list.

17 Switch to **Design** view, and in the **Field Properties** area, click the **Lookup** tab. Notice on the **Lookup** page for the **fLookup** field that the **Limit To List** property is set to **Yes**, but the **Allow Value List Edits** property is also set to **Yes**, meaning that users can change the list.

Let's ensure that users can select values from the list but cannot change it.

18 Click the **Allow Value List Edits** property, click the arrow that appears, and then click **No**.

19 Save the table, and switch to **Datasheet** view. Then enter Utah in the **fLookup** field of the first record, and press **Tab**. Notice that the message that appears now has no option to edit the list.

Access will not accept your entry and won't allow you to change the lookup list.

20 Click **OK** to close the message box. Then click **BC** in the list, and press **Tab**.

❌ CLEAN UP Close the FieldTest table. Keep the GardenCompany06 database open for use in the last exercise.

Multicolumn lookup lists

If you want people to be able to select a friendly name from a list but you want the database to store a different name or even a number, create a two-column lookup list that associates the two types of entries. For example, you might want to associate employees' first names or nicknames with their employee ID numbers.

To set up a multicolumn lookup list:

1   Create a new lookup field, and indicate on the first page of the **Lookup** wizard that you want to enter the values.

2   On the second page, change the **Number of columns** setting to **2**. Then enter the data you want Access to store in **Col1** and the friendly name in **Col2**, and click **Next**.

3   On the third page, designate the column in which the data to be stored is located—in this case, **Col1**—and then click **Next**.

4   On the last page, assign a name to the field, select the **Limit To List** check box if appropriate, and click **Finish**.

Clicking the field's arrow will then display a two-column list from which the user can select an entry. The stored value will be displayed in the field.

To display only the friendly name in the list and in the table:

1   Switch to **Design** view.

2   In the **Field Properties** area, on the **Lookup** tab for the multicolumn field, change the **Column Widths** property from **1";1"** to **0;1"**.

3   Save the table.

Allowing only values in other tables

In "Defining relationships between tables" in Chapter 2, "Create databases and simple tables," you learned how to link tables in such a way that a user could not enter a CustomerID that did not exist in the Customers table or an EmployeeID that did not exist in the Employees table. These relationships are critical to ensuring that any specific item of data is stored in the database only once. But relationships also provide a powerful means to improve the accuracy of the database's data.

If you ask a dozen sales clerks to enter the name of a specific customer, product, and shipper in an invoice, it is unlikely that all of them will enter the same thing. In cases like this, in which the number of correct choices is limited (to actual customer, actual product, and actual shipper), providing the means to choose the correct information from a list derived from the Customers table, the Products table, and the Shippers table will improve your database's accuracy and consistency.

One of the key concerns when looking up information in another table is the efficiency of the process. Looking up an employee in an Employees table with 9 records is not very difficult. Looking up a customer in a Customers table with 200 records, however, could be quite tedious. If you use an intuitive CustomerID instead of relying on an autogenerated number as the primary key of the Customers table, database users can enter the CustomerID and then verify it in the list. For example, using the first three letters of a customer's last name plus the first two of his or her first name will almost certainly result in unique CustomerID values. These values will not only serve as the primary key for the Customers table but will be easy for users to intuit when working in other tables linked to the Customers table.

In this exercise, you'll use the Lookup wizard to create a list of possible field values from the entries in a field in a related table. You'll also change the primary key in a table to facilitate the lookup process.

➡️ SET UP You need the GardenCompany06 database you worked with in the preceding exercise to complete this exercise. If necessary, open the database. Then follow the steps.

1 On the **Database Tools** tab, in the **Relationships** group, click the **Relationships** button. On the **Relationships** page, notice that there are relationships between the **Customers** and **Orders** tables and between the **Employees** and **Orders** tables.

We want to create Customer and Employee lookup fields in the Orders table, so first let's delete the existing relationships and fields.

2 Right-click the diagonal part of the line between the **Customers** and **Orders** tables, and click **Delete**, clicking **Yes** to confirm the deletion. Repeat this step for the line between the **Employees** and **Orders** tables. Then close the **Relationships** page.

TIP If you want to remove a table's box from the Relationships page, right-click the box and click Hide Table. If you want to remove all the boxes, click the Clear Layout button in the Tools group on the Design tool tab.

3   Open the **Orders** table, and drag across the **CustomerID** and **EmployeeID** field names to select those fields. On the **Fields** tool tab, in the **Add & Delete** group, click the **Delete** button. Then click **Yes** to permanently delete the fields and **Yes** to delete their indexes.

Now let's add a new Employee lookup field.

4   At the right end of the table, click the **Click to Add** field. On the **Fields** tool tab, in the **Add & Delete** group, click the **More Fields** button, and then click **Lookup & Relationship** to start the **Lookup** wizard.

5   With **I want the lookup field to get the values from another table or query** selected, click **Next**.

6   To identify the table on which the lookup field will be based, click **Table: Employees** in the list. Then click **Next**.

7   On the third page, in the **Available Fields** list, double-click **EmployeeID**, then **FirstName**, and then **LastName** to transfer those fields to the **Selected Fields** list. Then click **Next**.

8   On the fourth page, click the arrow for the first sort box, and click **LastName** in the list. Then click **Next**. Notice on the fifth wizard page that by default, the **EmployeeID** field (the key column) is hidden.

You can adjust the column widths to fit the values the same way you would adjust field widths.

9   Click **Next**. On the wizard's last page, enter Employee as the name of the field, and select the **Enable Data Integrity** check box. Then click **Finish**.

Let's test the list.

10 Click in the **Employee** field of the first record, and then click the arrow at the right end of the field to display a list of possible entries.

Employee ▾	
Kim	Akers
Nancy	Anderson
Karen	Berg
Chase	Carpenter
Molly	Dempsey
Michael	Entin
Kari	Furse
Tom	O'Neill
Naoki	Sato

The list is in alphabetical order by last name.

11 Click **Nancy Anderson** to enter the name **Nancy** as the salesperson for this order.

Next let's change the CustomerID field of the Customers table so that it accepts manually entered, intuitive IDs.

12 Open the **Customers** table in **Design** view. Then on the **Design** tool tab, in the **Tools** group, click the **Primary Key** button to turn it off.

13 Change the **Data Type** setting for the **CustomerID** field to **Short Text**.

14 Change the **Field Size** property to **5**, and enter an **Input Mask** property of >LLLLL;; to force Access to display the **CustomerID** value in capital (uppercase) letters, no matter how it is entered.

15 Click the **CustomerID** field in the **Field Name** column, and in the **Tools** group, click the **Primary Key** button. Then save the table.

Let's test the new field.

16 Switch to **Datasheet** view. For each customer, assign a **CustomerID** that consists of the first three letters of the last name and the first two letters of the first name. Try entering an ID in all lowercase letters and notice that Access displays them in uppercase.

17   Sort the table in ascending order on the **CustomerID** field, and then close it, clicking **Yes** to save your changes.

Now let's create a new lookup field in the Orders table.

18   In the **Orders** table, use the **Lookup** wizard to create a new lookup field based on the **CustomerID**, **FirstName**, and **LastName** fields of the **Customers** table. Sort the lookup list on **LastName**, and then click **Next**.

19   On the page that asks you to adjust the width of the columns in the lookup field, point to the right border of the **FirstName** field name, and when the pointer changes to a double-headed arrow, drag all the way to the left to hide that column. Click **Next**.

20   Name the field Customer, and select the **Enable Data Integrity** check box. Then click **Finish**.

Let's test the new field by entering an order for Pilar Ackerman.

21   In the **Customer** field of the first record, enter ack. Notice that because **Ackerman** is the only **LastName** value beginning with those letters, Access completes the entry for you.

22   Click the field in the record below it to enter the name **Ackerman** as it appears in the **Customers** table.

23   In the active record, enter c, which Access completes as **campbell**, the first **LastName** value beginning with **c** in the **Customers** table.

24   This is not the customer we want, so click the arrow at the right end of the field to display the list of possible values with **Campbell** highlighted.

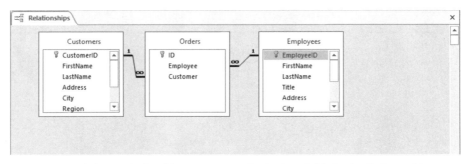

*Because Access has scrolled the list to the Campbell entry,
it is easy to select the name you want.*

25   Click **Cox**, and press **Tab**. Then close the **Orders** table.

Let's take a look at the one-to-many relationships between the Customers and Orders tables and between the Employees and Orders tables that make the lookup lists possible.

26   On the **Database Tools** tab, in the **Relationships** group, click the **Relationships** button.

Access created these relationships to support the lookup fields in the Orders table.

✖ CLEAN UP Close the GardenCompany06 database.

Multivalued fields

Usually, you will be able to build database tables in which each field holds only one value. However, sometimes you might need to store more than one value in a single field. For example, in a Projects table, you might need to store multiple employee names in a Team field.

To set up a multivalued field that restricts values to those in a table:

1 Create a new lookup field, and indicate on the first page of the **Lookup** wizard that you want to look up the values in a table.
2 On the second page, select a table from the list.
3 On the third page, select the fields you want to include.
4 On the fourth page, indicate any sorting.
5 On the fifth page, make any necessary adjustments to the column width.
6 On the last page of the wizard, enter a name for the field, and select the **Allow Multiple Values** check box.

When the table is open in Datasheet view, clicking the field's arrow displays a list from which users can choose entries by selecting their check boxes. Clicking OK then displays the selected values in the field.

TIP Think carefully about how your database will be used before creating multivalued fields. They are not easy to change, and they can produce unexpected results in filters and queries.

Key points

- The Data Type setting restricts the data that can be entered into a field to a specific type.

- The Field Size property for the Short Text, Number, and AutoNumber data types restricts the number of characters allowed in a Short Text field or the number of digits allowed in a Number or AutoNumber field.

- The Input Mask property controls the format in which data can be entered.

- You can use a validation rule to precisely define acceptable data. Access tests entries against the rule and rejects any that don't comply.

- For fields with a fixed set of possible entries, a lookup list ensures consistent data entry.

- If it is important that values in one table match values in another, you can create a lookup field based on that table to keep entries accurate.

6

Chapter at a glance

Create

Create queries manually,
page 203

Summarize

Summarize data by using queries,
page 208

Update

Update records by using queries,
page 218

Delete

Delete records by using queries,
page 222

Create queries

IN THIS CHAPTER, YOU WILL LEARN HOW TO

- Create queries by using a wizard.

- Create queries manually.

- Summarize data by using queries.

- Calculate by using queries.

- Update records by using queries.

- Delete records by using queries.

Microsoft Access 2013 provides a variety of tools you can use to locate specific items of information. In Chapter 4, "Display data," you learned how to sort and filter tables and forms. With a little more effort, you can create two basic types of queries:

- **Select** Finds records in the database that match the criteria you specify and then display those records in a datasheet, form, or report. You can use select queries to display specific fields from specific records from one or more tables.

- **Action** Finds records in the database that match the criteria you specify and then do something with those records. You can use action queries to ensure the ongoing accuracy of a database—for example, by updating information or deleting selected records from a table.

You can save both types of queries and run the saved queries at any time to generate updated results when data changes.

In this chapter, you'll use different methods to create queries that locate information matching multiple criteria. Then you'll create queries to summarize data and perform calculations. Finally, you'll create an update query and a delete query.

Creating queries by using a wizard

In Chapter 4 "Display data," you learned how to retrieve information from a database table by filtering it. These techniques are effective, but limited in the following ways:

- The filters are not saved, or are saved only temporarily.

- The filters are applied only to the table or form that is currently open.

If you want a filter to be permanently available, or if you want to filter more than one table or tables that are not open, you need to move beyond filters and into the realm of queries.

The most common type of query is the select query. The easiest way to set up a select query, especially when you are first learning about them, is to use a query wizard. Four wizards are available:

- **Simple** Sets up a query to retrieve data from one or more tables and displays the results in a datasheet. For example, you could use a simple query to extract the name and address of every customer who has ever placed an order.

- **Find Duplicates** Sets up a query to locate records that have the same information in one or more fields that you specify. For example, you could use this type of query to extract the name and address of every customer who has placed more than one order.

- **Find Unmatched** Sets up a query to locate records in one table that don't have related records in another table. For example, you could use this type of select query to locate people in the Customer table who have never placed an order.

- **Crosstab** Sets up a query to calculate and restructure data for easier analysis. You can use a crosstab query to calculate a sum, average, count, or other type of total for data that is grouped by two types of information, one down the left side of the datasheet and one across the top. The cell at the junction of each row and column displays the results of the query's calculation.

For a query to work effectively with multiple tables, Access must understand the relationships between the fields in those tables.

SEE ALSO For more information about creating relationships, see "Defining relationships between tables" in Chapter 2, "Create databases and simple tables."

Regardless of whether you create a query by using a wizard or manually, what you create is a statement describing the conditions that must be met for records to be matched in one or more tables. When you run the query, the matching records appear in a new datasheet.

In this exercise, you'll use the Simple Query wizard to create a query that combines information from two tables that are related through a common field. You'll then look at the underlying structure of the query, hide some fields, and sort the query results.

SET UP You need the GardenCompany07 database located in the Chapter07 practice file folder to complete this exercise. Be sure to use the practice database for this chapter rather than continuing on with the database from an earlier chapter. Open the database, and if you want, save your own version to avoid overwriting the original. Then follow the steps.

1   On the **Create** tab, in the **Queries** group, click the **Query Wizard** button to open the **New Query** dialog box.

7

In this dialog box, you choose which of the four query wizards you want to use.

2   With **Simple Query Wizard** selected in the list, click **OK** to start the wizard.

If no table is selected in the Navigation pane when you click the Query Wizard button, the first table in the list is selected on the wizard's first page.

3   Display the **Tables/Queries** list, and click **Table: Customers**. Then click the **Move All** button to move all the fields from the **Available Fields** list to the **Selected Fields** list.

4   In the **Selected Fields** list, click the **PhoneNumber** field, and then click the **Remove** button.

    TIP The quickest way to move all but one or two fields to the Selected Fields list, especially if a table has many fields, is to move them all and then remove those you don't want.

5   Display the **Tables/Queries** list, and click **Table: Orders.**

6   In the **Available Fields** list, double-click the **OrderID**, **OrderDate**, **ShippedDate**, and **RequiredDate** fields to move them to the **Selected Fields** list. Then click **Next**.

    TIP If a relationship between the tables hasn't already been defined, you will be prompted to define it. You will then need to restart the wizard.

7   We want to display detailed query results, so with **Detail** selected, click **Next**.

    SEE ALSO For information about using a query to summarize data, see "Summarizing data by using queries" later in this chapter.

8   On the wizard's last page, change the query title to Customer Orders. Then with **Open the query to view information** selected, click **Finish** to run the query and display the results in a datasheet.

9   Scroll the datasheet to the right, and notice that the requested order information is displayed to the right of each customer's information.

Region	PostalCode	Country	OrderID	OrderDate	ShippedDate	RequiredDate
WA	88004	USA	11080	1/5/2012	1/6/2012	
BC	V4T 1Y9	Canada	11140	2/1/2012	2/2/2012	
BC	V4T 1Y9	Canada	11149	2/2/2012	2/3/2012	2/7/2012
WA	88052	USA	11092	1/16/2012	1/19/2012	
WA	88072	USA	11094	1/22/2012	1/23/2012	
WA	88277	USA	11093	1/19/2012	1/21/2012	
WA	88053	USA	11110	1/24/2012	1/25/2012	
WA	88902	USA	11139	1/31/2012	2/1/2012	
MT	49707	USA	11103	1/23/2012	1/24/2012	1/28/2012
OR	87008	USA	11105	1/23/2012	1/25/2012	
WA	88121	USA	11081	1/6/2012	1/7/2012	
CA	84112	USA	11125	1/29/2012	1/30/2012	2/3/2012
CA	84306	USA	11129	1/30/2012	1/31/2012	
BC	V7L 1L3	Canada	11153	2/3/2012	2/7/2012	
BC	V7L 5A6	Canada	11151	2/3/2012	2/5/2012	
WA	88119	USA	11152	2/3/2012	2/7/2012	
WA	88007	USA	11096	1/22/2012	1/23/2012	
ID	73844	USA	11084	1/12/2012	1/14/2012	
WA	88115	USA	11131	1/30/2012	1/31/2012	

Record: 1 of 87 • No Filter • Search

Only the customers who have placed orders appear in the query results.

Let's make a few adjustments to the query in Design view.

10   Switch to **Design** view to display the query in the **Query Designer**.

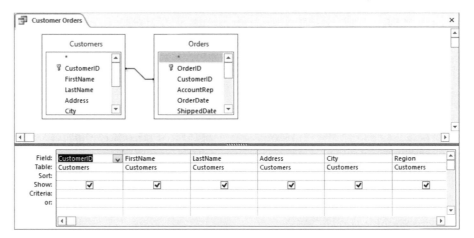

The top pane identifies the tables used by the query and the relationship between them. In the design grid, the Field row identifies the fields used, the Table row identifies each field's table, and selected check boxes in the Show row indicate the fields to display in the results.

SEE ALSO For more information about the Query Designer, see the next section, "Creating queries manually."

Suppose we want to use the CustomerID, Address, Country, and OrderID fields in the query, but we don't want to display these fields in the results datasheet. Let's hide them, and also sort the results.

11   In the **Show** row, clear the check boxes for **CustomerID**, **Address**, **Country**, and **OrderID**.

12   In the **Sort** row, click the **PostalCode** field, click the arrow that appears, and then click **Ascending** to sort the results on this field.

Field:	Address	City	Region	PostalCode	Country	OrderID
Table:	Customers	Customers	Customers	Customers	Customers	Orders
Sort:				Ascending		
Show:	☐	☑	☑	☑	☐	☐
Criteria:						
or:						

The fields with cleared check boxes will not appear in the query's results.

13   On the **Design** tool tab, in the **Results** group, click the **Run** button to display the datasheet with the new results.

FirstName	LastName	City	Region	PostalCode	OrderDate	ShippedDate	RequiredDate
Luciana	Ramos	Helena	MT	49624	1/12/2012	1/13/2012	
Randall	Boseman	Butte	MT	49707	1/23/2012	1/24/2012	1/28/2012
Scott	Gode	Pocatello	ID	73204	1/30/2012	1/31/2012	
Richard	Lum	Boise	ID	73704	2/2/2012	2/3/2012	2/7/2012
Brian	Cox	Moscow	ID	73844	1/12/2012	1/14/2012	
Parul	Manek	Provo	UT	74606	2/6/2012	2/7/2012	
Kathie	Flood	Glendale	CA	81203	1/29/2012	1/30/2012	2/3/2012
Ben	Miller	Granada Hills	CA	81344	2/7/2012	2/9/2012	
Scott	Mitchell	Escondido	CA	82029	2/7/2012	2/8/2012	
Patricia	Doyle	Carmel Valley	CA	83924	1/26/2012	1/29/2012	
David	Campbell	San Francisco	CA	84112	1/29/2012	1/30/2012	2/3/2012
Patrick	Sands	San Francisco	CA	84140	2/6/2012	2/8/2012	
Chris	Cannon	Palo Alto	CA	84306	1/30/2012	1/31/2012	
Ted	Bremer	Beaverton	OR	87008	1/23/2012	1/25/2012	
Sydney	Higa	Portland	OR	87201	1/22/2012	1/23/2012	1/27/2012
Andrew R.	Hill	Portland	OR	87210	1/29/2012	1/30/2012	
Modesto	Estrada	Burns	OR	87710	1/14/2012	1/16/2012	1/19/2012
Anne	Hellung-Larsen	Elgin	OR	87827	1/26/2012	1/29/2012	1/31/2012
Karan	Khanna	Auburn	WA	88001	1/6/2012	1/8/2012	1/12/2012

Record: I◄ ◄ 1 of 87 ► ►I ►☰ No Filter Search

Four fields no longer appear in the results datasheet, and the extracted records are sorted on the PostalCode field.

TIP When a query is open, you can also simply switch to Datasheet view to run the query.

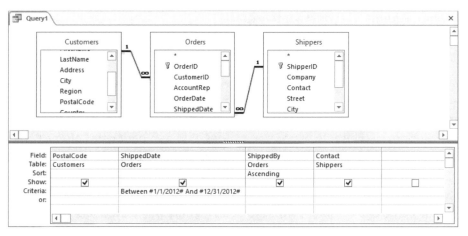 **CLEAN UP** Close the Customer Orders query, saving your changes. Keep the GardenCompany07 database open for use in later exercises.

Creating queries manually

The query wizards guide you through the creation of common queries, but you create less common queries manually in the Query Designer.

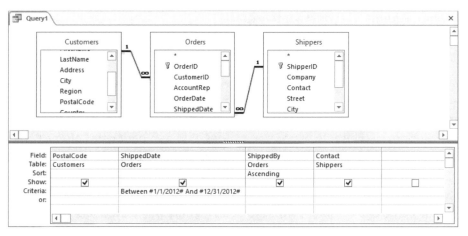

This query was created manually in the Query Designer.

Let's review the features of the Query Designer:

- In the top pane are field lists for the tables that can be included in the query.

- Lines connecting the field lists indicate that the tables are related by common fields.

- A table's primary key field is indicated in its field list by a key icon.

- The Field row of the design grid contains the names of the fields actually included in the query.

- The Table row shows which table each field belongs to.

- The Sort row indicates which field(s) the query results will be sorted on, if any.

- A selected check box in the Show row means that the field will be displayed in the results datasheet. (If the check box isn't selected, the field can be used in determining the query results, but it won't be displayed.)

- The Criteria row can contain criteria that determine which records will be displayed.

- The Or row sets up alternate criteria.

When you create a query manually, you add field lists for the tables you want to use to the top pane of the Query Designer and either double-click or drag fields from the lists to consecutive columns of the design grid. You then indicate which field to sort the matched records on and which field values to show in the results datasheet. As with filters, the power of queries lies in the criteria you set up in the Criteria and Or rows. This is where you specify precisely which information you want to extract.

SEE ALSO For information about filters, see Chapter 4, "Display data."

If you want to run an existing query with a variation of the same basic criteria, you can display the existing query in Design view, modify the criteria, and then rerun the query. However, it would be tedious to do this more than a couple of times. If you know you will often run variations of the same query, you can set it up as a parameter query. Parameter queries display a dialog box to prompt for the information to be used in the query. For example, suppose you know you are getting low on the stock of an item and you need to place an order for more of that product with the supplier. You might use a parameter query to request the name of a supplier so that you can identify other products you purchase from that supplier before placing the order. This type of query is particularly useful when used as the basis for a report that you run periodically.

In this exercise, you'll create a query by manually setting it up in the Query Designer. You'll add criteria to extract the records for specific dates, and then convert the query into a parameter query that requests the dates to extract at run time.

 SET UP You need the GardenCompany07 database you worked with in the preceding exercise to complete this exercise. If necessary, open the database. Then follow the steps.

1   On the **Create** tab, in the **Queries** group, click the **Query Design** button to display a blank **Query Designer** and open the **Show Table** dialog box.

You select the tables you want to work with on the Tables page. You can also use existing queries or a combination of tables and queries as the basis for a new query.

Let's manually recreate the Customer Orders query from the previous exercise.

2   In the dialog box, double-click **Customers**, double-click **Orders**, and then click **Close**.

TIP To add the field list for another table to an existing query, display the Show Table dialog box at any time by clicking the Show Table button in the Query Setup group on the Design tool tab. You can also drag the table from the Navigation pane to the top pane of the Query Designer. To delete a table from a query, right-click the table's field list, and then click Remove Table.

3   Double-click the title of the **Customers** field list to select all the fields in the list. Then point to the selection, and drag down to the **Field** row of the first column in the design grid. Notice that the fields occupy consecutive columns and that the **Table** row of each column designates the **Customers** table as the source of the field.

TIP The asterisk at the top of each field list represents all the fields in the table. Dragging the asterisk to a column in the Field row inserts a single field that represents all the fields, meaning that you cannot then manipulate the fields individually.

4   Scroll the grid to the right, and click in the **Field** row of the next blank column. Then in the **Orders** field list, in turn double-click the **OrderID**, **OrderDate**, **ShippedDate**, and **RequiredDate** fields to add those fields to the next four columns.

Field:	Country	PhoneNumber	OrderID	OrderDate	ShippedDate	RequiredDate
Table:	Customers	Customers	Orders	Orders	Orders	Orders
Sort:						
Show:	☑	☑	☑	☑	☑	☑
Criteria:						
or:						

You have added fields from two tables to the design grid.

5   Point to the gray field selector above the **PhoneNumber** field, and when the pointer changes to a black down arrow, click to select the column. Then in the **Query Setup** group, click the **Delete Columns** button.

KEYBOARD SHORTCUT Press Delete to delete the selected column. For a list of keyboard shortcuts, see "Keyboard shortcuts" at the end of this book.

6   In the **Show** row, clear the check boxes of the **OrderID**, **Country**, **Address**, and **CustomerID** fields.

7   In the **Sort** row, set the **PostalCode** field to **Ascending**.

8   In the **Results** group, click the **Run** button. Check the datasheet to ensure that the query produces the correct results.

Let's make this query return the records for a specific range of dates.

9   Switch to **Design** view. In the **Criteria** row of the **OrderDate** field, enter the following, and then press the **Enter** key:

Between 1/1/2012 And 1/8/2012

TIP When you enter the *A* of *And*, Access displays a list of operators you might be intending to use. You can click an option in the list to save yourself a few keystrokes. In this case, ignore the list, and it will disappear.

10   Widen the **OrderDate** field to fit its contents, so that the entire criterion is visible in this field.

Field:	PostalCode	Country	OrderID	OrderDate	ShippedDate
Table:	Customers	Customers	Orders	Orders	Orders
Sort:	Ascending				
Show:	☑	☐	☐	☑	☑
Criteria:				Between #1/1/2012# And #1/8/2012#	
or:					

Access has added # signs to designate a date format.

11   Run the query to extract the matching records.

FirstName ▾	LastName ▾	City ▾	Region ▾	PostalCode ▾	OrderDate ▾	ShippedDate ▾	RequiredDate ▾
Karan	Khanna	Auburn	WA	88001	1/6/2012	1/8/2012	1/12/2012
Pilar	Ackerman	Bellevue	WA	88004	1/5/2012	1/6/2012	
Eric	Lang	Bothell	WA	88011	1/5/2012	1/7/2012	
Reed	Koch	Seattle	WA	88103	1/8/2012	1/9/2012	1/12/2012
Kevin F.	Browne	Seattle	WA	88121	1/6/2012	1/7/2012	

Only five orders were placed in the requested period.

Now let's have the query request the range of dates each time you run it.

12   Switch to **Design** view. In the **Criteria** row of the **OrderDate** field, replace the existing criterion with the following, entering this criterion exactly as shown and then pressing the **Enter** key:

Between [Enter the beginning date:] And [Enter the ending date:]

13   Run the query, which opens the **Enter Parameter Value** dialog box.

The first Enter Parameter Value dialog box requests the beginning date in the range.

14   In the text box, enter 1/8/12, and click **OK**.

15   In the second **Enter Parameter Value** dialog box, enter 1/15/12, and click **OK**. Notice that the results datasheet lists only the nine orders placed between the specified dates.

16   Save the query as Orders By Date.

❌ CLEAN UP Close the query. Keep the GardenCompany07 database open for use in later exercises.

Summarizing data by using queries

You typically use a query to locate all the records that meet some criteria. But sometimes you are not as interested in the details of all the records as you are in summarizing the query results in some way. For example, you might want to know how many orders have been placed this year or the total dollar value of all orders placed.

The easiest way to extract summary information is by creating a query that groups the necessary fields and does the math for you. The calculations are performed by using one of the following aggregate functions:

- **Sum** Calculates the total of the values in a field

- **Avg** Calculates the average of the values in a field

- **Min** Extracts the lowest value in a field

- **Max** Extracts the highest value in a field

- **Count** Counts the number of values in a field, not counting Null (blank) values

- **StDev** Calculates the standard deviation of the values in a field

- **Var** Calculates the variance of the values in a field

When you use the Simple Query wizard to create a query based on a table that has fields containing numeric data, the wizard gives you the option of creating a summary query. If you select Summary on the wizard's second page and then click Summary Options, the wizard displays a dialog box in which you can specify the aggregate function you want to use.

If you are using the Simple Query wizard to build a query with fields that contain numeric data, you can have the wizard add an aggregate function to the query.

When creating a query manually, or modifying an existing query, you can click the Totals button in the Show/Hide group on the Design tool tab to add a Total row to the grid. You can then select the aggregate function you want from a list. The list also allows you to group fields, select the first or last record that meets the specified criteria, enter an expression, or make additional criteria refinements.

TIP You don't have to create a query to summarize all the data in a table. You can display the table in Datasheet view and then on the Home tab, in the Records group, click the Totals button to add a Total row at the bottom of the table. (Clicking the Totals button again removes the row from the table.) In the Total row of each field, you can select the type of summary data you want to appear from a list. The types available for each field depend on its data type. For example, you can count all fields, but you can only calculate the sum or average of fields containing numeric data.

In this exercise, you'll create a query that calculates the total number of products in an inventory, the average price of all the products, and the total value of the inventory.

→ **SET UP** You need the GardenCompany07 database you worked with in the preceding exercise to complete this exercise. If necessary, open the database. Then follow the steps.

1 Open the **Query Designer**, and add the **Products** table to the query.

2 In the **Products** field list, double-click **ProductID**, and then double-click **UnitPrice**.

3 On the **Design** tool tab, in the **Show/Hide** group, click the **Totals** button to add a **Total** row below the **Table** row in the design grid, with the **Group By** aggregate function in the **Total** row of each field.

   TIP If you need to adjust the height of the design grid after adding the Total row, drag the bar that separates the design grid and the top pane upward.

4 Click in the **Total** row of the **ProductID** field, click the arrow, and then in the list, click **Count** to replace **Group By** with the **Count** aggregate function.

5 Display the **Total** list for the **UnitPrice** field, and click **Avg**.

Field:	ProductID	UnitPrice				
Table:	Products	Products				
Total:	Count	Avg				
Sort:						
Show:	✔	✔	☐	☐	☐	☐
Criteria:						
or:						

This simple query summarizes the data in two fields in different ways.

Let's run the query to count the number of records containing a value in the ProductID field and the average of all the UnitPrice values.

6 Run the query.

CountOfProductID ▾	AvgOfUnitPrice ▾
189	$17.92

The results show that the average price of 189 products is $17.92.

Now let's add a new field that uses data from two fields in the Products table to perform a calculation.

7   Switch to **Design** view.

8   In the **Field** row of the third column, enter UnitPrice*UnitsInStock, and press the **Enter** key.

9   Widen the third column so that its entire contents are displayed. Notice that the expression you entered has changed to the following:

Expr1: [UnitPrice][UnitsInStock]*

Field:	ProductID	UnitPrice	Expr1: [UnitPrice]*[UnitsInStock]		
Table:	Products	Products			
Total:	Count	Avg	Group By		
Sort:					
Show:	☑	☑	☑	☐	☐
Criteria:					
or:					

This expression will multiply the price of each product by the number of units in stock.

10   Double-click **Expr1**, and enter Value of Inventory as the expression's label.

11   Display the **Total** list for the third column, and then click **Sum**.

12   Save the query with the name Product Analysis.

13   Run the query, which returns the sum of all the values calculated by the expression.

14   Widen the columns of the results datasheet so that their entire contents are displayed.

Product Analysis			✕
CountOfProductID ▾	AvgOfUnitPrice ▾	Value of Inventory ▾	
189	$17.92	$27,405.41	

This query now summarizes the data in three ways.

 CLEAN UP Close the query, saving your layout changes. Keep the GardenCompany07 database open for use in later exercises.

Calculating by using queries

As you saw in the previous exercise, you can not only use a query to summarize data by using built-in aggregate functions but you can also perform a calculation and create a new field in which to store it. For example, you might want to calculate an extended price or how long employees have worked for the company.

One of the basic tenets of good database design is that you should never store information that can be calculated from existing data. Instead of creating a new field in a table and increasing the size of the database with redundant information, use an expression in a query to compute the desired information from existing data whenever you need it.

TIP It is possible to use the results of one query as a field in another query. The nested query involves use of a Structured Query Language (SQL) Select statement and is called a *subquery*. For more information about subqueries, search for *Nest a query inside another query* in Access Help.

In this exercise, you'll create a query that combines information from two tables into a datasheet and calculates the extended price of an item based on the unit price, quantity ordered, and discount.

SET UP You need the GardenCompany07 database you worked with in the preceding exercise to complete this exercise. If necessary, open the database. Then follow the steps.

1 Open the **Query Designer**, and add the **Order Details** and **Products** tables to the query.

2 Drag the following five fields from their field lists to consecutive columns in the design grid.

From this field list	Drag this field
Order Details	OrderID
Products	ProductName
Order Details	UnitPrice
Order Details	Quantity
Order Details	Discount

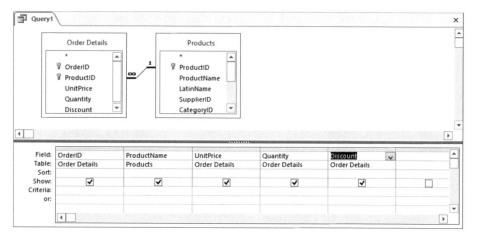

The results datasheet will display the extracted information in the order of the fields in the design grid.

3   Run the query.

OrderID	Product Name	UnitPrice	Quantity	Discount
11091	Autumn Crocus	$18.75	4	0
11079	Compost bin	$58.00	1	0
11083	Compost bin	$58.00	1	0
11138	Compost bin	$58.00	1	0
11152	Compost bin	$58.00	1	0
11085	Cactus sand potting m	$4.50	2	0
11093	Cactus sand potting m	$4.50	2	0
11121	Cactus sand potting m	$4.50	1	0
11132	Cactus sand potting m	$4.50	1	0
11148	Cactus sand potting m	$4.50	1	0
11114	Weeping Forsythia	$18.00	3	0
11147	Weeping Forsythia	$18.00	1	0
11082	Bat box	$14.75	3	0
11086	Bat box	$14.75	2	0
11159	Bat box	$14.75	3	0.1

Record: 1 of 215   No Filter   Search

The results show that the query is working correctly.

4   Save the query with the name Order Details Extended.

5   Switch to **Design** view. Then in the **OrderID** column, display the **Sort** list, and click **Ascending**.

Now in a new field in the design grid, let's use the Expression Builder to insert an expression that computes the extended price by multiplying the unit price by the quantity sold, minus any discount.

6   In the **Field** row, right-click in the first blank column, and then click **Build** to open the **Expression Builder** dialog box.

In the Expression Builder dialog box, the Order Details Extended query is selected in the Expression Elements box, and the Expression Categories box displays the fields from the query.

Here is the expression you are going to build in the expression box:

CCur([Order Details]![UnitPrice]*[Order Details]![Quantity]*
(1-[Order Details]![Discount]))

The CCur function converts the results of the math inside its parentheses to currency format.

TIP If you wanted to enter this expression directly into the field, you could simplify it to this:

CCur([Order Details]![UnitPrice]*[Quantity]*(1-[Discount]))

The [Order Details]! part is required only for the UnitPrice field, which appears in both tables. It tells the query which table to use.

7   In the **Expression Elements** list, double-click **Functions**, and then click **Built-In Functions**.

8   In the **Expression Categories** list, click **Conversion**. Then in the **Expression Values** list, double-click **CCur**.

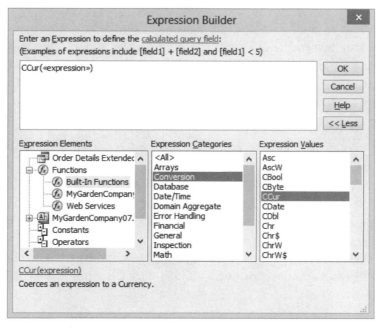

The <<expression>> inside the parentheses represents the expressions that will eventually result in the number Access should convert to currency format.

9   In the expression box, click **<<expression>>** to select it, so that the next thing you enter will replace it. (The next expression element is the UnitPrice field from the Order Details table.)

10   In the **Expression Elements** list, click the minus icon to the left of **Functions** to collapse that element. Then click the plus icon to the left of **GardenCompany07. accdb** (or your version of that file—ours is **MyGardenCompany07**), double-click **Tables**, and click **Order Details**.

11   In the **Expression Categories** list, double-click **UnitPrice** to replace the **<<expression>>** placeholder with the table/field information.

Now let's multiply the amount in the UnitPrice field by the amount in the Quantity field.

12   With the cursor after **[UnitPrice]** in the expression box, click **Operators** in the **Expression Elements** list; click **Arithmetic** in the **Expression Categories** list; and double-click ***** (multiply) in the **Expression Values** list.

13   In the expression box, click <<**Expr**>> to select it. In the **Expression Elements** list, in
      the **Tables** area of the **GardenCompany07.accdb** list, click **Order Details**. Then in the
      Expression Categories list, double-click **Quantity**.

      So far, we have entered an expression that calculates the total cost by multiplying
      the price of an item by the quantity ordered. However, suppose the sale price is dis-
      counted due to quantity or another factor. The discount, which is stored in the Order
      Details table, is expressed as the percentage to deduct. But it is easier to compute
      the percentage to be paid than it is to compute the discount and subtract it from the
      total cost.

      TIP The Discount field values are displayed in the Order Details table as percentages,
      but they are stored in the database as decimal numbers between 0 and 1. (For ex-
      ample, a discount displayed as 10% is stored as 0.1). So if the discount is 10 percent,
      the percentage to be paid is 1-Discount, or 0.9. In other words, the expression will
      multiply the unit price by the quantity and then multiply that result by 0.9.

14   With the cursor to the left of the closing parenthesis in the expression box, enter
      *(1-. In the **Expression Categories** list, double-click **Discount**. Then enter) (closing
      parenthesis).

The entire expression now appears in the expression box.

TIP If the entire expression isn't visible in the expression box, you can widen the Expression Builder dialog box by dragging its left or right border.

15   In the **Expression Builder** dialog box, click **OK** to insert the expression into the design grid.

16   Press **Enter** to complete the entry of the expression. Then widen the column so that the entire expression is visible.

Access has assigned the label *Expr1* to the field. (This label is known as the *field alias*.) Let's change the label to something more meaningful.

17   In the design grid, double-click **Expr1**, and then enter ExtendedPrice.

18   Run the query.

OrderID	Product Name	UnitPrice	Quantity	Discount	ExtendedPrice
11079	Crushed rock	$62.50	1	0	$62.50
11079	Compost bin	$58.00	1	0	$58.00
11080	Douglas Fir	$18.75	1	0	$18.75
11080	Fortune Rhododendrc	$24.00	2	0.1	$43.20
11081	Golden Larch	$27.00	1	0	$27.00
11081	Lawn cart	$85.00	1	0.1	$76.50
11082	Bat box	$14.75	3	0	$44.25
11083	Compost bin	$58.00	1	0	$58.00
11083	GrowGood potting soi	$6.35	1	0	$6.35
11083	QwikRoot	$18.00	1	0	$18.00
11083	Grass rake	$11.95	1	0	$11.95
11084	Gooseberries	$7.50	3	0	$22.50
11084	Ambrosia	$6.25	1	0	$6.25
11084	Blackberries	$4.50	6	0	$27.00
11085	Cactus sand potting m	$4.50	2	0	$9.00

Record: 1 of 215   No Filter   Search

The orders are sorted by the OrderID field, and the extended price is calculated in the last field.

19   In the few records with discounts, verify that the query calculates the extended price correctly.

⊗ CLEAN UP Close the query, saving it when prompted. Keep the GardenCompany07 database open for use in later exercises.

Updating records by using queries

As you use a database and as it grows, you might discover that errors creep in or that some information becomes out of date. You can tediously scroll through the records looking for those that need to be changed, but it is more efficient to use the tools and techniques provided by Access for that purpose.

If you want to find or replace multiple instances of the same word or phrase, you can use the Find and Replace commands in the Find group on the Home tab. These commands work much like the same commands in Microsoft Word or Microsoft Excel.

If you want to manipulate information stored in the database only under certain circumstances, you need the power of an action query. An action query finds records that match the selection criteria and performs an action on them. For example, you can increase the price of all products in one category by a certain percentage, or remove all the items belonging to a specific product line. This type of data manipulation is easy to do with an action query. Not only does using a query save time, but it helps to avoid errors.

Four types of actions are available:

- **Append** Adds records from one or more tables to the end of one or more other tables.

- **Delete** Deletes records from one or more tables.

- **Make-table** Creates a new table from all or part of the data in one or more tables.

- **Update** Makes changes to records in one or more tables. Running an update query makes irreversible changes to the underlying table, so you should always create a backup copy of the table before running this type of query. You can quickly create a copy of a table by displaying the **Tables** list in the **Navigation** pane, clicking the table you want to copy, pressing **Ctrl+C**, and then pressing **Ctrl+V** to paste a copy. In the **Paste Table As** dialog box, enter a name for the new table, and then click **OK**. The backup table then becomes part of the database. You can delete it when you are sure that the update query produced the results you want.

TIP In addition to these queries, you can create SQL queries, including union, pass through, and data definition queries. SQL queries are beyond the scope of this book.

You can't create an action query directly; you must first create a select query and then convert it. With an existing select query open in the Query Designer, click the appropriate button in the Query Type group on the Design tool tab. (You can also right-click the query in the Query Designer, click Query Type, and then click the type of query you want.)

In this exercise, you'll create an update query to increase the price of selected items by 10 percent.

 SET UP You need the GardenCompany07 database you worked with in the preceding exercise to complete this exercise. If necessary, open the database. Then follow the steps.

1   In the **Navigation** pane, copy and paste the **Categories** table, naming the new object **Copy Of Categories**, so that you have a backup in the event that your query produces unexpected results.

2   On the **Create** tab, in the **Queries** group, click the **Query Wizard** button. Then with **Simple Query Wizard** selected in the **New Query** dialog box, click **OK**.

3   Display **Table: Categories** in the **Tables/Queries** list, and in the **Available Fields** list, double-click **CategoryName** to move it to the **Selected Fields** list.

4   Display **Table: Products** in the **Tables/Queries** list, and in the **Available Fields** list, double-click **ProductName** and **UnitPrice** to move them to the **Selected Fields** list.

5   Click **Finish** to create the query by using the default detail setting and title and to run the query.

Categories Query			✕
Category Name	Product Name	Unit Price	
Bulbs	Magic Lily	$44.00	
Bulbs	Autumn Crocus	$20.63	
Bulbs	Anemone	$30.80	
Bulbs	Lily-of-the-Field	$41.80	
Bulbs	Siberian Iris	$14.25	
Bulbs	Daffodil	$14.25	
Bulbs	Peony	$21.95	
Bulbs	Lilies	$11.55	
Bulbs	Begonias	$20.85	
Bulbs	Bulb planter	$7.65	
Cacti	Prickly Pear	$3.30	
Ground covers	Crown Vetch	$12.95	
Ground covers	English Ivy	$5.95	
Ground covers	European Ginger	$6.25	
Ground covers	St. John's Wort	$9.75	

Record: 1 of 189 ▶ ▶ ▶ ▼ No Filter Search

Only the Category Name, Product Name, and Unit Price fields are displayed.

The current query results include the products in all categories. We want to raise the prices of the products in only the Bulbs and Cacti categories, so let's change the query to select only those categories.

6   Switch to **Design** view.

This Categories Query was created and named by the Simple Query wizard.

7   In the **Criteria** row of the **CategoryName** field, enter bulbs, and in the **or** row of the same field, enter cacti. Then press the **Enter** key.

8   Run the query to confirm that only bulbs and cacti are listed, and then return to **Design** view.

The query now selects the records we want to change. Let's convert this select query to an update query so that we can make a change to the selected records.

9   On the **Design** tool tab, in the **Query Type** group, click the **Update** button.

In the design grid, the Sort and Show rows disappear and an Update To row appears.

10   In the **Update To** row of the **UnitPrice** column, enter [UnitPrice]*1.1. Then press the **Enter** key.

TIP Enclosing UnitPrice in square brackets indicates that it is a database object—in this case, a field in a table. If you use the Expression Builder to insert this expression, it looks like this:

*[Products]![UnitPrice]*1.1*

Because this description of the field includes the table in which it is found, you can insert this expression in other tables.

11   Without running the query, switch to **Datasheet** view to display a list of the same unit prices you viewed earlier; they have not been changed yet.

TIP In a select query, clicking the View button on the Home tab or the Datasheet View button on the View Shortcuts toolbar is the same as clicking the Run button. But in an update query, clicking the View button or the Datasheet View button simply displays a list of the fields that will be updated.

12   Switch to **Design** view. Then run the query, which displays a message box asking you to confirm that you want to update the records.

7

This message box cautions that you can't undo the changes you are about to make.

13   In the message box, click **Yes**, and then switch to **Datasheet** view. Notice that the prices in the **UnitPrice** field have been increased by **10** percent.

✖ CLEAN UP Close the Categories Query, saving your changes. Keep the GardenCompany07 database open for use in the last exercise.

Deleting records by using queries

Over time, some of the information stored in a database might become obsolete. For example, the Products table lists all the products the company currently offers for sale or has sold in the past. You can indicate that a product is no longer available for sale by placing a check mark in a Discontinued field. Discontinued products aren't displayed in the catalog or offered for sale, but they are kept in the database for a while in case it becomes practical to sell them again. A similar situation could exist with customers who haven't placed an order in a long time or who have asked to be removed from a mailing list but might still place orders.

To maintain an efficient database, it is a good idea to discard outdated records from time to time. You could scroll through the tables and delete records manually, but if all the records you want to delete match some pattern, you can use a delete query to quickly get rid of all of them.

It is important to keep two things in mind when deleting records from a database:

- You can't recover deleted records.
- The effects of a delete query can be more far-reaching than you intend.

If the table from which you are deleting records is related to another table, and the Cascade Delete Related Records option for that relationship is selected, records in the second table will also be deleted. (*Cascade Delete* essentially means that the deletion is also applied to related records.) Sometimes this is what you want, but sometimes it isn't. For example, you probably don't want to delete records of previous sales at the same time that you delete discontinued products.

As a precaution, before actually deleting records, you might want to display the Relationships page by clicking the Relationships button in the Relationships group on the Database Tools tab. If the table you are deleting data from has a relationship with any table containing information that shouldn't be deleted, right-click the relationship line, click Edit Relationship, and make sure that if the Enforce Referential Integrity check box is selected, the Cascade Delete Related Records check box is *not* selected.

As a further safeguard against potential problems, you will want to back up your database before deleting the records. You might also want to create a new table (perhaps named *Deleted<file name>*) and then move the records you want to delete to the new table, in which you can review them before deleting them permanently.

SEE ALSO For information about backing up a database, see "Preventing database problems" in Chapter 12, "Protect databases."

In this exercise, you'll create a delete query that will remove the records of discontinued products from a table.

→ SET UP You need the GardenCompany07 database you worked with in the preceding exercise to complete this exercise. If necessary, open the database. Then follow the steps.

1 Open the **Query Designer**, and add the **Products** table to the query.

2 In the **Products** field list, double-click * (the asterisk) to enter **Products.*** in the **Field** row and **Products** in the **Table** row of the first column of the design grid.

   TIP Double-clicking the asterisk in the field list is a quick way to move all the fields to the query, without each field taking up a column in the design grid and possibly making it necessary to scroll from side to side to view them all. However, selecting all the fields in this way prevents you from setting Sort, Show, and Criteria values for individual fields. To set these values, you have to add the specific fields to the design grid, thereby adding them twice. To avoid displaying the fields twice in the results, clear the check box in the Show row of the duplicate individual fields.

3 In the **Products** field list, double-click **Discontinued** to copy it to the next available column in the design grid.

   Let's convert this select query to a delete query and then use criteria to identify the records we want to delete.

4 On the **Design** tool tab, in the **Query Type** group, click the **Delete** button to convert this select query to a delete query.

Field:	Products.*	Discontinued				▲
Table:	Products	Products				
Delete:	From	Where				
Criteria:						
or:						▼

In the query design grid, the Sort and Show rows disappear, and a Delete row appears.

In the first column, which contains the reference to all fields in the Products table, the Delete row contains the word *From*, indicating that this is the table from which records will be deleted. When you add individual fields to the remaining columns, as you did with the Discontinued field, the Delete row displays *Where*, indicating that this field can include deletion criteria. The Discontinued field is set to the Yes/ No data type, which is represented in the datasheet as a check box that is selected to indicate Yes and cleared to indicate No. To locate all discontinued products, you need to identify records with the Discontinued field set to Yes.

5   In the **Criteria** row of the **Discontinued** field, enter **Yes**, and then press the **Enter** key.

Before we do anything else, let's test the query.

6   Without running the query, switch to **Datasheet** view, which displays the 18 discontinued products that will be deleted if you run the query.

7   Scroll to the right to verify that for all records, the **Products.Discontinued** check box is selected.

8   Switch back to **Design** view, and run the query.

Before deleting the records, Access warns you of the permanence of this action.

9   In the message box, click **Yes**, which displays another warning.

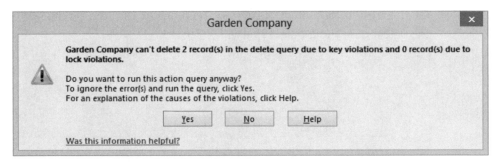

Access cannot delete two of the discontinued records.

10   In the message box, click **No** to cancel the deletion. Two discontinued records cannot be deleted because they have entries in the **Order Details** table. If this were a real database, you would need to decide whether to set the **Discontinued** field of these products to **No** (clear their check boxes) or to delete the entries from the **Order Details** table before allowing the query to delete the product records.

Suppose you are concerned that someone might accidentally run this delete query and destroy records you aren't ready to destroy. Let's change the query back to a select query before saving it.

11   On the **Design** tool tab, in the **Query Type** group, click the **Select** button. Notice that in the query design grid, the **Delete** row has disappeared and the **Sort** and **Show** rows are now displayed.

12   Save the query with the name **Delete Discontinued Products**.

TIP If you want to delete obsolete records in the future, open the select query in Design view, convert it to a delete query, and then run it.

❌ CLEAN UP Close the query, and then close the GardenCompany07 database.

7

Key points

- Create a query to display specific fields from specific records from one or more tables. You can save the query for later use.

- You can use wizards or create queries manually in the Query Designer.

- Queries can use aggregate functions such as Sum and Avg to summarize data, and they can perform calculations on matched data.

- An update query performs an updating action on its results, such as replacing the contents of a field.

- A delete query deletes records that meet specific criteria. Use caution with this type of query; the effects can be far reaching, and you can't recover deleted records.

Chapter at a glance

Modify

Modify forms created by using a wizard,
page 228

Add

Add controls,
page 237

Display

Display subforms,
page 245

Create custom forms

8

IN THIS CHAPTER, YOU WILL LEARN HOW TO

- Modify forms created by using a wizard.

- Add controls.

- Display subforms.

Every form has three basic sections: Form Header, Detail, and Form Footer. When you use the Form tool or a wizard to create a form, a logo placeholder and a title is added to the Form Header section, a set of text box and label controls for each field in the underlying table is added to the Detail section, and the Form Footer section is left blank. You can customize any form by adding controls to its sections and by rearranging controls to make the form easy to work with.

Ease of data entry is the major consideration when designing a form, because the easier this process is, the less likely people are to make mistakes. One of the ways to eliminate mistakes is to have Microsoft Access 2013 enter data automatically based on existing entries. Another is to make it possible to enter data in more than one table at a time by using subforms.

In this chapter, you'll control a form's function and appearance by inserting controls and modifying the form and control properties. You'll also present information from multiple tables in one form by using subforms.

TIP This chapter builds on the discussion of forms in Chapter 3, "Create simple forms."

PRACTICE FILES To complete the exercises in this chapter, you need the practice files contained in the Chapter08 practice file folder. For more information, see "Download the practice files" in this book's Introduction.

Modifying forms created by using a wizard

When a form is intended as the primary method of entering new records, it usually includes all the fields from the underlying table. As demonstrated in Chapter 3, "Create simple forms," the quickest way to create a form that includes all the fields from one table is to use the Form tool. Another method, which provides more control over the creation of the form, is to use a wizard. In either case, you can easily customize the form after it is created.

In Chapter 3, we showed you how to work with forms in Layout view. Because the data in the underlying table or tables is displayed in this view, you can more easily gauge the effects of moving and sizing the controls and their labels. You can display the Property Sheet pane and adjust properties to fine-tune form elements, and you can make most of the adjustments you are likely to want in the custom form.

When you want more control over the layout of a form, you can work in Design view. In this view, you can modify the structure of the form on a design grid, but the data from the underlying table or tables is not visible.

In Design View, Access displays horizontal and vertical rulers and a grid to help you position controls and labels.

The form design grid is divided into three sections:

- **Form Header** Contains information to be displayed at the top of the form, such as a title.

- **Detail** Contains a text box control and an associated label control for each of the fields you selected for inclusion in the form.

- **Form Footer** Can contain information to be displayed at the bottom of the form. By default, this section is blank, so it is closed.

In Design view, you can work with the form in the following ways:

- Adjust the size of sections.

- Apply a theme.

- Change the size of controls.

- Arrange controls logically to facilitate data entry.

- Adjust the properties of form elements in the Property Sheet pane.

- Add fields from the Field List pane.

- Add controls to limit data entry choices or add functionality to the form.

  SEE ALSO For information about adding controls to forms, see "Adding controls" later in this chapter.

In this exercise, you'll use the Form wizard to create a form that displays a list of product categories. You'll then modify the form in Design view by formatting its title, making a control inaccessible to users, changing a label, and adding and resizing a control for a new field.

Different types of forms

Most forms facilitate data entry—adding or editing records in one or more tables. However, some forms are more specialized than others, and some serve purposes other than data entry. The following is an overview of the types of forms you can create by clicking buttons in the Forms group on the Create tab:

- **Form Design** Displays a blank design grid in Design view, in which you can design a form from scratch.

- **Blank form** Displays a blank canvas in Layout view and opens the Field List pane, from which you can drag fields from the database tables onto the form.

- **Navigation** Displays a gallery of predefined navigation form layouts.

  SEE ALSO For information about navigation forms, see "Designing navigation forms" in Chapter 11, "Make databases user friendly."

Clicking the More Forms button displays a gallery of additional types of forms:

- **Multiple items** Displays more than one record at a time on a single form page. Sometimes called a *continuous form*.

- **Datasheet** Looks and behaves like a datasheet (table).

- **Split** Provides two synchronized views of the same data, one in a form and the other in a datasheet. This greatly simplifies the process of finding and editing records.

- **Modal dialog** Looks and behaves like a dialog box. It has default OK and Cancel buttons. When the form is active, nothing else can be done until it is closed.

SET UP You need the GardenCompany08 database located in the Chapter08 practice file folder to complete this exercise. Be sure to use the practice database for this chapter rather than continuing on with the database from an earlier chapter. Open the database, and if you want, save your own version to avoid overwriting the original. Then follow the steps.

1 In the **Navigation** pane, in the **Tables** group, click **Customers**. Then on the **Create** tab, in the **Forms** group, click the **Form Wizard** button to start the **Form** wizard.

If a table is selected in the Navigation pane when you click the Form Wizard button, that table's information populates the wizard's first page.

2 Display the **Tables/Queries** list, and click **Table: Categories**. In the **Available Fields** list, double-click **CategoryID** to move it to the **Selected Fields** list, and double-click **CategoryName**. Then click **Next** to move to the next page, where you choose a layout for the new form.

TIP The preview area on the left shows how the form will look with the selected option applied.

3 Explore the layout options, and then with **Columnar** selected, click **Next**.

4   With **Open the form to view or enter information** selected, click **Finish** to accept
     the suggested title and open the form.

The new form displays the first record in the Categories table.

5   Scroll through a few records by using the controls on the record navigation bar at
     the bottom of the form.

     Let's make a few changes in Design view.

6   Switch to **Design** view.

*The design grid for the Categories form includes a Form Header that contains the title, a Details
area that contains label and text box controls for two fields, and an empty Form Footer.*

7   On the **Design** tool tab, in the **Themes** group, click the **Themes** button. Then in the **Themes** gallery, click the **Whisp** thumbnail to make the color scheme of that theme available to the form.

8   Click the **Form Header** section bar to select that section. Then on the **Format** tool tab, in the **Control Formatting** group, click the **Shape Fill** button. In the top row of the **Theme Colors** palette, click the third swatch (**Light Green, Background 2**).

9   Point to the bottom of the **Form Header** section (just above the **Detail** section bar), and when the pointer changes to a two-headed arrow, drag downward to enlarge the section until the entire **Categories** title control is visible.

10   Click the **Categories** title control. On the **Arrange** tool tab, in the **Sizing & Ordering** group, click the **Size/Space** button to display a list of sizing and spacing options.

Size

- To Fit
- To Tallest
- To Shortest
- To Grid
- To Widest
- To Narrowest

Spacing

- Equal Horizontal
- Increase Horizontal
- Decrease Horizontal
- Equal Vertical
- Increase Vertical
- Decrease Vertical

Grid

- Grid
- Ruler
- Snap to Grid

Grouping

- Group
- Ungroup

The list includes commands for adjusting the size and spacing of controls, in addition to grid and grouping options.

11   In the **Size** area of the list, click **To Fit**.

12   Make the **Form Header** section just tall enough to contain the title control.

Next, suppose we don't want users to be able to change the value in the CategoryID text box control. Let's disable it so that its text and background are gray.

13   In the **Detail** section, click the **CategoryID** text box control, and on the **Design** tool tab, in the **Tools** group, click the **Property Sheet** button.

KEYBOARD SHORTCUT Press F4 to open and close the Property Sheet pane. For a list of keyboard shortcuts, see "Keyboard shortcuts" at the end of this book.

14   In the **Property Sheet** pane, click the **Data** tab. Click the **Enabled** property, click its arrow, and click **No**. Then close the **Property Sheet** pane.

15   Click the **Category Name** label control, double-click **Category**, and then delete it and the following space.

Now let's add the category description from the Categories table to this form.

16   Drag the bottom of the **Detail** section down until the section is about **2.5** inches tall. Then drag the right border until the form design grid is about **5** inches wide.

TIP You cannot change the width of sections independently; widening one section widens the entire form.

17   On the **Design** tool tab, in the **Tools** group, click the **Add Existing Fields** button to open the **Field List** pane.

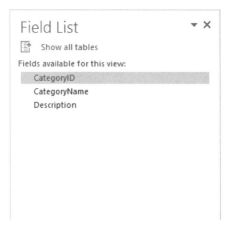

You can click Show All Tables to display the fields from other tables in the database.

18   In the **Field List** pane, click **Description**, drag the field below the **Category Name** text box control in the **Detail** section, and then close the **Field List** pane.

19   Point to the border of the **Description** text box control, and drag the control so that its left edge is aligned with the **Category Name** control and its top edge sits at the **1** inch mark on the vertical ruler.

20   Click the **Description** label control, and drag the large handle in the upper-left corner to the left until the control is aligned with the labels above it. Then widen the control to match the other controls.

21   With the **Description** label control still selected, hold down the **Ctrl** key, and click the **Name** and **CategoryID** label controls to add them to the selection. Then on the **Format** tool tab, in the **Font** group, click the **Align Right** button.

22   On the **Arrange** tool tab, in the **Sizing & Ordering** group, click **Size/Space**. Then in the **Spacing** area of the list, click **Equal Vertical**.

23   Display the **Size/Space** list again, and in the **Size** area, click **To Tallest** to make all the label controls the same size.

24   Select all the text box controls, display the **Property Sheet** pane, and on the **Format** page, set **Left** to **2"**.

25   Make the **Detail** section just tall enough to contain its controls so that the form occupies the smallest possible amount of space.

8

You have added a text box control and its associated label control, and changed the controls' alignment, size, and spacing.

TIP If you point to the border of a text box control and drag it to a new location, the associated label moves with it. Similarly, if you point to the border of a label control and drag, the associated text box control also moves. If you want to move either control independently of the other, you must drag the large gray square in the control's upper-left corner.

Let's look at the results of the changes.

26   Switch to **Form** view.

The labels and their controls now look neater on the form.

27   Scroll through a few category records. Try to edit entries in the **CategoryID** field to confirm that you can't.

The record selector bar down the left side of this form isn't needed right now, so let's turn it off.

28   Switch to **Design** view, and click the form selector (the box in the upper-left corner at the junction of the horizontal and vertical rulers) to display the properties for the entire form **in the Property Sheet** pane .

29   On the **Format** page of the **Property Sheet** pane, change the **Record Selectors** property to **No**. Then close the **Property Sheet** pane.

30   Switch to **Form** view to verify that the form no longer has a record selector.

❌ CLEAN UP Close the Categories form, saving your changes. Keep the GardenCompany08 database open for use in later exercises.

Adding controls

Although text box and label controls are the most common controls found in forms, you can also enhance your forms with many other types of controls. For example, you can add combo boxes, check boxes, and list boxes to present people with choices instead of having them make entries in text boxes.

When a form is displayed in Layout view or Design view, the controls available in that view are located in the Controls gallery on the Design tool tab. Each control is one of the following types:

- **Bound** A control that is linked to a field in a table or the datasheet created by a query. These controls include:
  - Text boxes and labels
  - Option groups and buttons, combo boxes, list boxes, and check boxes
  - Charts
  - Subforms/subreports
- **Unbound** A control that is not bound to any underlying data. These controls include:
  - Buttons and toggle buttons
  - Tabs and page breaks
  - Hyperlinks, web browser controls, and navigation controls
  - Attachments
  - Frames
  - Lines and images

8

In this exercise, you'll insert a picture into the Form Header of a form and replace the default title with a custom one. You'll also replace a text box control in the Detail section with a combo box control.

SET UP You need the GardenCompany08 database you worked with in the preceding exercise and the Hydrangeas graphic located in the Chapter08 practice file folder to complete this exercise. If necessary, open the database. Then open the Customers form in Design view, and follow the steps.

1 In the **Customers** form, make the **Form Header** section about **1.5** inches tall.

2 In the **Form Header** section, select the logo control, hold down the **Ctrl** key, and select the label control. Then press the **Delete** key.

3 On the **Design** tool tab, in the **Controls** group, click the **More** button to display a menu containing the **Controls** gallery.

From the Controls gallery, you can insert bound and unbound controls.

4 In the gallery, click the **Image** thumbnail, and then on the left side of the **Form Header** section, draw a control approximately **1** inch high and **1.5** inches wide. When you release the mouse button, the **Insert Picture** dialog box opens.

5 In the dialog box, navigate to your **Chapter08** practice file folder, and double-click **Hydrangeas**.

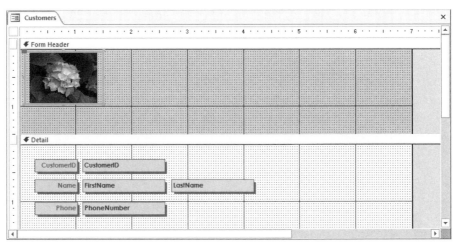

The hydrangeas photo has been inserted into the Form Header section.

TIP How an image fits into an image control is determined by the Size Mode property of the control. If the property is set to Clip and the control isn't large enough to display the entire image, the image is cropped. If the property is set to Stretch, you can enlarge the control to display the entire image. If the property is set to Zoom (the default), the image automatically resizes to fit the control.

Now let's add a label control so that we can enter a title for the form.

6   In the **Controls** group, display the **Controls** gallery, and then click the **Label** thumbnail.

7   To the right of the picture in the **Form Header** section, drag diagonally to draw a control about **2** inches wide and **0.5** inch tall.

8   In the active label control, enter Garden Company. Press **Shift+Enter** to insert a line break, and then enter Customers.

9   Click the **Form Header** section bar. On the **Format** tool tab, in the **Control Formatting** group, click the **Shape Fill** button. Then in the top row of the **Theme Colors** palette, click the third swatch (**Light Green, Background 2**).

10 Select the label text, and in the **Font** group, make the text **20** points, bold, and any dark green color. Then center the text.

11 If **Garden Company** wraps to two lines, drag the sizing handle in the middle of the right side of the label frame to the right until the two words fit on one line. Then on the **Arrange** tool tab, in the **Sizing & Ordering** group, click the **Size/Space** button, and in the **Size** area of the **Size/Space** list, click **To Fit**.

12 Reduce the height of the **Form Header** section so that it is just big enough to contain its controls.

You have completed all the adjustments to the controls in the Form Header section.

Next let's create a combo box that displays a list of possible countries but that also allows users to enter the country if it is not already in the list. First we'll turn off the Control Wizards feature so that we can add a control with all its default settings, without having to work through the associated wizard's pages.

13 On the **Design** tool tab, in the **Controls** group, click the **More** button. At the bottom of the menu, do one of the following:

- If the icon associated with **Use Control Wizards** is not orange (inactive), press **Esc** to close the menu.

- If the icon is orange (active), click **Use Control Wizards** to deactivate the command.

14 Enlarge the **Detail** section to create at least an inch of space below the **Country** controls.

15 Display the **Controls** gallery, and click the **Combo Box** thumbnail. Then drag diagonally to draw a control below the **Country** text box control. Make it approximately **1.5** inches wide and **0.25** inch tall.

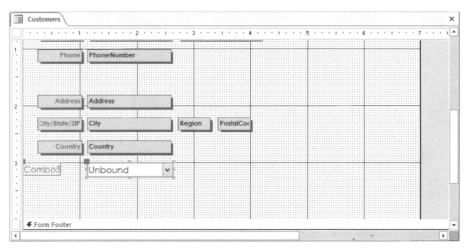

Because the combo box control is not attached to a field in the Customers table, its name is Unbound.

TIP Access assigns a number to each control when it is created. Don't be concerned if the numbers associated with the controls you create are different from those in our graphics.

16 Click the **Country** text box control. On the **Format** tool tab, in the **Font** group, click the **Format Painter** button, and then click the combo box control.

TIP The formatting of the Country text box is copied to both the combo box control and its label.

Now let's create a simple query that extracts one example of every country in the Country field of the Customers table and displays the results as a list when users click the combo box arrow.

17 Right-click the combo box, and then click **Properties** to open the **Property Sheet** pane.

18   In the pane, click the **Data** tab. Then click the **Control Source** arrow, and in the list, click **Country** to bind the combo box control to the **Country** field in the **Customers** table.

19   Verify that the **Row Source Type** property is set to **Table/Query**. Then in the **Row Source** box, enter the following:

SELECT DISTINCT Customers.Country FROM Customers;

Be sure to include the period (but no space) between *Customers* and *Country*, and the semicolon at the end of the text. (The words in capital letters are instructions and the remaining words are variables that identify the field and the table to which the instructions should be applied.)

Property Sheet	▾ ✕
Selection type: Combo Box	

Combo55	⌄

Format	Data	Event	Other	All

Control Source	Country
Row Source	SELECT DISTINCT Customers.Country FROM Customers; ⌄ …
Row Source Type	Table/Query
Bound Column	1
Limit To List	No
Allow Value List Edits	Yes
List Items Edit Form	
Inherit Value List	Yes
Show Only Row Source Value	No
Input Mask	
Default Value	
Validation Rule	
Validation Text	
Enabled	Yes
Locked	No
Auto Expand	Yes

To display the entire query, you can widen the Property Sheet pane by dragging its left border to the left.

20   Click the combo box label control. Click the **Format** tab of the **Property Sheet** pane, and change the **Caption** property to Country.

21   Click the original **Country** text box control, and press **Delete** to delete the control and its associated label. Then move the new combo box and label into their places, sizing them as needed.

> **TIP** To ensure that new controls are aligned with existing controls, you can click an existing control and make a note of its Width, Height, Top, and Left properties. Then use whichever of those settings is relevant to fine-tune the new control. You can also use the Arrow keys to nudge the controls into place.

22   Shrink the size of the **Detail** section until it is only as tall as it needs to be to hold its controls. Also shrink the width of the form so that the contents of all the sections fit neatly.

Let's draw a dark green line across the form, below the Phone control, and make sure that no matter what size the program window is, the line always stretches across the width of the form.

23   If the entire form design grid is not visible, close the **Property Sheet** pane. Then from the **Design** tool tab, display the **Controls** gallery, click the **Line** thumbnail, and drag a line across the width of the form design grid to separate the name and phone number information from the address.

24   If the **Property Sheet** pane is closed, open it, and set the **Height** property to 0 and the **Border Width** property to **2 pt**. Then close the pane.

> **TIP** Setting the height to 0 does not make the line invisible; it ensures that the line is straight.

25   With the line still selected, on the **Format** tool tab, in the **Control Formatting** group, click the **Shape Outline** button, and set the line color to the same dark green color as the title in the **Form Header** section.

26   On the **Arrange** tool tab, in the **Position** group, click the **Anchoring** button to display the **Anchoring** gallery.

8

Top Left	Stretch Across Top	Top Right	
Stretch Down	Stretch Down and Across	Stretch Down and Right	
Bottom Left	Stretch Across Bottom	Bottom Right	

You can anchor a control in four positions and make it stretch in five directions.

27 In the gallery, click **Stretch Across Top**.

28 Switch to **Form** view, and try making the program window various sizes. Notice that although the width of the form was only about **7** inches in **Design** view, the form header and the line always span the width of the window, no matter what its size.

As a last step, let's test the combo box control.

29 Scroll through a couple of records, and then click the **Country** combo box arrow to display the country list.

Selecting possible entries is quick and easy with a combo box.

CLEAN UP Close the Customers form, saving your changes. Keep the GardenCompany08 database open for use in the last exercise.

Displaying subforms

As you saw in "Exploring forms" in Chapter 1, "Explore Microsoft Access 2013," if a one-to-many relationship exists between two tables, you can display information from both the "one" and the "many" sides of the relationship by using a main form and a subform. For example, the main form for related Customers and Orders tables might display information about a customer (the "one" side), and the subform might list all the orders that the customer has placed (the "many" side).

Suppose you want to create a main form that includes all the fields of one table with a subform that includes all the fields of another table. As long as there is only one one-to-many relationship between the tables already defined on the Relationships page, the fastest way to create the form and its subform is by using the Form tool. Simply click the primary table in the Navigation pane, and then on the Create tab, in the Forms group, click the Form button. The Form tool creates and displays a main form and subform, each containing all the fields of its source table.

Selecting fields for main forms and subforms

If you want to create a main form and subform that include only some of the fields in their underlying tables, use the Form wizard, as follows:

1 Ensure that there is a relationship between the tables. Then on the **Create** tab, in the **Forms** group, click the **Form Wizard** button.

2 On the wizard's first page, in the **Tables/Queries** list, click the table on which you want to base the form.

3 In the **Available Fields** list, double-click the fields you want to include in the main form to move them to the **Selected Fields** list.

4 In the **Tables/Queries** list, click the table on which you want to base the subform.

5 In the **Available Fields** list, double-click the fields you want to include in the subform, and then click **Next**.

6 On the wizard's second page, with the primary table and **Form with subform(s)** selected, click **Next**.

7 On the third page, select the layout you want, and then click **Next**.

8 On the last page, enter the titles you want for your forms, and with **Open the form to view or enter information** selected, click **Finish**.

8

If you have already created a main form and you now want to add a subform to it, you can add a subform/subreport control to the main form.

In this exercise, you'll add a subform to an existing form in Design view, and you'll then modify its appearance in Layout view.

SET UP You need the GardenCompany08 database you worked with in the preceding exercise to complete this exercise. If necessary, open the database. Then open the Categories form in Design view, and follow the steps.

1   Enlarge your workspace by expanding the **Detail** section until it is approximately **3** inches tall.

2   On the **Design** tab, display the **Controls** menu. If the **Use Control Wizards** icon near the bottom of the menu is not active (orange), click the command.

3   In the **Controls** gallery, click the **Subform/Subreport** thumbnail. Then in the **Detail** section, below the **Description** label and text box controls, drag a control, which starts the **SubForm** wizard.

On the first page of the SubForm wizard, you select the source of the subform data.

4   With **Use existing Tables and Queries** selected, click **Next**.

5   Display the **Tables/Queries** list, and click **Table: Products**.

6   In the **Available Fields** list, double-click the **ProductName**, **CategoryID**, **Quantity-PerUnit**, **UnitPrice**, and **UnitsInStock** fields to add them to the **Selected Fields** list. Then click **Next**.

On the third page of the SubForm wizard, you specify how the main form and subform are linked.

TIP Because there is a relationship between the Products table and the Categories table that is based on the CategoryID field, the wizard selects Choose From A List and indicates the relationship it will use. If the wizard can't identify which fields are related, it selects the Define My Own option and displays list boxes in which you can specify which fields should be related.

7   With **Choose from a list** selected, click **Next**, and then click **Finish** to accept the suggested name for the subform and embed it in the **Categories** form.

The subform control has its own Form Header, Detail, and Form Footer sections, and can be scrolled independently of the main form.

8   Above the upper-left corner of the subform control, click the **Products subform** label, and press **Delete**.

Let's explore the subform in various views.

9   Switch to **Form** view, where by default, the subform looks like a datasheet.

The subform has its own scroll bars and record navigation bar.

TIP This main form and subform are ideal for checking which products are assigned to which categories and for looking up information about the products in a category. But if you want to create a form whose main purpose is data entry, be sure to include all the fields in which the database user will need to enter information.

10 Right-click the subform, point to **Subform**, and then click **Form**. Notice that when the subform is in **Form** view, it reflects its layout in **Design** view.

The form layout is not as useful as the datasheet layout.

11   Switch the subform back to **Datasheet** view.

Let's modify the layout of the subform.

12   Switch to **Layout** view. Then click any field in the subform, and on the **Home** tab, in the **Text Formatting** group, change the font size to **9**.

13   Double-click the right border of each field name to adjust the column to its widest entry.

14   Widen the subform so that **Units in Stock** is visible, by dragging the subform's right border to the right.

Adjusting field widths is often easier in Layout view, where the underlying data from the table is visible.

Let's test the subform.

15 Switch to **Form** view. Then use the record navigation bar for the main form to display each category in turn, verifying that the products in that category are listed in the datasheet in the subform.

16 Click the **First record** button to return to the first category (**Bulbs**). Then in the subform, click **Bulbs** in the **Category** column to the right of the first product (**Magic Lily**).

   TIP Because the Category field is a combo box control, an arrow appears at the right end of the field to indicate that you can select a field value from a list.

17 Click the field's arrow to display the list of categories, and then change the category to **Cacti**.

18   On the main form's record navigation bar, click the **Next record** button to move to the **Cacti** category. Notice that the subform now includes the **Magic Lily** record.

19   Display the **Category** list for the **Magic Lily** record, and return it to the **Bulbs** category.

Let's delete the product category from the subform to ensure that it can't be changed.

20   Switch to **Design** view, and click **Yes** when prompted to save the form and the subform.

21   In the subform, click the **CategoryID** combo box control, and then press **Delete**.

22   Save the form, switch back to **Layout** view, and then adjust the width of the subform, allowing space for the scroll bar.

23   Switch to **Form** view, and scroll through the main form categories to view the results.

Categories				✕

Categories

Category ID   1

Name   Bulbs

Description   Spring, summer and fall, forced

Product Name	Quantity Per Unit	Unit Price	Units In Stock
Magic Lily	One dozen	$48.40	40
Autumn Crocus	One dozen	$22.69	37
Anemone	One dozen	$33.88	26
Lily-of-the-Field	One dozen	$45.98	34
Siberian Iris	6 per pkg.	$15.67	30
Daffodil	6 per pkg.	$15.67	24
Peony	6 per pkg.	$24.14	20
Lilies	6 per pkg.	$12.71	18
Begonias	6 per pkg.	$22.93	12

Record: I◄ ◄ 1 of 10 ► ►I ►* 🔽 No Filter   Search

Record: I◄ ◄ 1 of 18 ► ►I ►* 🔽 No Filter   Search

You can easily use this form to check the assignments of products to categories.

❌ CLEAN UP Close the Categories form, and click Yes twice to save your changes. Then close the GardenCompany08 database.

Key points

- Forms have three main sections: Form Header, Detail, and Form Footer. You can size them to suit the needs of the form.

- You can customize any section of your form's layout by adding and deleting labels, moving labels and text box controls, and adding graphics.

- After you define a relationship between tables, you can add a subform to a main form.

8

Chapter at a glance

Create

Create reports manually,
page 256

Modify

Modify report content,
page 262

Add

Add subreports,
page 270

Create custom reports

IN THIS CHAPTER, YOU WILL LEARN HOW TO

- Create reports manually.

- Modify report content.

- Add subreports.

Reports often include sets of information that are related to the topic of the report, but not necessarily related to each other. For example, a report might include information about the production, marketing, and sales activities of a company. Or it might include information about compensation and the company's pension plan. Each topic is related to a particular aspect of running the business, but the topics don't all fit nicely into the structure of an individual Microsoft Access 2013 report.

One solution to this problem is to create separate reports, print them, and store them together in a binder. Another is to save them in electronic format in a folder or on a network. An easier and more sophisticated solution is to combine them by using subreports.

In this chapter, you'll build a fairly complex report. You'll start by creating the report shell (the main report) manually in Design view. Then you'll modify the layout and content of the shell report. Finally, you'll provide detailed information by embedding a subreport within the main report.

TIP This chapter builds on the discussion of reports in Chapter 5, "Create simple reports."

PRACTICE FILES To complete the exercises in this chapter, you need the practice file contained in the Chapter09 practice file folder. For more information, see "Download the practice files" in this book's Introduction.

Creating reports manually

When a report includes controls that are bound to specific fields in one or more tables, usually the most efficient way to create the report is by using the Report wizard. When you include more than one table in a report, the wizard evaluates the relationships between the tables and offers to group the records in any logical manner available. As with multitable forms, if you haven't already established the relationships between the tables, you have to cancel the wizard and establish them before continuing.

TIP If you are using more than two tables in a report, or if you will be using the same combination of tables in several reports or forms, you can save time by creating a query based on those tables and then using the results of that query as the basis for the report or form. For information about queries, see Chapter 7, "Create queries."

When a report will include mostly unbound controls, which don't pull information from underlying tables, it is easier to create the report manually in Design view. In this view, the structure of the report is laid out on a design grid, in much the same arrangement as a form in Design view.

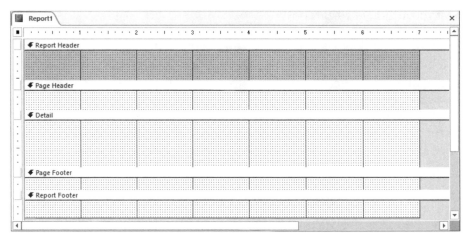

Reports have five main sections and can include additional grouping sections.

The report design grid is divided into five main sections:

- **Report Header** Contains information to be displayed at the top of the first page of the report, such as the report title.

- **Page Header** Contains information to be displayed at the top of every page of the report, like the header in a Microsoft Word document.

- **Detail** Usually contains the controls that make up the main body of the report.

- **Page Footer** Contains information to be displayed at the bottom of every page, such as a page number.

- **Report Footer** Contains information to be displayed at the bottom of the last page of the report.

By default, the Report Header and Report Footer sections are not present on the report. You can hide and display the Report Header, Report Footer, Page Header, or Page Footer sections by right-clicking the design grid and then clicking the respective command. You can also close a section without removing it by setting the Height property in its Property Sheet pane to 0". (This technique can be useful if you want to concentrate on one section without being distracted by another.)

To organize a report, you can group and sort its contents. When you group information, such as grouping all customers by region or all products by category, a Group Header section is added to the report for each grouping level you specify. Group headers are identified by the field name in their section bars.

As with forms, you can work with reports in Design view in the following ways:

- Apply a theme.

- Adjust the size of sections.

- Add, size, and arrange controls.

- Adjust the properties of report elements in the Property Sheet pane.

9

Adding hyperlinks, charts, and buttons

A variety of additional controls are available to enhance the usefulness of reports and forms, such as the following:

▪ **Hyperlink**   Clicking the **Hyperlink** button in the **Controls** gallery displays the **Insert Hyperlink** dialog box. You can insert a static link to a file, a webpage, another object in the database, or an email message window by using the same techniques you would use to insert a hyperlink in other Microsoft Office 2013 programs. For example, you might want to add a link to your organization's website.

> **TIP** In forms, you can use a Web Browser control to insert a dynamic hyperlink that changes depending on the data displayed. To set up dynamic links, click Hyperlink Builder in the Link to bar of the Insert Hyperlink dialog box to separate the target address into its component parts. For more information about the Web Browser control, search for *Add Web browsing to a form* in Access Help.

▪ **Chart**   You can use the **Chart** wizard to plot the data in an existing table or query (or both). In the **Controls** gallery, click the **Chart** button, and then drag to create the control that will hold the chart and start the **Chart** wizard. Follow the wizard's instructions to select the data that will be plotted, the type of chart, and the layout. When you click **Finish**, the chart appears in the control, which you can move and size like any other control.

▪ **Button**   You can create a button that performs a specific task, such as displaying the **Print** dialog box. To add a button to a report, click the **Button** button, and click to create the button control. Right-click the control, and click **Build Event**. Double-click **Macro Builder**, and in the **Actions** area in the **Action Catalog** pane, expand the type of action you want. Double-click the action to open a page on which you can add any information the macro needs, and then close the page. You can assign a name and picture to the button on the **Format** page of its **Property Sheet** pane.

> **TIP** Adding a button to a form is much easier than adding one to a report. In the Controls gallery, click the Button button, and then click to create the button control and start the Command Button wizard. Follow the wizard's instructions to select the action, icon, and name for the button. Click Finish to insert the button in the location you clicked. You can then move and size it like any other control. Behind the scenes, the wizard embeds a macro in the control's On Click property. To view the macro, display the Event page of the button's Property Sheet pane, and then click the Ellipsis button to open the page containing the macro.

In this exercise, you'll manually create a shell report that contains a Report Header section, a Page Footer section, and a section in which you will add grouped data in a later exercise.

SET UP You need the GardenCompany09 database located in the Chapter09 practice file folder to complete this exercise. Be sure to use the practice database for this chapter rather than continuing on with the database from an earlier chapter. Open the database, and if you want, save your own version to avoid overwriting the original. Then follow the steps.

1 Without selecting a table or query in the **Navigation** pane, on the **Create** tab, in the **Reports** group, click the **Report Design** button to display a blank report design grid that has the default sections for a new report: **Page Header**, **Detail**, and **Page Footer**.

2 Right-click anywhere in the design grid, and then click **Report Header/Footer** to enclose the default sections with **Report Header** and **Report Footer** sections.

Now let's add the category name from the Categories table to this form.

3 On the **Design** tool tab, in the **Tools** group, click the **Add Existing Fields** button to open the **Field List** pane, which is currently empty because no source table or query is selected in the **Navigation** pane.

KEYBOARD SHORTCUT Press Alt+F8 to open and close the Field List pane. For a list of keyboard shortcuts, see "Keyboard shortcuts" at the end of this book.

4 In the **Field List** pane, click **Show all tables**

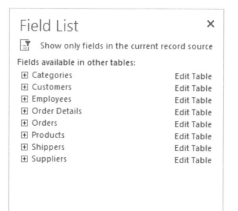

The Field List pane displays a list of all the tables whose fields you can add to the report.

5   In the **Field List** pane, expand the **Categories** table by clicking the adjacent plus sign.

6   Double-click the **CategoryName** field to add label and text box controls for that field to the **Detail** section of the report design grid.

7   Close the **Field List** pane and resize the **Details** section of the report until all the sections are visible.

Let's group the records in the report by category.

8   On the **Design** tool tab, in the **Grouping & Totals** group, click the **Group & Sort** button to open the **Group, Sort, and Total** pane at the bottom of the report page.

9   In the **Group, Sort, and Total** pane, click **Add a group** to add a **Group on** bar with the **select field** list displayed.

10   In the **select field** list, click **CategoryName** to add a **CategoryName Header** section to the report.

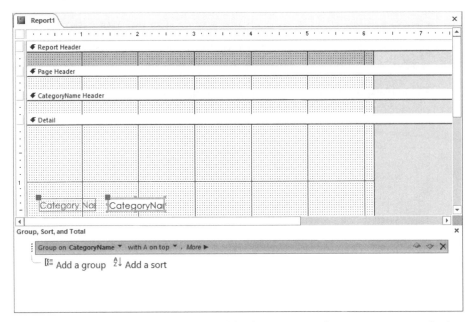

In the final report, records will be grouped by the category whose name appears in the CategoryName Header section.

11   Close the **Group, Sort, and Total** pane.

12   Save the report as *Sales By Category*.

Let's make a few changes to the report layout.

13   Point to the border of the **CategoryName** text box control (not the gray handle), and drag the control into the **CategoryName Header** section, which also moves the associated label control.

14   In the **Tools** group, click the **Property Sheet** button.

KEYBOARD SHORTCUT Press F4 to open and close the Property Sheet pane.

15   Click the **Report Header** section bar, and then on the **Format** page of the **Property Sheet** pane, set the **Height** property to 1″.

TIP You complete the setting of a property by clicking another property or by pressing Enter.

16   Repeat step 15 to set the **Height** property for the other sections of the report as follows:

PageHeader	0″ (closes the section)
CategoryName Header	2.2″
Detail	0″ (closes the section)
Page Footer	0.2″
Report Footer	0″ (closes the section)

TIP You can manually set the height of a section by dragging its bottom edge up or down.

17   Close the **Property Sheet** pane.

9

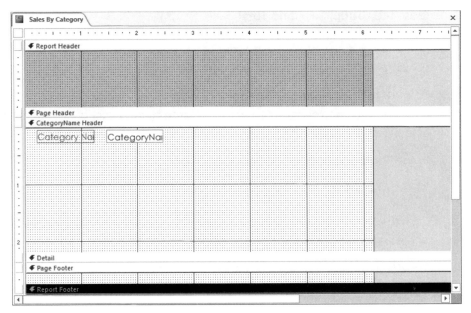

Only the Report Header, CategoryName Header, and Page Footer sections are now open.

18   Switch to **Print Preview** to display the results of your work.

⊗ CLEAN UP Close the Sales By Category report, saving your changes. Keep the
GardenCompany09 database open for use in later exercises.

Modifying report content

Reports are like forms in the following ways:

- You can create them by using wizards and then modify them in Layout view or
  Design view.

- You can display information from one or more records from one or more tables
  or queries.

- You can have multiple sets of headers and footers to group and describe their
  contents.

Whether you create a report with the Report wizard or manually, you can always modify it by adding controls or changing the layout or formatting of the existing controls. As with forms, you can modify reports in either Layout view or Design view. Layout view is more intuitive because the data is visible while you make adjustments, but Design view gives you more control. In Design view, refining a report can be an iterative process, and you will often find yourself switching back and forth between Design view and Print Preview to evaluate each change and plan the next.

In this exercise, you'll modify the content of a report by inserting a title and date in the report header and page numbers in the report footer. You'll also insert and remove labels and change the appearance of text.

 SET UP You need the GardenCompany09 database you worked with in the preceding exercise to complete this exercise. If necessary, open the database. Then open the Sales By Category report in Design view, and follow the steps.

1   In the upper-left corner of the report, double-click the report selector (the box at the junction of the horizontal and vertical rulers), which both selects the entire report and opens the **Property Sheet** pane.

2   On the **Format** page of the **Property Sheet** pane, set the **Grid X** and **Grid Y** properties to 10 to make the grid larger. Then close the **Property Sheet** pane.

    TIP You can quickly turn the grid or the rulers on and off by right-clicking the report and then clicking Grid or Ruler.

    Let's make some formatting changes.

3   Click the **Report Header** section bar, and on the **Format** tool tab, in the **Control Formatting** group, click the **Shape Fill** button. Then in the top row of the **Theme Colors** palette, click the third swatch (**Light Green, Background 2**).

4   On the **Design** tool tab, in the **Header/Footer** group, click the **Title** button to insert a control layout containing the following cells and controls:

    ▪ In the cell on the left, a logo placeholder

    ▪ In the cell in the center, a label control containing the report title

    ▪ In the upper-right cell, a date placeholder

    ▪ In the lower-right cell, a time placeholder

9

Layouts

Layouts are optional mechanisms for constraining the alignment of controls. By default, Access provides two layout formats:

- **Tabular** Inserts controls in cells arranged in columns and rows. The label controls are always in the section above the text box controls so that they resemble column headings. By default, Access uses the Tabular layout for reports created with the Report tool and for blank reports populated by dragging fields from the Field List pane.

- **Stacked** Inserts controls in cells arranged in two columns, with label controls in the left column's cells and text box controls in the right column's cells. By default, Access uses the Stacked layout for forms created with the Form tool and for blank forms populated by dragging fields from the Field List pane.

To impose a layout or switch from one layout to the other:

- On the **Arrange** tool tab, in the **Table** group, click the button for the layout you want.

To remove a layout so that you can place controls where you want them:

- Select all the controls in the layout. Then click the **Remove Layout** button in the **Table** group.

- Right-click the selection, click **Layout**, and then click **Remove Layout**.

To add a row of controls to an existing layout:

- Select an adjacent cell, and in the **Rows & Columns** group, click the **Insert Above** or **Insert Below** button.

To add a column of controls to an existing layout:

- Select an adjacent cell, and in the **Rows & Columns** group, click the **Insert Left** or **Insert Right** button.

To delete a row or column from a layout:

- Right-click a cell in the row or column, and click **Delete Row** or **Delete Column**.
- Select the row or column, and then press **Delete**.

To merge two cells in a layout (so that one control can span two columns or two rows):

- Select the cells, and in the **Merge/Split** group, click the **Merge** button.

To split a cell in a layout (so that two controls can fit in one column or one row):

- Select the cell, and in the **Merge/Split** group, click the **Split Horizontally** or **Split Vertically** button.

5   With the title selected, on the **Format** tool tab, in the **Font** group, make the title **20** points, bold, and any dark green color.

6   On the **Arrange** tool tab, in the **Sizing & Ordering** group, click the **Size/Space** button, and then click **To Fit** to make the label control fit the title.

Now let's add the date.

7   On the **Design** tool tab, in the **Header/Footer** group, click the **Date and Time** button to open the **Date and Time** dialog box.

You can specify options for both date controls and time controls in this dialog box.

8   With the **Include Date** check box and the first date format option selected, clear the **Include Time** check box. Then click **OK** to insert a control containing the =**Date()** function in the upper-right cell of the layout in the **Report Header** section.

Because the layout constrains the controls, the control containing the title shrinks to make room for the control containing the date.

TIP If you insert a date and time control in a report that doesn't have a Report Header section, Access adds the section and inserts the control. This control's function will insert the current date whenever you generate the report.

Let's remove the layout from the Report Header section so that we have more options for arranging the controls.

9   Hold down the **Ctrl** key, and select all the controls and placeholders in the **Report Header** section. Then right-click the selection, click **Layout**, and click **Remove Layout**.

10   Point to the alert button that appears, and read the warning about the two controls in this section not being associated with each other. Then click the button, and in the list, click **Dismiss Error**.

TIP It is always wise to investigate these alerts, but in this exercise, you can dismiss any alerts displayed about unassociated controls.

11   Click a blank area of the section to release the selection. Then drag the date control below the title control.

TIP When you release the mouse button, the date control snaps into position against the grid. You can prevent grid snapping by clicking the Size/Space button in the Sizing & Ordering group on the Arrange tab, and then clicking Snap To Grid to turn it off. If you want to override Snap To Grid and position a control precisely, set the Top and Left properties in the Property Sheet pane.

12   Right-click the title control, click **Size**, and click **To Fit**. Then Use the **Width** and **Left** properties to adjust the width and position of the date control to match the title control.

13   Center the date control, and then click away from the control.

The Report Header section now contains only two controls.

TIP If you need to format or move several controls in a section, first group them together. Select the controls, click the Size/Space button in the Sizing & Ordering group on the Arrange tool tab, and then in the Grouping area of the list, click Group. Grouped controls can be manipulated as a unit, but not individually. To change just one of the controls, you must first ungroup all the controls.

Now let's turn our attention to the CategoryName Header section.

14   In the **CategoryName Header** section, delete the **Category Name** label.

15   Select the **CategoryName** text box control, and make it **16** points, bold, and the same dark green you used previously. Then open the **Property Sheet** pane, set the **Height** property to 0.3" and the **Width** property to 2.0", and close the **Property Sheet** pane.

16   Move the control so that its top sits against the top of the section and its left border sits two grid points in from the left edge of the section.

17   On the **Design** tool tab, display the **Controls** gallery, and click the **Label** thumbnail. Then click directly below the lower-left corner of the **CategoryName** text box control.

TIP To precisely align the left edge of one control with that of another, set their Left properties to the same value.

18   In the label control, enter Product: (including the colon), and then press **Enter**. Notice that, because this label is unassociated, an alert button appears.

19   Click the alert button, and then in the list, click **Ignore Error**.

20   Make the label **12** points, bold, and italic. Then if necessary, size the control to fit its contents.

The CategoryName Header section now contains a text box control and a label control.

Now let's add a page number to the Page Footer section.

21   On the **Design** tool tab, in the **Header / Footer** group, click the **Page Numbers** button to open the **Page Numbers** dialog box.

You can set the format, position, and alignment of page numbers all in one dialog box.

22   In the **Format** area, click **Page N of M**. In the **Position** area, click **Bottom of Page [Footer]**. Then with **Center** as the **Alignment** setting and the **Show Number on First Page** check box selected, click **OK**. Notice that a control containing **"Page " & [Page] & " of " & [Pages]** appears in the center of the **Page Footer** section.

TIP In this expression, "Page" and " of " are literal strings of characters, & is the Concatenate operator, and [Page] and [Pages] are two identifiers derived from the report itself. For information about expressions and operators, see "Validating the data" in Chapter 6, "Maintain data integrity."

23   Save the report, and then switch to **Print Preview**.

You can page through the report to view all the product categories.

✖ CLEAN UP Close the Sales By Category report. Keep the GardenCompany09 database open for use in the last exercise.

9

Adding subreports

When you want to be able to show data from two related tables in a report, you can insert a subreport into a main report. You create the main report as you would any other report. Then you use a wizard to insert either the subreport itself or a subreport control into the main report. In either case, both the main report and the subreport appear as objects in the Reports group of the Navigation pane.

TIP After establishing the correct table relationships, you can quickly insert an existing report as a subreport of another by opening the main report in Design view and then dragging the second report from the Reports group of the Navigation pane to the appropriate section of the main report.

Depending on the nature of the information in a report or subreport, you might be able to enhance the usefulness of both types of reports by performing calculations in them. You can insert unbound controls and then use the Expression Builder to create expressions that tell Access what to calculate and how, thereby making summary information and statistics readily available in one report.

In this exercise, you'll select a query as a record source for a report and insert a subreport into a main report to display sales per product and per category. Then you'll display calculated totals for each category.

SET UP You need the GardenCompany09 database you worked with in the preceding exercise to complete this exercise. If necessary, open the database. Then open the Sales By Category report in Design view, and follow the steps.

1 Double-click the report selector to select the report and open the **Property Sheet** pane.

2 On the **Data** page, click the **Record Source** arrow, and in the list, click **Sales By Category** to base the report on the results of that existing query. Then close the **Property Sheet** pane.

3 On the **Design** tool tab, display the menu containing the **Controls** gallery, and ensure that **Use Control Wizards** is active. Next click the **Subform/Subreport** button. Then click in the **CategoryName Header** section approximately two grid points below the lower-left corner of the **Product** label control to insert a blank, unbound subreport control into the main report and start the **SubReport** wizard.

The first step is to choose the object on which the subreport will be based.

4 With **Use existing Tables and Queries** selected, click **Next**.

5 In the **Tables/Queries** list, click **Query: Sales By Category**.

6 Move **CategoryID**, **ProductName**, and **ProductSales** from the **Available Fields** list to the **Selected Fields** list, and then click **Next**.

7 With **Choose from a list** and **Show Sales By Category for each record in Sales By Category using CategoryID** selected, click **Next**.

   TIP The option selected in the list box is displayed in its entirety below the list box.

8 Click **Finish** to replace the unbound subreport control with a control named **Sales by Category subreport**.

   Let's adjust the size of the subreport and delete the controls we don't need.

9 With the entire subreport control selected, open the **Property Sheet** pane.

   TROUBLESHOOTING If the subreport control is not selected, click its top edge to select it.

10 On the **Format** page, set the **Width** property to **6.6"** and the **Height** property to **2.0"**. Then close the **Property Sheet** pane.

11   Delete all the controls in the **Report Header** section of the subreport.

12   In the main report, delete the partially hidden **Sales by Category subreport** label control.

> **TIP** If you accidentally delete a control, click the Undo button on the Quick Access Toolbar to undo the deletion.

13   In the **Detail** section of the subreport, delete the **CategoryID** text box control.

The sales for each product will appear in the subreport's Detail section.

Now let's make some formatting changes to the controls in the Detail section.

14   Select the **ProductName** text box control, display the **Format** page of the **Property Sheet** pane, change the **Font Size** property to **9**, and change the **Width** property to **2.125"**.

15   At the top of the **Property Sheet** pane, change the control selection to **ProductSales**, change the **Font Size** property to **9**, change the **Left** property to **3.5"**, and change the **Width** property to **1"**.

You have formatted the two controls in the Detail section of the subreport.

Next let's create a summarizing function that will calculate the total of the ProductSales values in the subreport's Report Footer section.

16   In the **Property Sheet** pane, change the control selection to **Report Footer**, set its **Height** property to $0.333''$, and press **Enter**. Then scroll the subreport until the entire **Report Footer** section is visible.

17   On the **Design** tool tab, display the **Controls** gallery, click the **Text Box** thumbnail, and click in the center of the **Report Footer** section to insert an unbound control and its label.

18   Select the label of the unbound control, and in the **Property Sheet** pane, set the following properties:

Caption	Total:
Font Size	9
Font Weight	Bold

19   In the subreport, click the unbound control, and then on the **Data** page of the **Property Sheet** pane, in the **Control Source** property, click the **Ellipsis** button to open the **Expression Builder** dialog box.

20   In the **Expression Elements** list, double-click **Functions**, and then click **Built-In Functions**.

21   In the **Expression Values** list, double-click **Sum** to display **Sum (<<expression>>)** in the expression box.

9

22   Click **<<expression>>**. In the **Expression Elements** list, click **Sales By Category subreport**, and then in the **Expression Categories** list, double-click **ProductSales**.

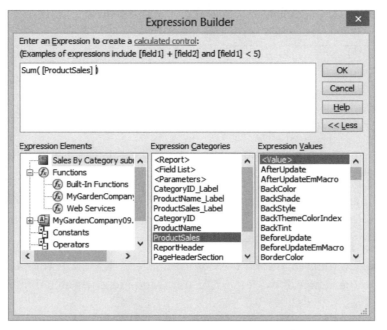

You have built an expression that calculates the total of the ProductSales values.

23   Click **OK** to close the **Expression Builder** and enter the calculation both in the unbound control and as the **Control Source** property in the **Property Sheet** pane.

Let's make the two controls in the Report Footer section match the locations and sizes of the controls in the Detail section.

24   With the calculated control still selected, on the **Format** page, set **Font Size** to **9** and **Font Weight** to **Bold**.

25   Set the **Format** property to **Currency**, and change the **Left** property to 3.5".

26   Click the **Total** label control, and change its **Left** property to 1.3" and its **Width** property to 2.125".

27   Switch to **Print Preview** to examine the results.

For each product category, the report shows the total of the sales per product and per category.

As a final touch, let's adjust the position of the Product label control and remove the subreport's border.

28 Switch back to **Design** view, cut and paste the **Product:** label control from the **CategoryName Header** section to the subreport's **Report Header** section, and then align it with the **ProductName** control in the **Detail** section.

29 Click the top edge of the subreport to select it. Then on the **Format** page of the **Property Sheet** pane, change the **Border Style** property to **Transparent**.

30 Preview the report.

> **TIP** Several factors affect the layout of the subreport. The width of the subreport sets the width of the space available for the display of text. The minimum height of the area in which field values (in this case, product information) are displayed is the height you set for the subreport (because the Can Shrink property for the subreport is set to No). The maximum height of the field value display area is the length of the list (because the Can Grow property is set to Yes) plus the space between the bottom of the subreport and the bottom of the Detail section. You might want to experiment with these settings to understand how they interact.

✖ CLEAN UP Close the Sales By Category report, saving both the main report and subreport when prompted. Then close the GardenCompany09 database.

Key points

- When a report includes mostly unbound controls, it is easier to create the report manually in Design view.

- Refining a report in Design view gives you more control than working in Layout view, but be prepared to switch back and forth between Design view and Print Preview to evaluate each change.

- Insert a subreport within another report to show grouped information in meaningful ways.

- You can often enhance the usefulness of a subreport by performing calculations in unbound controls to summarize its data.

Database management and security

Chapter at a glance

Import

Import information,
page 280

Export

Export information,
page 295

Copy

Copy to and from other Office programs,
page 306

Import and export data 10

IN THIS CHAPTER, YOU WILL LEARN HOW TO

- Import information.

- Export information.

- Copy to and from other Office programs.

Good database design saves keystrokes when you're entering new information and maintaining a database. But when you are populating a database, you can save even more time and effort in another way: by importing data from existing files in other formats.

When you import information into a Microsoft Access 2013 database, the data being imported usually needs to match certain patterns, or the import process might fail. There aren't any such restrictions when exporting data from an Access database, and the process rarely fails. However, some exported database objects aren't very useful in certain formats.

All the methods of importing and exporting data described in this chapter work well, but they aren't the only ways to share information with other programs. Sometimes simple copy and paste techniques are the most efficient methods, especially when you want to make Access data available to other Microsoft Office 2013 programs.

TIP Importing from and exporting to Microsoft SQL Server (the OBDC Database options in the Import & Link group on the External Data tab) is beyond the scope of this book. For information, search for *SQL Server* in Access Help.

In this chapter, you'll experiment with getting information into and out of an Access database. After an overview of the import processes for different types of files, you'll import data from various sources. Then you'll export data to other Office 2013 programs. Finally, you'll copy and paste data directly from an Access database into a Microsoft Word document and a Microsoft Excel worksheet.

Importing information

If the information you intend to store in an Access database already exists in almost any other electronic document, it is quite likely that you can move it into Access without re-entering it, by using the Get External Data wizard. With this wizard, the standard steps for importing data into an Access 2013 database are as follows:

1   On the **External Data** tab, in the **Import & Link** group, click the button for the type of source file you want to import, which starts the **Get External Data** wizard.

   TIP Clicking the Data Services button doesn't start the wizard. Instead, it opens the Create Link To Data Services dialog box. A discussion of Data Services is beyond the scope of this book.

2   On the wizard's first page, specify the source file's location. Depending on the source type, also specify whether to import the source file as a new table, to append the source file's data to an existing table, or to create a linked table. Then click **OK** to open the appropriate import wizard or open the dialog box necessary to complete the next step.

   TIP If you want to import data into an existing table but the data structure isn't the same as the table structure, it's often easier to import the data into Excel, manipu-late it there, and then import it into Access.

3   Follow the instructions for selecting data from the source file, formatting the data, choosing a primary key, and naming the target object. Then click **Finish**.

When the import process is complete, you return to the Get External Data wizard, which gives you the opportunity to save the import steps so that you don't have to repeat them for other similar import processes. To save the import steps:

1   In the **Get External Data** wizard, select the **Save Import Steps** check box to display the settings necessary to save the process.

2   Name the saved import process, and enter a description (optional).

3   If you use Microsoft Outlook and want to create an Outlook task to remind you to run the import process at some specific time in the future, select the **Create Outlook Task** check box.

4   Click **Save Import**.

> **TIP** If you chose to create an Outlook task, Outlook opens a task window that already contains information about the task. You simply set a due date, make any other necessary adjustments to the settings, and click Save & Close in the Actions group on the Task tab.

To run a saved import operation:

1   In the **Import & Link** group on the **External Data** tab, click the **Saved Imports** button.

2   Click the import you want to run, and then click **Run**.

> **TIP** If you have created an Outlook task for the import process, you can click Run Import in the Microsoft Access group on the Task tab of the task window.

In the sections that follow, we discuss some of the issues to bear in mind when importing data from a specific source.

Importing from other Access databases

Suppose you have one Access database that includes tables of information about products and orders and another that includes customer contact information. You want just one database containing all the information. You can save time by importing the product and order information into the contacts database (or vice versa), rather than re-creating it all.

You can easily import any of the standard Access objects: tables, queries, forms, and reports. (Macros and modules can also be imported, but they are beyond the scope of this book.) When you import a table, you have the option of importing only the table definition (the structure displayed in Design view), or both the definition and the data. When you import a query, you can import it as a query or you can import the results of the query as a table.

> **TIP** If you need only some of the fields or records from a table in another database, you can create a query in the other database to select only the information you need and then import the results of the query as a table. Alternatively, you can import the table and either edit it in Design view or clean it up by using queries.

10

When you import an Access object, the entire object is imported as an object with the same name into the active database. You can't import only selected fields or records. If the active database already has an object with the same name, Access imports the new object with a number appended to the end of the name.

Importing from Excel worksheets

Access works seamlessly with Excel. You can import an entire worksheet or a named range from a worksheet into either a new table (one that is created during the import process) or an existing table. You can also import specific fields from a worksheet or range.

Excel is a good intermediate format to use when importing information that isn't set up to import directly into Access. For example, if you want to add or remove fields, combine or split fields, or use complex mathematical functions to manipulate data before importing it into Access, Excel is a great place to do it.

Importing from text files

Text files are the common denominator of all document types. Almost every program that works with words and numbers can generate some kind of text file. Access can import tabular data (tables and lists) from text files that contain data structured in two ways:

- **Delimited text file** Each record ends with a paragraph mark, and each field in the table or list is separated from the next by a comma or some other special character, called a *delimiter*. If the data in a field includes the delimiting special character, the entire field must be enclosed in quotation marks. (Some people enclose all fields in quotation marks to avoid having to locate those containing the special character.)

- **Fixed-width text file** In every record, the data in a particular field includes the same number of characters. If the actual data doesn't fill the field, the field is padded with spaces so that the starting point of the data in the next field is the same number of characters from the beginning of every record. For example, if the first field contains 12 characters, the second field always starts 13 characters from the beginning of the record, even if the actual data in the first field is only 4 characters.

  Fixed-width text files used to be difficult to import into databases because you had to carefully count the number of characters in each field and then specify the field sizes in the database or in the import program. If the length of any field was even one character off, all records from that point on would be jumbled. That is no longer a problem with Access, because the Import Text wizard makes importing a fixed-width text file simple.

Importing from other database programs

Importing information from databases created in programs other than Access is usually an all-or-nothing situation, and quite often, what you get isn't in the exact format you need. For example, you might find that transaction records include redundant information, such as the name of the product or purchaser, in every record. A database containing information about people might include the full name and address in one field, when you would prefer to have separate fields for the first name, last name, street address, and so on. You can choose to import information as it is and manipulate it in Access, or you can move it into a program such as Excel or Word and manipulate it there before importing it into Access.

TIP The only way to import the data from some older database programs is to export the data from that program to a fixed-width text file and then import that file into Access.

Importing from Outlook folders

You can import address books and other folders from Outlook into an Access database. This can be particularly useful if you want to import contact information.

Importing from SharePoint lists

If your organization uses a Microsoft SharePoint site, you can import content from SharePoint lists into Access in two ways:

- **Importing** Creates a copy of the list in the Access database. During the import operation, you select the lists you want to copy, and for each selected list, you specify whether you want to import the entire list or only a specific view. The import operation creates a table in Access and then copies the source list (or view) into that table as fields and records. Changes made to the imported data in either Access or SharePoint are not replicated.

- **Linking** Creates a table in Access containing data that is linked to the source data. This process is more efficient than importing if you want to work with data from a SharePoint list in Access but keep the information in both locations current. Linked tables are indicated in the Access Navigation pane by a blue arrow pointing to a yellow table. Information you update in Access is reflected in the SharePoint list when you refresh the view, and vice versa.

10

Whichever method you choose, before you import a SharePoint list into a new table in an Access database, it is a good idea to do the following:

1   Make a note of the SharePoint site's URL.

2   On the SharePoint site, identify the lists you want to copy to the database, and then decide whether you want the entire list or just a particular view.

    TIP You can import multiple lists in a single import operation, but you can import only one view of each list. If one of the standard views doesn't fit your needs, create a custom view containing only the fields and list items you want before proceeding with the import process.

3   Review the columns in the source list or view, and identify the database into which you want to import the lists.

    TIP When you import a SharePoint list, Access creates a table with the same name as the source list. If that name is already in use, Access appends a number to the new table name—for example, Contacts1. Access will not overwrite a table in the destination database or append the contents of a list or view to an existing table.

To import the SharePoint list or lists you have identified, follow these steps:

1   Open a new blank database.

2   On the **External Data** tab, in the **Import & Link** group, click the **More** button. Then click **SharePoint List** to start the **Get External Data** wizard, which displays a list of known SharePoint sites. (You are not limited to the sites in this list.)

3   On the **Select the source and destination of the data** page, in the **Specify a SharePoint site** area, click the address of the site you want to connect to, or enter it in the box.

4   Click either **Import the source data** or **Link to the data source**. Then click **Next**.

5   If prompted to enter your site credentials, do so.

6   On the **Import data from list** page, in the **Import** column, select the check box of each list you want to import into the database.

7   In the **Items to import** column, for each of the selected lists, select the view (arrangement of data) you want to import into the database.

8   With the **Import display values instead of IDs for fields that look up values stored in another list** check box selected, click **OK**.

TROUBLESHOOTING No progress bar appears while Access imports the lists, and this process can take some time. Resist clicking the OK button more than once.

9   When the last page of the wizard appears, click **Close**. Or choose to save the import steps, provide the necessary information, and then click **Save Import**.

After you import or link to a list, you should open the resulting table in Datasheet view to verify that all of the fields and records were imported and that there were no errors. You can review the data type and other field properties by switching to Design view.

Importing from .html files

HTML is used to create webpages. It uses tags to control the appearance and alignment of the content displayed in a web browser. For a table to display correctly on a webpage, the table's rows and cells must be enclosed in appropriate HTML tags. For example, a simple HTML table might look like the following.

```
...<table><tr>    <td>LastName</td><td>FirstName</td></tr>    <td>Anderson</td>
<td>Nancy</td></tr></table>...
```

In an .html file, the <table>, <tr> (table row), and <td> (table data) tags and their corresponding </table>, </tr>, and </td> end tags make the data look like a structured table when it is viewed in a web browser.

All the Office 2013 programs can save a document in HTML format, and to a limited extent, they can read or import a document that was saved in HTML format by another program. When you import an .html file into Access, the program scans the document and identifies anything that looks like structured data. You can then evaluate what Access has found and decide whether to import it.

10

Importing from .xml files

XML format is often used for exchanging information between programs, both on and off the web. XML format is similar to HTML format in two ways: both are plain text that indicate formatting within tags, and both use start and end tags. However, HTML tags describe how elements should look, whereas XML tags specify the structure of the elements in a document. Also, as its name implies, the XML tag set is extensible—there are ways to add your own tags. The following is an example of a simple .xml file.

```
<?xml version="1.0"?><ORDER>    <CUSTOMER>Michele Martin</CUSTOMER>
<PRODUCT>        <ITEM>Sterilized soil</ITEM>       <PRICE>$8.65</PRICE>
<QUANTITY>1 bag</QUANTITY>    </PRODUCT></ORDER>
```

This simple file describes an order that Michele Martin (the customer) placed for one bag (the quantity) of Sterilized soil (the item) at a cost of $8.65 (the price). Because XML tags the data's *structure* rather than its *appearance*, you can easily import the data from an .xml file into a database table. An actual file created for this purpose would contain one instance of the <ORDER> through </ORDER> block for each order.

An.xml file might store both the data and the structure for a table; or the data might be stored in an .xml file for which the structure is defined by an accompanying schema stored in an .xsd file. If the structure is defined by a scheme, be sure the schema's .xsd file is in the same folder as the corresponding .xml file; otherwise Access will import only the data and assign default properties to all fields.

TIP Access 2013 can apply a transform to XML data as you import or export it. A *transform* is a type of template used to convert XML data to other formats. When you apply a transform during the import process, the data is transformed before it enters the table, so you can adapt an .xml file to a different table structure. In-depth coverage of transforms is beyond the scope of this book.

In this exercise, you'll populate a database from multiple sources. You'll import three tables and a form from an Access database. Then you'll import data from a comma-delimited text file into an existing table. Finally, you'll import information from an Excel worksheet into a new table.

→ SET UP You need the GardenCompany10 database, the Customers workbook, the Employees text file, and the ProductsAndSuppliers database located in the Chapter10 practice file folder to complete this exercise. Be sure to use the practice database for this chapter rather than continuing on with the database from an earlier chapter. Open the GardenCompany10 database, and if you want, save your own version to avoid overwriting the original. Then follow the steps.

1   On the **External Data** tab, in the **Import & Link** group, click the **Access** button to start the **Get External Data** wizard.

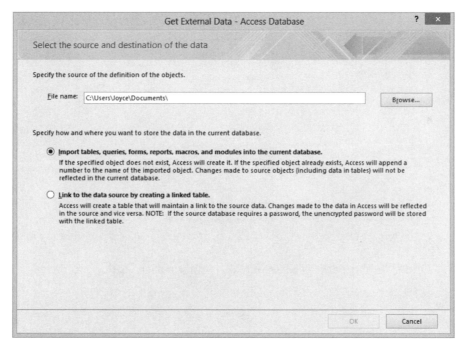

Access Database appears in the title bar because the pages of the wizard are specific to the import process you selected.

2   On the **Select the source and destination of the data** page, click **Browse**.

3   In the **File Open** dialog box, navigate to the **Chapter10** practice file folder, click the **ProductsAndSuppliers** database, and then click **Open**.

4   With **Import tables, queries, forms, reports, macros, and modules into the current database** selected in the wizard, click **OK** to open the **Import Objects** dialog box.

In the Import Objects dialog box, you select the Access objects you want to import.

5   On the **Tables** page, click **Select All**, and then click **Options** to display additional choices.

Import Objects

Tabs: Tables | Queries | Forms | Reports | Macros | Modules

Tables list:
- Categories
- Products
- Suppliers

Buttons: OK | Cancel | Select All | Deselect All | Options >>

Import
- ☑ Relationships
- ☐ Menus and Toolbars
- ☐ Import/Export Specs
- ☐ Nav Pane Groups
- ☐ All Images and Themes

Import Tables
- ⦿ Definition and Data
- ○ Definition Only

Import Queries
- ⦿ As Queries
- ○ As Tables

On the expanded Tables page, the default settings will import relationships that exist between the selected tables, their data, and their structure.

6   Click the **Forms** tab, click **Categories**, and then click **OK** to close the dialog box and begin the import process.

7   When the import process is complete, on the **Save Import Steps** page, click **Close**.

8   From the **Navigation** pane, open the **Categories**, **Products**, and **Suppliers** tables, review their records to verify that all three tables have been successfully imported into the database, and then close them.

10

Now let's populate the empty Employees table.

9   On the **External Data** tab, in the **Import & Link** group, click the **Text File** button to start the **Get External Data** wizard.

> **TIP** Text files typically have a .txt extension. However, some programs save delimited text files with a .csv or .tab extension. You will also occasionally find text files with an .asc (for ASCII) extension. Some programs save fixed-width text files with a .prn (for printer) extension, which Access doesn't recognize; you would need to change this extension to one that Access does recognize. Access treats text files with all acceptable extensions the same way.

10 Browse to the **Chapter10** practice file folder, click the **Employees** text file, and then click **Open**.

11 Click **Append a copy of the records to the table**. Display the adjacent list, and click **Employees**. Then click **OK**, which starts the **Import Text** wizard and displays the content of the selected delimited text file.

Each field is enclosed in quotation marks, and the fields are separated by commas.

TIP When information is imported into an existing table, all the field names and data types must match exactly; otherwise, Access displays an error. If the structure matches but data in a field is too long or has some other minor problem, Access might import the record containing the field into an ImportError table, rather than into the intended table. You can fix the problem in the ImportError table and then copy and paste the record into the correct table.

12   In the lower-left corner of the page, click **Advanced** to open the **Employees Import Specification** dialog box.

You can make changes to the default settings in this dialog box.

TIP If you want to import several files by using the same custom settings, you can specify the settings and save them. Then as you open each file, you can click Specs in this dialog box to apply the saved specifications.

13   In the **Employees Import Specification** dialog box, click **Cancel**. Then in the **Import Text** wizard, click **Next**.

The wizard separates the file into fields at the commas.

TIP If the columns are jumbled, you can choose a different delimiter from the options at the top of the page to view that delimiter's results.

14   Select the **First Row Contains Field Names** check box, and click **Next**. Then click **Finish**.

15   On the **Save Import Steps** page, click **Close**.

16   Open the **Employees** table to confirm that Access successfully imported the records from the text file. Then close the table.

Now let's import customer information from an Excel worksheet into a new table.

17   On the **External Data** tab, in the **Import & Link** group, click the **Excel** button to start the **Get External Data** wizard.

18   Browse to the **Chapter10** practice file folder, click the **Customers** workbook, and then click **Open**.

19   With **Import the source data into a new table in the current database** selected, click **OK**, which starts the **Import Spreadsheet** wizard.

Sample data from the selected worksheet or named range appears in a tabular format.

20   With **Show Worksheets** and **Customers** selected, click **Next**.

21   Select the **First Row Contains Column Headings** check box, and then click **Next**.

You can set the Data Type and Indexed properties of each field. You can also exclude a field from the import process.

22   Click **Next**.

23   On the page that sets the primary key, click **Choose my own primary key**. Then with the **CustomerID** field selected in the adjacent box, click **Finish**.

24   On the **Save Import Steps** page, click **Close**.

25   Open the **Customers** table to confirm that Access imported the customer records correctly.

✕ CLEAN UP Close the Customers table. Keep the GardenCompany10 database open for use in later exercises.

Linking to information

If your information is still being actively maintained in another program and you want to bring it into Access to analyze it, create reports, or export it to another format, you should consider linking your Access database to the existing information in its original program rather than importing the information. Although working with data that is stored in your own database is faster, safer, and more flexible, sometimes linking is preferable, especially if it is important that the data in Access is always up to date.

The most common reason for linking to data in another Access database or a different program is because you don't own the data. Perhaps another department in your organization maintains the data in a SQL database, and that department is willing to give you permission to read the tables and queries but not to change them. Other reasons are security and ease of data distribution.

You can usually link to information in any application from which you can import information. The only difference in the process is that you select the Link To The Data Source By Creating A Linked Table option on the Select The Source And Destination Of The Data page of the Get External Data wizard. Access indicates a linked table by an arrow to the left of the table icon.

TIP If you link to a file stored on your network, be sure to use a universal naming convention (UNC) path, rather than a mapped network drive, because a UNC path is less likely to change.

Exporting information

You can export Access database objects in all the file formats from which you can import data. You can also export information in Portable Document Format (PDF) and XML Paper Specification (XPS) format.

The specific formats available depend on the object you are exporting, as shown in the following table.

Database object	Valid export format
Table	ACCDB, XLS, XLSB, XLSX, SharePoint List, PDF, XPS, RTF, TXT, XML, ODBC, HTML, Word Merge
Query	ACCDB, XLS, XLSB, XLSX, SharePoint List, PDF, XPS, RTF, TXT, XML, ODBC , HTML, Word Merge
Form	ACCDB, XLS, XLSB, XLSX, PDF, XPS, RTF, TXT, XML, HTML
Report	ACCDB, XLS, PDF, XPS, RTF, TXT, XML, HTML

TIP To display a list of the export file formats available for a specific Access object, right-click the object in the Navigation pane, and then point to Export.

Like the import process, the export process for most file types is orchestrated by an easy-to-follow wizard by using these standard steps:

1 In the **Navigation** pane, select the object you want to export.

2 On the **External Data** tab, in the **Export** group, click the button for the program or type of file you want to create, which starts the **Export** wizard.

3 On the wizard's first page, depending on the export format, specify one or all of the following:

- The destination file's location and format

- Whether to export just data, or data with formatting

- Whether to open the file when the export process is complete

- Whether to export only selected records

4 Click **OK**.

When the export process is complete, you return to the Export wizard, which gives you the opportunity to save the export steps so that you don't have to repeat them for future similar export processes. The process for saving export steps is nearly identical to the process for saving import steps.

The steps for exporting Access database objects in PDF or XPS format or as email attachments are slightly different but are still quite automated. You can also use an Access table or query as the data source for the Word 2013 mail merge process; this process is not covered in this topic, but if you are familiar with mail merge in Word, it is relatively straightforward.

In the sections that follow, we discuss some of the issues to bear in mind when exporting data to a specific type of file.

Exporting to other Access databases

It is very simple to export any single object from one Access 2013 database to either another Access 2013 database or to a database in an earlier version of Access. You can't, however, export multiple objects in one operation.

Exporting to Excel worksheets

You can export a single table, form, report, or query from an Access 2013 database to an Excel 2013 workbook, or to a workbook that can be opened by earlier versions of Excel.

When you export a table that contains a subdatasheet or a form that contains a subform, Access exports only the main datasheet or form. To export a subdatasheet or subform, you must perform another export operation on that object.

To combine multiple Access objects into a single Excel workbook, first export the individual objects to different workbooks. Then merge all the worksheets in Excel.

Exporting to Word documents

If you need to move a table or the results of a query to an existing Word document, it is often easiest to simply copy and paste the records from the datasheet. But if you want to work with the contents of a report in Word, you need to export the report.

When you export information from Access 2013 to Word, Access creates a Rich Text Format (RTF) document, which can be opened by Word and several other applications.

Exporting to text files

Text files are the lowest-common-denominator file format. Most applications can open, display, and save information in text format. The downside to text files is that they don't contain any formatting information, so they look consistently plain in all applications.

Depending on what type of content you are trying to export from a database, you might have the option to export the layout with the data. If you select this option, the unformatted text will be arranged in the text file much as it is in the Access object. If you don't choose this option, the information will be saved in either delimited or fixed-length lines.

Exporting to .pdf and .xps files

If you want people to be able to view a database object but not change it, save the object in the Portable Document Format (PDF) or the XML Paper Specification (XPS) format. Both the PDF and XPS formats are designed to deliver objects as electronic representations of the way they look when printed. The data in .pdf and .xps files is essentially static, and content cannot be easily edited, so these formats are ideal for objects that will be part of legal documents. Both types of files can easily be sent by email to many recipients and can be made available on a webpage for downloading by anyone who wants them. However, .xps files cannot be opened, viewed, or edited in Office 2013 programs

When you indicate that you want to export a database object in PDF or XPS format by clicking the PDF Or XPS button in the Export group on the External Data tab, the Publish As PDF Or XPS dialog box opens so that you can select the destination location and format, assign a name, and optimize the size of the file for your intended distribution method. Click Options to display a dialog box in which you can specify the records or pages to include in the PDF or XPS version of the object and whether to include or exclude accessibility structure tags. When you click Publish, the object is saved with your specifications, and the Export wizard gives you the opportunity to save the export steps.

TIP Another way to create a .pdf or .xps file is to display the Save As page of the Backstage view, and in the File Types pane, click Save Object As to display the available formats in the right pane. Clicking PDF Or XPS and then clicking the Save As button displays the Publish As PDF Or XPS dialog box, in which you can save the file in the usual way.

Exporting to SharePoint lists

If you have permission to create content on a SharePoint site, you can export a table or query database object to the site as a SharePoint list. The list content is static and will not reflect changes made to the source table or query after the export operation. You can't overwrite or add data to an existing list.

TIP You can export only one object to a SharePoint list at a time. However, when Access exports a table, it also exports all related tables.

Exporting to .html files

Many organizations that store accounting, manufacturing, marketing, sales, and other information on their computers have discovered the advantages of sharing this information within the company or with the rest of the world through a website. With Access, you can export tables, queries, forms, and reports as web-ready .html files. You can then view the objects in a web browser, such as Windows Internet Explorer.

When you export a table, query, or form, Access converts it to an HTML table. When you export a report, Access converts it to a series of linked .html files (one for each page of the report).

TIP To display the HTML tags that define the structure of the file, you can either view the file in a web browser or open it in a text editor.

Exporting to .xml files

You can export tables, queries, forms, and reports from Access in an XML format that can be used by other applications. To export to an .xml file:

1 In the **Export** group on the **External Data** tab, click the **XML File** button to start the **Export** wizard, in which you specify the destination location and assign a name.

2 Click **OK** to open the **Export XML** dialog box, in which you can do one of the following:

   ■ Select the **Data (XML)** check box to export the data.

   ■ Select the **Schema of the data (XSD)** check box to create a separate .xsd schema that contains the structure of the XML data.

   ■ Select the **Presentation of your data (XSL)** check box to export an .xls stylesheet that describes how to display the XML data.

   TIP To export a table as a combined data/schema file, in the Export XML dialog box, click More Options, click the Schema tab, click Embed Schema In Exported XML Data Document, and then click OK.

3 Click **OK** to save the object with your specifications. The **Export** wizard then gives you the opportunity to save the export steps.

You can view the tagged .xml file in Internet Explorer and the .xsd file in any text editor.

In this exercise, you'll export an Access table to another Access database and to an Excel workbook. Then you'll export the table as both a formatted and an unformatted text file.

➜ SET UP You need the GardenCompany10 database you worked with in the preceding exercise to complete this exercise. Create a blank desktop database named Exported in the Chapter10 practice file folder, and close the open table. Then if necessary, open the GardenCompany10 database, and follow the steps.

1 In the **Navigation** pane, in the **Tables** group, click **Suppliers**.

   TIP When you export an entire table, there is no need to open it first.

2 On the **External Data** tab, in the **Export** group, click the **Access** button to start the **Export – Access Database** wizard.

3 On the wizard's first page, click **Browse**.

4 In the **File Save** dialog box, navigate to the **Chapter10** practice file folder, click **Exported**, and then click **Save**.

5 In the **Export – Access Database** wizard, click **OK**, which opens the **Export** dialog box.

You can export the table's structure and data or only the structure.

6 With **Suppliers** displayed in the **Export Suppliers to** box and **Definition and Data** selected in the **Export Tables** area, click **OK** to export the selected table.

7 On the **Save Export Steps** page, click **Close**.

   Let's check that the export was successful.

8 Display the **Exported** database in a separate instance of Access.

TIP You can open only one database at a time in a single instance of Access. If you open a second database without first closing the one you are working in, Access prompts you to save recent changes and then closes the first database before opening the second. To open two databases at the same time, start a second instance of Access from the Start screen (Windows 8) or the Start menu (Windows 7), and then open the second database from the Backstage view. You can also double-click the database file in File Explorer (Windows 8) or Windows Explorer (Windows 7).

9   In the **Navigation** pane, in the **Tables** group, double-click **Suppliers**, verify that the table exported correctly, and then close the **Exported** database.

Now suppose we need to provide the information in the Suppliers table to someone who doesn't have Access installed on her computer. Let's export the same table as an Excel workbook.

10   In the **GardenCompany10** database, open the **Suppliers** table in **Datasheet** view. Then on the **External Data** tab, in the **Export** group, click the **Excel** button to start the **Export – Excel Spreadsheet** wizard.

11   On the wizard's first page, click the **Browse** button. Then verify that the **Chapter10** practice file folder is selected in the **File Save** dialog box, and click **Save**.

By default, the spreadsheet has the same name as the table it's based on and will be saved in the Excel Workbook (*.xlsx) format.

TIP You can change the name and format in the File Save dialog box, or you can edit the name and select a different format in the wizard.

12 Select the **Export data with formatting and layout** check box and the **Open the destination file after the export operation is complete** check box. Then click **OK**, which starts Excel and opens the exported workbook.

The Suppliers table has been exported to the Suppliers sheet in the workbook.

13 Close the workbook and Excel, and then on the **Save Export Steps** page of the **Export – Excel Spreadsheet** wizard, click **Close**.

TIP If you want to make the data in a table available in Outlook, you can export the table as an attachment to an email message by clicking the Email button in the Export group.

Now let's export data from Access to a text file.

14 With the **Suppliers** table open in **Datasheet** view, on the **External Data** tab, in the **Export** group, click the **Text File** button to start the **Export – Text File** wizard.

15   With the path to the **Chapter10** practice file folder displayed in the **File name** box, change the default file name from **Suppliers.txt** to Suppliers_fixed.txt.

16   Select the **Export data with formatting and layout** and **Open the destination file after the export operation is complete** check boxes. Then click **OK**, which opens the **Encode 'Suppliers' As** dialog box.

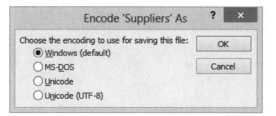

In this dialog box, you can select the encoding format options you want.

17   With **Windows (default)** selected, click **OK** to start your default text editor and open the exported text file.

```
Suppliers_fixed - Notepad                                            _ □ ×
File   Edit   Format   View   Help
-------------------------------------------------------------------------
|      SupplierID    |    SupplierName    |    ContactName    |    ContactTitle    |    Add
-------------------------------------------------------------------------
|             1 | Garden Hardware   | Don Richardson    | Purchasing Manager | 45 Tandy
-------------------------------------------------------------------------
|             2 | The Shrub Club    | Jonathan Mollerup | Order              | 1234 Lap
-------------------------------------------------------------------------
|             3 | NoTox Pest Control| Brad Sutton       | Sales              | P.O. Box
-------------------------------------------------------------------------
|             4 | Cover Up Stuff    | Stuart Munson     | Marketing Manager  | 4567 Gra
-------------------------------------------------------------------------
|             5 | Rosie's Roses     | Heather Murchison | Export             | 76543 Ba
-------------------------------------------------------------------------
|             6 | Soil and Sand     | Robert O'Hara     | Marketing          | 321 E. H
-------------------------------------------------------------------------
|             7 | Wholesale Rock &  | Josh Barnhill     | Marketing Manager  | 43 Magno
-------------------------------------------------------------------------
|             8 | The Herb House    | Douglas Groncki   | Sales              | 987 Colm
-------------------------------------------------------------------------
|             9 | Green Things      | Jason Carlson     | Sales Agent        | 12 Orche
-------------------------------------------------------------------------
|            10 | The Grass Factory | Scott Seely       | Marketing Manager  | 1098 Ast
-------------------------------------------------------------------------
|            11 | Green Thumb       | Richard Carey     | Sales Manager      | 5432 Moo
-------------------------------------------------------------------------
|            12 | The Complete      | Paul West         | International       | 9876 Ang
```

In Notepad, the rows and columns of the table are separated by dashes and pipe characters.

18   Close the text file, and then close the wizard without saving the export steps.

10

19   Repeat steps 14 through 18 to export the table again, but this time change the name to **Suppliers_delim.txt**, and don't select the **Export data with formatting and layout** and **Open the destination file after the export operation is complete** check boxes.

Because you didn't select the formatting and layout option on the wizard's first page, you can refine the export results.

TIP You can experiment with different wizard options, moving as far as the last page and then backing up to try a different approach. At any point, you can click Finish to accept the default settings for all the wizard's remaining options.

20   Switch between the **Delimited** and **Fixed Width** options, noticing the difference in the data in the **Sample export format** box.

21   With **Delimited** selected, click **Next**.

> **TIP** The options on the wizard's next page vary depending on whether you are exporting a delimited or fixed-width file.

22   Leave **Comma** selected, select the **Include Field Names on First Row** check box, and click **Finish** to export the table as an unformatted text file.

23   Close the wizard without saving the export steps.

24   To check the exported file, navigate to the **Chapter10** practice file folder in File Explorer or Windows Explorer, and double-click **Suppliers_delim**.

```
Suppliers_delim - Notepad
File  Edit  Format  View  Help
"SupplierID","SupplierName","ContactName","ContactTitle","Address","City","State","PostalCode"
1,"Garden Hardware Mfg.","Don Richardson","Purchasing Manager","45 Tandy St.","Washington","DC
2,"The Shrub Club","Jonathan Mollerup","Order Administrator","1234 Lapis Ave.","Chevy Chase",
3,"NoTox Pest Control","Brad Sutton","Sales Representative","P.O. Box 555","Lander","WY","7252
4,"Cover Up Stuff","Stuart Munson","Marketing Manager","4567 Grand Army Plaza","Brooklyn","NY"
5,"Rosie's Roses","Heather Murchison","Export Administrator","76543 Bayou Dr.","Plaquemine","L
6,"Soil and Sand Supplier","Robert O'Hara","Marketing Representative","321 E. Houston St. #6",
7,"Wholesale Rock & Gravel","Josh Barnhill","Marketing Manager","43 Magnolia Way","Plains","GA
8,"The Herb House","Douglas Groncki","Sales Representative","987 Colman Dr.","San Luis Obispo"
9,"Green Things Galore","Jason Carlson","Sales Agent","12 Orchestra Terrace","Walla Walla","WA
10,"The Grass Factory","Scott Seely","Marketing Manager","1098 Asbury St.","Carmel Valley","CA
11,"Green Thumb Fertilizers","Richard Carey","Sales Manager","5432 Mockingbird Ln.","Louisburg
12,"The Complete Garden Supplier","Paul West","International Marketing Mgr.","9876 Angeles Ave
13,"Evergreen Emporium","John Y. Chen","Coordinator Foreign Markets","567 Bartlett Blvd.","Bal
14,"The Carnivorous Connection","Robert Lyon","Sales Representative","21098 Baker Dr.","Eugene
15,"The Bulb Basket","Brian Perry","Marketing Manager","456 Breezewood Ave.","San Diego","CA",
16,"Itty Bitty Bonsai","Mindy Martin","Regional Account Rep.","234 Green Grass Hills St.","Gre
17,"Flower Heaven","Ben Smith","Sales Representative","2345 N.W. 99th St.","Seattle","WA","881
18,"The Tree Farm","Jim Kim","Sales Manager","7654 SW Clinton Ave.","Lewiston","ID","73501","(
19,"The Berry Bush Barn","TiAnna Jones","Wholesale Account Agent","432 Bryn Mawr Ave.","Cedar
20,"Liven Right Rhodies","Cat Francis","Owner","89 Maple Dr.","Carlisle","PA","97013","(717) 5
```

In Notepad, the fields of the table are separated by commas.

❌ CLEAN UP   Close the text file and the Suppliers table. Keep the GardenCompany10 database open for use in the last exercise.

10

Copying to and from other Office programs

Sometimes the quickest and easiest way to get information into or out of a database is to just copy it and paste it where you want it. This technique works particularly well for getting data out of an Access table and into Word or Excel. Information that you paste into a Word document becomes a Word table, complete with a heading row containing the field captions as column headings. Information that you paste into an Excel worksheet appears in the normal row-and-column format.

Getting data into another Access table by using this technique is a little more complicated. The data you are pasting must meet all the criteria for entering it by hand (input mask, validation rules, field size, and so on), and you must have the correct table cells selected when you use the Paste command. If Access encounters a problem when you attempt to paste a group of records, it displays an error message and pastes the problem records into a Paste Errors table. You can then troubleshoot the problem in that table, fix whatever is wrong, and try copying and pasting again.

TIP To copy an entire table from one Access database to another, open both databases, copy the table from the source database to the Microsoft Office Clipboard, and then paste it into the destination database. You can paste the table data and/or table structure as a new table or append the data to an existing table.

In this exercise, you'll copy and paste records between an Access database table, an Excel worksheet, and a Word document.

➜ SET UP You need the GardenCompany10 database you worked with in the preceding exercise and the Shippers workbook located in the Chapter10 practice file folder to complete this exercise. Start Excel and open a blank workbook. Then if necessary, open the GardenCompany10 database, open the Customers table in Datasheet view, and follow the steps.

1 Point to the row selector of the first record in the table, and when the pointer changes to a right arrow, drag through six records to select them.

2 On the **Home** tab, in the **Clipboard** group, click the **Copy** button.

KEYBOARD SHORTCUT Press Ctrl+C to copy a selection to the Clipboard. For a list of keyboard shortcuts, see "Keyboard shortcuts" at the end of this book.

3   Display the blank Excel worksheet. Then with cell **A1** selected, on the Excel **Home** tab, in the **Clipboard** group, click the **Paste** button.

KEYBOARD SHORTCUT Press Ctrl+V to paste a cut or copied item from the Clipboard.

	A	B	C	D	E	F	G	H	I	J	K
1	CustomerID	FirstName	LastName	Address	City	Region	PostalCode	Country	PhoneNumber		
2	ACKPI	Pilar	Ackerman	8808 Backbay St.	Bellevue	WA	88004	USA	(425) 555-0194		
3	ADATE	Terry	Adams	1932 52nd Ave.	Vancouver	BC	V4T 1Y9	Canada	(604) 555-0193		
4	ALLMI	Michael	Allen	130 17th St.	Vancouver	BC	V4T 1Y9	Canada	(604) 555-0192		
5	ASHCH	Chris	Ashton	89 Cedar Way	Redmond	WA	88052	USA	(425) 555-0191		
6	BANMA	Martin	Bankov	78 Riverside Dr.	Woodinville	WA	88072	USA	(425) 555-0190		
7	BENPA	Paula	Bento	6778 Cypress Pkwy.	Oak Harbor	WA	88277	USA	(360) 555-0189		
8											
9											

The Access field names have become Excel column headings.

4   Switch back to the Access database.

Now let's copy and paste only a few fields of a few records.

5   In the **FirstName** field, point to the left border of the value **Ted**, and when the pointer changes to a thick cross, drag down and to the right until the **FirstName** through **Region** fields are selected for six records.

6   In the **Clipboard** group, click the **Copy** button.

7   Switch back to Excel, click cell **A9**, and then in the Excel **Clipboard** group, click the **Paste** button to paste in the new selection, again with column headings.

8   Start Word, and create a new blank document. Then on the **Home** tab, in the **Clipboard** group, click the **Paste** button to create a nicely formatted table.

The Customers title reflects the name of the table from which this data came.

9   Exit Word and Excel, without saving your changes. Then close the **Customers** table.

Now let's copy the data from an Excel worksheet and paste it into a new table in the current database.

10   In File Explorer or Windows Explorer, navigate to the **Chapter10** practice file folder, and double-click the **Shippers** Excel workbook.

11   In Excel, select cells **A1:H6** of the active worksheet, and on the **Home** tab, in the **Clipboard** group, click the **Copy** button.

12   Switch back to Access, right-click in the **Tables** group of the **Navigation** pane, and click **Paste**.

13   When Access asks whether the first row of data contains column headings, click **Yes**.

14   Click **OK** to acknowledge that the import process was successful, and then notice that the new **Shippers** table has been added to the **Tables** group of the **Navigation** pane.

15   Double-click the **Shippers** table to open it, and verify that all records were successfully copied.

❌ CLEAN UP Exit Excel. Then close the Shippers table and the GardenCompany10 database.

Key points

- Importing information into Access 2013 from other programs is an easy way to add data without reentering it.

- If data is actively maintained in another program and you want to work with it in Access, you can link the Access database to the data without actually importing it.

- You can export information from an Access database in a variety of formats, depending on the object you are exporting.

- Copying and pasting information from an Access database is often the easiest way to make the data available to other Office programs.

- If the data in other Office programs is set up appropriately, you can copy and paste it into an Access database.

10

Chapter at a glance

Design

Design navigation forms,
page 312

Create

Create custom categories,
page 319

Garden Company

Forms
- Customer List
- Customer Records
- Home Page
- New Customer

Reports
- Alphabetical List of Products
- Sales By Category

Unassigned Objects

Control

Control which features are available,
page 323

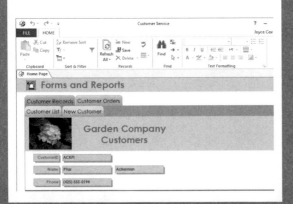

Make databases user friendly

IN THIS CHAPTER, YOU WILL LEARN HOW TO

- Design navigation forms.

- Create custom categories.

- Control which features are available.

A Microsoft Access 2013 database can be a complex combination of objects and the tools for managing and manipulating them. If information will be entered and retrieved from your database by people who aren't proficient with Access, the information will be safer and the database users happier if you insulate them from the inner workings of Access. When you turn your collection of objects and information into an application that organizes related tasks, users can focus on the job at hand, rather than on learning how to use the program the database is running in. With a little extra effort on your part, you can make it easier for them to access and manipulate data, and more difficult for them to unintentionally change or delete it.

In Access 2013, the most common way to control access to a database is either by creating a navigation form or by creating custom categories and groups in the Navigation pane. You can also control which commands and which parts of the database users can interact with.

In this chapter, you'll create a simple navigation form, create a custom category and groups, and set various startup options that control the users' working environment.

PRACTICE FILES To complete the exercises in this chapter, you need the practice files contained in the Chapter11 practice file folder. For more information, see "Download the practice files" in this book's Introduction.

Designing navigation forms

A navigation form appears as a set of navigation buttons that the user can click to display and work with forms and reports. You can add a navigation form to any database to make it easier for users who don't have extensive Access knowledge to enter information and find exactly what they need.

TIP You cannot work with tables and queries directly from a navigation form. If you want users to be able to view a table or the results of a query in a navigation form, you need to create datasheet forms based on those objects and then insert those forms into the navigation form.

You can choose from the following six navigation form layouts:

- **Horizontal Tabs** Assigns each object to a button, which looks like a tab, across the top of the form.

- **Vertical Tabs, Left** Assigns each object to a button down the left side of the form.

- **Vertical Tabs, Right** Assigns each object to a button down the right side of the form.

- **Horizontal Tabs, 2 levels** Assigns each primary object to a button in the first row across the top of the form, and assigns each secondary object to a button on the second row. For example, if you assign the Customers form to a button at the first level, you might assign the New Customer form to a button at the second level. Users can refer to the Customers form to find out whether a customer record already exists. If it doesn't, they can click the button for the New Customer form to display a new blank record, in which they can enter the customer's information.

- **Horizontal Tabs and Vertical Tabs, Left** Assigns each object to a button across the top or down the left side of the form, depending on where you insert it. With this arrangement, you can have one navigation form that satisfies the needs of two separate groups—for example, order-related buttons across the top, and inventory-related buttons down the side.

- **Horizontal Tabs and Vertical Tabs, Right** Assigns each object to a button across the top or down the right side of the form, depending on where you insert it.

The layout you choose depends on the number and type of database objects you want to be available from the form, and the way you want to arrange them.

When you create a navigation form, it is displayed in Layout view so that you can begin to design it. The functionality of the form is supplied by a navigation control that consists of a placeholder for a navigation button and a subform or subreport control. When you drag a form or report from the Navigation pane to the button placeholder, the Navigation Target Name property on the Data page of the button's Property Sheet pane is set to the name of the form or report, and that name is also displayed on the button. (You can change the name on the button by changing its Caption property.) The form or report itself is displayed in the subform or subreport control. A new placeholder navigation button is added to the navigation bar, ready to receive the next form or report you insert.

This navigation form has the Horizontal Tabs layout, three buttons, and a subform.

A navigation form makes a convenient "home page" for a database, especially if it is displayed automatically when the database is opened. Providing a default startup page makes it easy for users of the database to quickly access the database objects they are most likely to need to work with.

In this exercise, you'll create a datasheet form for viewing existing customers and a form for entering new customer information. You'll create a simple two-level navigation form to provide easy access to the customer information, and you'll add three forms and a report to it.

SET UP You need the GardenCompany11 database and the Logo graphic located in the Chapter11 practice file folder to complete this exercise. Be sure to use the practice database for this chapter rather than continuing on with the database from an earlier chapter. Open the database, and if you want, save your own version to avoid overwriting the original. Then with All Access Objects displayed in the Navigation pane, follow the steps.

1   In the **Tables** group in the **Navigation** pane, click **Customers**. Then on the **Create** tab, in the **Forms** group, click **More Forms**, and in the list, click **Datasheet** to create a datasheet form that looks like the **Customers** table.

2   Save the form as Customer List. Then open the **Property Sheet** pane, and on the **Data** page, set the **Allow Additions, Allow Deletions,** and **Allow Edits** properties to **No**.

3   Close the **Property Sheet** pane, and then close the form, saving your changes.

4   In the **Forms** group in the **Navigation** pane, right-click **Customer Records**, and click **Copy**. Then right-click anywhere in the **Forms** group, and click **Paste**. In the **Paste As** dialog box, enter New Customer as the name of the form, and click **OK**.

5   Open the **New Customer** form in **Layout** view, right-click the form's title, and click **Form Properties** to open the **Property Sheet** pane for the form. On the **Data** page, set the **Data Entry, Allow Additions, Allow Deletions,** and **Allow Edits** properties to **Yes**.

6   Close the **Property Sheet** pane, and then close the form, saving your changes.

We've now created two new forms, one exclusively for data lookup and the other exclusively for data entry. Now let's create a navigation form so that the new forms are easy to identify and access.

7   On the **Create** tab, in the **Forms** group, click the **Navigation** button, and then click **Horizontal Tabs, 2 Levels**. If Access opens the **Field List** pane, close it.

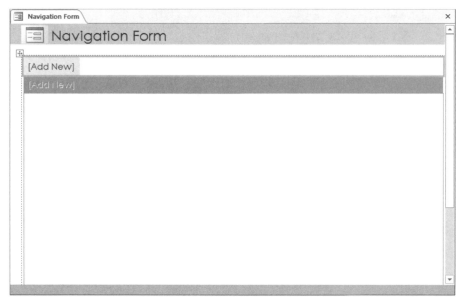

In Layout view, you can view the two levels of navigation controls.

First let's customize the form's tab and title.

8   Display the **Property Sheet** pane for the form. On the **Format** page, in the **Caption** property, enter Home Page, and press the **Enter** key. Then close the **Property Sheet** pane.

9   In the **Form Header**, click the **Navigation Form** title, click it again to activate it for editing, change the title to Forms and Reports, and press **Enter**. Then make the title 20 points, bold, and any dark green color.

10   Click in the **Form Header** away from the title control and logo placeholder, and apply the **Light Green, Background 2** color.

11   On the **Design** tool tab, in the **Header / Footer** group, click the **Logo** button, and insert the **Logo** graphic from the **Chapter11** practice file folder.

11

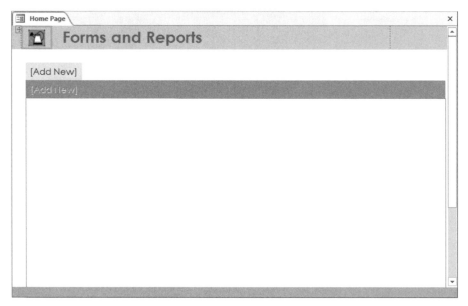

The fonts and colors available for formatting the form are provided by the object's theme.

12   Save the form with the name Home Page.

Now let's populate the navigation form by adding forms and reports to it. You can do this by assigning the forms and reports to the two rows of buttons on the navigation bar above the subform control.

13   In the **Forms** group in the **Navigation** pane, click **Customer Records**, and drag it to the first-level placeholder button at the top of the navigation control. Notice that the first-level button is now labeled **Customer Records**, and because the button is active, the **Customer Records** form is displayed in the subform control. Also notice that an **Add New** button has been added to the first-level navigation bar.

The Customer Records form displays the first record in the Customers table.

14 In the **Forms** group in the **Navigation** pane, click **Customer List**, and drag it to the second-level placeholder button below **Customer Records**. Notice that the second-level button is now labeled **Customer List**, and because the button is active, the datasheet form appears in the subform control.

15 Drag the **New Customer** form to the second-level placeholder button to the right of **Customer List**. The first-level **Customer Records** button now has two second-level buttons and a second-level placeholder button.

16 In the **Reports** group in the **Navigation** pane, drag **Customer Orders** to the first-level placeholder button to the right of **Customer Records**.

Let's test the work we have done so far.

17 Switch to **Form** view.

11

Customer Orders has a second-level placeholder button in Layout view, but the placeholder button is not visible in Form view.

18 Click the **Customer Records** button, and then in turn click the **Customer List** and **New Customer** buttons, observing the effect in the form.

Now let's format the navigation buttons to more clearly define the hierarchy.

19 Switch back to **Layout** view. Then click the **Customer Records** button, hold down the **Ctrl** key, and click the **Customer Orders** button.

20 On the **Format** tool tab, in the **Control Formatting** group, click the **Change Shape** button, and then click the second shape in the second column (**Round Same Side Corner Rectangle**).

21 Without changing the selection, in the **Control Formatting** group, click the **Quick Styles** button, and then click the fourth thumbnail in the rightmost column (**Subtle Effect – Orange, Accent 6**).

22 Repeat steps 20 and 21 for the first **Customer Records** second-level button (**Customer List**), making it the same shape as the first-level buttons but applying the fourth thumbnail in the second column (**Subtle Effect – Green, Accent 1**).

23 Use **Format Painter** to copy the formatting of **Customer List** to **New Customer**.

24 Switch to **Form** view, where the buttons now resemble colored tabs. Then click the **Customer Records** button.

You can use shapes and colors to categorize forms and reports.

⊗ CLEAN UP Close the Home Page form, saving your changes. Keep the Garden-Company11 database open for use in later exercises.

Creating custom categories

The Navigation pane is organized into categories and groups to make it easy to select the database object you want to work with. A number of built-in categories are available, and you can filter by group in various ways.

To provide database users with access to specific database objects, you can create custom categories, each containing multiple custom groups. You can drag and drop any valid Access object into a custom group to create a shortcut to the object; the object itself remains in its original group. This combination of categories, groups, and object shortcuts can be used to make frequently used objects more accessible. For example, if the accounting department runs a set of reports on the last day of each month, you could create an Accounting category containing a Month End Reports group and then add shortcuts to the reports to that group. Or if the Marketing department routinely works with several forms, queries, and reports, you could create a Marketing category containing either a group holding shortcuts to all the objects, or a group for each object type. There are no restrictions on the mix of objects you can place in a group.

In this exercise, you'll create a custom category, add two groups to it, and then add short-cuts to database objects to the groups.

 SET UP You need the GardenCompany11 database you worked with in the preceding exercise to complete this exercise. If necessary, open the database, and then follow the steps.

1   At the top of the **Navigation** pane, right-click **All Access Objects**, and then click **Navigation Options** to open the **Navigation Options** dialog box.

You can hide a group by clearing its check box in the list on the right.

2   In the **Grouping Options** area, below the **Categories** list, click **Add Item** to add a new category named **Custom Category 1** to the list.

3   Replace **Custom Category 1** with Garden Company, and press **Enter**. Notice that the heading above the list on the right changes to **Groups for "Garden Company"** to reflect the category selected in the list on the left.

4   Below the **Groups for "Garden Company"** list, click **Add Group**. Then replace **Custom Group 1** with Forms, and press **Enter**.

TIP Every custom category contains a default group named *Unassigned Objects*. This group contains all the objects in the database and is the source for the shortcuts you create in your custom groups.

5   Repeat step 4 to add a group named Reports. Then click **OK**.

Although it's not visible yet, the Garden Company category has been added to the Navigation pane. Let's assign a few forms and reports to the groups of the new category.

6   At the top of the **Navigation** pane, click **All Access Objects** to display the list of available categories, and then click **Garden Company**. Notice that this category contains an empty **Forms** group, an empty **Reports** group, and the **Unassigned Objects** group.

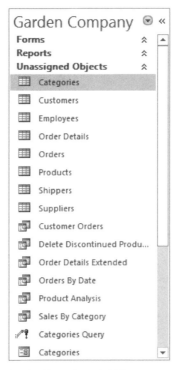

In the Unassigned Objects group, the object icons distinguish items of the same name.

7   In the **Unassigned Objects** group, click the **Customer List** form. Then hold down the **Shift** key, and click the **New Customer** form to select the **Customer List**, **Customer Records**, **Home Page**, and **New Customer** forms.

8   Drag the selection up to the top of the **Navigation** pane, releasing the mouse button when the selection is on top of the **Forms** group header. Notice that the selected forms no longer appear in the **Unassigned Objects** group; instead, shortcuts for them appear in the custom **Forms** group.

9   In the **Unassigned Objects** group, select the **Alphabetical List of Products** and **Sales By Category** reports.

10   Right-click the selection, click **Add to group**, and then click **Reports**.

11   Click the chevron at the right end of the **Unassigned Objects** group header to hide its objects.

This uncluttered Navigation pane makes it easy for users to spot what they need.

TIP To remove the Unassigned Objects group from the Navigation pane, display the Navigation Options dialog box, click Garden Company, clear the Unassigned Objects check box, and then click OK.

12   Test the new shortcuts by opening each form and report.

❌ CLEAN UP Keep the GardenCompany11 database open for use in the last exercise.

Controlling which features are available

If your database will be used by people with little or no experience with Access, you might want to control which features are available when a database opens. You can control the user environment by setting startup options for the database. For example, you can use startup options to control whether ribbon tabs and the Navigation pane are available, whether a specified object (such as a navigation form) is displayed on startup, and other features.

TIP Additional control can be achieved by the use of macros and Microsoft Visual Basic for Applications (VBA) procedures. These topics are beyond the scope of this book. For information, search for *Introduction to Access Programming* on the Office website.

In this exercise, you'll set startup options that create a version of the database that is appropriate for inexperienced users. You'll give the database the appearance of being a custom application, display the Home Page form when the database is opened, and hide program elements that users don't need. Then you'll find out how to bypass the startup options.

➡ SET UP You need the GardenCompany11 database you worked with in the preceding exercise and the Icon image located in the Chapter11 practice file folder to complete this exercise. If necessary, open the database, and then follow the steps.

1   Display the **Backstage** view, and click **Options** to open the **Access Options** dialog box. Then in the left pane, click **Current Database** to display that page.

On the Current Database page, you can set options for controlling the active database.

SEE ALSO For information about the other pages of the Access Options dialog box, see "Changing default program options" in Chapter 13, "Work in Access more efficiently."

Let's change the title in the title bar and replace the Access icon with one that visually identifies this particular database.

2 In the **Application Options** area, in the **Application Title** box, change the **Garden Company** title to Customer Service, and then press the **Tab** key.

TIP By default, the name and path of the active database appears in the title bar. To avoid confusion, we assigned the title *Garden Company* to all the practice files for this book. If you want to show the name and path of any practice database, display the Current Database page of the Access Options dialog box, and delete the contents of the Application Title box.

3   To the right of the **Application Icon** box, click **Browse**. Then navigate to the **Chapter11** practice file folder, and double-click the **Icon** image to enter the path of the icon in the box.

4   Below the **Application Icon** box, select the **Use as Form and Report Icon** check box.

TIP Now the icon will appear not only at the left end of the title bar, but also adjacent to the names of form and report pages.

Next let's set a home page for the database and make it harder for users to inadvertently make changes to the design of database objects.

5   Display the **Display Form** list, and then click **Home Page**.

6   Clear the **Enable Layout View** and **Enable design changes for tables in Datasheet view** check boxes.

7   In the **Navigation** area, clear the **Display Navigation Pane** check box.

TIP When the Use Access Special Keys check box is selected in the Application Options area, database users can open and close the Navigation pane by pressing the F11 key. If you clear the Display Navigation Pane check box and the Use Access Special Keys check box, users can't open the Navigation pane at all.

8   In the **Ribbon and Toolbar Options** area, clear the **Allow Full Menus** and **Allow Default Shortcut Menus** check boxes to prevent users from using these tools to make inappropriate changes to the database. (Only the **File** and **Home** tabs will be visible to users.)

9   Click **OK** to implement the changes and close the **Access Options** dialog box.

10 When Access tells you that you must close and reopen the database for the changes to take effect, click **OK**.

Initially, the only visible change is that *Customer Service* and a colorful icon appear in the title bar. Let's close and reopen the database to view the other changes.

11 Close the **GardenCompany11** database, and then reopen it.

11

The database opens with the Home Page form displayed, the Navigation pane closed, and only the File and Home tabs on the ribbon.

12 Press the **F11** key. Notice that because you did not clear the **Use Access Special Keys** check box in the **Access Options** dialog box, pressing this keyboard shortcut still opens or closes the **Navigation** pane.

> **SEE ALSO** For a list of keyboard shortcuts, see "Keyboard shortcuts" at the end of this book.

13 Display the **Backstage** view, where only the **Print** page, a **Privacy Options** button, and an **Exit** button are available.

> **TIP** Clicking the Privacy Options button displays the Access Options dialog box, where you can easily reverse the changes you made on the Current Database page.

14   Click **Exit** to close the database and exit Access.

Let's open the database in such a way that we can make a change that ordinary users are restricted from making.

15   Restart Access, and in the **Recent** area of the **Backstage** view, hold down the **Shift** key, and click your **GardenCompany11** file to bypass all the startup options.

 CLEAN UP   If you want, reverse all the changes you made to settings in the Access Options dialog box. Then close the GardenCompany11 database.

Key points

- Navigation forms provide a web-like interface that makes it easy for people who are not familiar with Access to enter data in forms and view reports.

- Custom categories and groups provide users with access to the forms and reports they need, while restricting access to the objects they don't need.

- Setting startup options is another way to make it more difficult for users to unintentionally change or delete data.

11

Chapter at a glance

Assign

Assign passwords to databases,
page 330

Split

Split databases,
page 334

Prevent

Prevent database problems,
page 342

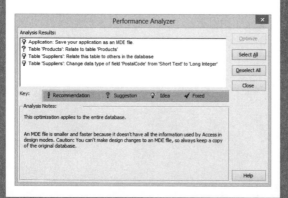

Protect databases

12

IN THIS CHAPTER, YOU WILL LEARN HOW TO

- Assign passwords to databases.

- Split databases.

- Secure databases for distribution.

- Prevent database problems.

Database protection takes two forms: ensuring that the database's data is secure, and ensuring that its data is available and useable.

The need for database security is an unfortunate fact of life. As with your house, car, office, or briefcase, the level of security required for your database depends on the value of what you have and whether you are trying to protect it from curious eyes, accidental damage, malicious destruction, or theft. The security of a company's business information can be critical to its survival. For example, you might not be too concerned if a person gained unauthorized access to your products list, but you would be very concerned if a competitor managed to obtain your customer list. And the destruction or deletion of your critical order information would be a disaster. Your goal is to provide adequate protection without imposing unnecessary restrictions on the people who need access to your database. The protection techniques you choose depend to a large extent on how many people are using the database and where it is stored.

In addition to ensuring that a database is secure, you need to ensure that it is well maintained. Normal usage can result in conditions that increase the size of a database and slow it down, so ongoing maintenance is essential for reliable performance. This is especially true if the database is stored on a network rather than on a local drive, and if it is accessed by multiple users.

In this chapter, you'll assign a password to a database, protect data from accidental or intentional corruption by splitting the database, and prepare the database for broader distribution. You'll also back up a database and run various utilities to assist with database maintenance.

PRACTICE FILES To complete the exercises in this chapter, you need the practice file contained in the Chapter12 practice file folder. For more information, see "Download the practice files" in this book's Introduction.

Assigning passwords to databases

You can keep unauthorized users out of a database by assigning it a password. Access then prompts anyone attempting to open the database for the password, and opens it only if the password is correct.

To assign a password to or remove a password from a database, you must first open the database for exclusive use, meaning that no one else can have the database open. This will not be a problem for a database stored on your own computer and used only by you, but if you want to set or remove a password for a database that is located on a network, you will first need to make sure nobody else is using it.

You can use any word or phrase as a database password, but to create a secure password, keep the following in mind:

- Passwords are case sensitive.

- You can include letters, accented characters, numbers, spaces, and most punctuation marks.

- A good password includes uppercase letters, lowercase letters, and symbols or numbers, and isn't a word found in a dictionary.

SEE ALSO For more information about creating secure passwords, search for the article "Create strong passwords" on the Microsoft website.

Assigning a password to a database has an important secondary benefit. A database created in Access is a *binary file* (a file that stores instructions and data in such a way that it can usually be understood only by a computer). If you open the file in a word processor or a text editor, its content is mostly unreadable, but if you look closely enough at the file, you can discover quite a bit of information. It is unlikely that enough information will be exposed to allow anyone to steal anything valuable. However, people can and do scan files with computer tools designed to look for key words that lead them to restricted information. When you assign a password to a database, the database is automatically encrypted each time it is closed, making it more unreadable. Opening the file in Access with the correct password decrypts the file and makes its data readable again.

A caveat: it is easy to assign a database password, and certainly better than providing no protection at all, in that it keeps most unauthorized people out of the database. However, many inexpensive password recovery utilities are available, theoretically to help people recover a lost password. Anyone can buy one of these utilities and "recover" the password to your database. Also, because the same password works for all users (and nothing prevents one person from giving the password to many other people), simple password protection is most appropriate for a database that has only a few users.

In this exercise, you'll assign a password to a database, test it, and then remove it.

SET UP You need the GardenCompany12 database located in the Chapter12 practice file folder to complete this exercise. Be sure to use the practice database for this chapter rather than continuing on with the database from an earlier chapter. Open the database, and if you want, save your own version to avoid overwriting the original. Then close the database without exiting Access, and follow the steps.

1 With Access running but no database open, display the **Open** page of the **Backstage** view.

2 Open the **Open** dialog box, navigate to the **Chapter12** practice file folder, and click (don't double-click) your version of the **GardenCompany12** database. (We saved our version as **MyGardenCompany12**.) Then click the **Open** arrow, and in the list, click **Open Exclusive**.

12

If other people need to work on the database, they cannot open it until you close it. So it's now safe to set a password.

3   Display the **Info** page of the **Backstage** view.

From this page, you can run utilities to help prevent database problems, assign a password, and assign file properties that help identify the file.

TIP Clicking View And Edit Database Properties in the right pane doesn't display the Property Sheet pane. It displays the Properties dialog box for the active database. In this dialog box, you can assign properties, such as a title, subject, and keywords, that help identify the file and make it easier to find in browsing dialog boxes and programs such as File Explorer.

4   Click **Encrypt with Password** to open the **Set Database Password** dialog box.

As you enter the characters of the password in this dialog box, Access disguises them as asterisks.

5   In the **Password** box, enter 2013D@t@b@se!, and then press the **Tab** key.

6   In the **Verify** box, enter 2013D@t@b@se!. Then click **OK**. A message box warns
    that row-level locking will be ignored.

*Row-level locking is one of the settings that prevent two people from making changes to the
same record (row) at the same time.*

TIP If you have not enrolled in the Microsoft Customer Experience Improvement Program, the Was This Information Helpful link will not be included in the message box.

7   Click **OK** to close the message box, and then close the database without exiting
    Access.

    Now let's test the password.

8   Try to open the database. Instead of displaying the **Home Page** navigation form,
    Access opens the **Password Required** dialog box.

You cannot work with the database unless you know the password.

9   In the **Enter database password** box, enter 2013Database, and click **OK**.

Access warns that the password is not valid.

10   In the message box, click **OK**.

11   When the **Password Required** dialog box is redisplayed, enter the correct password, 2013D@t@b@se!, and then click **OK**.

Now let's remove the password.

12   Display the **Info** page of the **Backstage** view, and click **Decrypt Database**. A message warns that the password cannot be removed unless the database is open for exclusive use.

13   Click **OK**, and then close the database without exiting Access.

14   Open the database for exclusive use, entering the password when prompted.

15   On the **Info** page of the **Backstage** view, click **Decrypt Database**. Then in the **Unset Database Password** dialog box, enter the password, and click **OK** to remove the password.

❌ CLEAN UP Close the database to release the exclusive use.

Splitting databases

When a database user works over a network on a database that is not stored on his or her own computer, Access has to move database objects over the network from the computer where the objects are stored to the computer where the user is working on them. If several people are working on the database at the same time, processing times can get noticeably slower. Under these circumstances, you might want to consider splitting the database to speed up performance.

Splitting a database involves organizing the database into two parts:

- **Back-end database** Contains the tables that store all the data. It remains on the network computer.

- **Front-end database** Contains the forms, queries, and reports that people use to work with the data. It is copied to the local computer of any user who needs to work with the database.

Because Access can move the data required by a database object over the network much faster than it can move the entire object, database performance is improved. But another major benefit of splitting the database is that it helps protect the core data in the tables from problems that might affect its reliability and usability.

You split a database by using the Database Splitter wizard, which you start by clicking the Access Database button in the Move Data group on the Database Tools tab.

In this exercise, you'll use the Database Splitter wizard to organize a database into back-end and front-end components.

➡ SET UP You need the GardenCompany12 database you worked with in the preceding exercise to complete this exercise. Open the database, and then follow the steps.

1   Close any open database objects, and then save the database as GardenCompany12_split.

    TIP You should ALWAYS make a local copy of a database you want to split. Then if the results are not what you expected, you have an unsplit version available for use.

2   When the new version of the database opens with the **Home Page** navigation form displayed, close the form.

3   On the **Database Tools** tab, in the **Move Data** group, click the **Access Database** button to start the **Database Splitter** wizard.

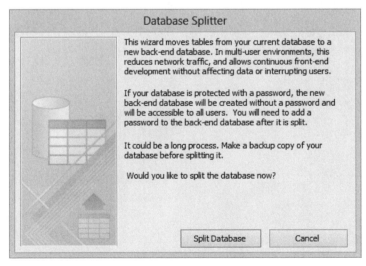

The wizard explains the process before you begin.

4   Click **Split Database**. The **Create Back-end Database** dialog box opens, with GardenCompany12_split_be (in our case, **MyGardenCompany12_split_be**) suggested as the name of the back-end part of the database.

5   If the contents of the **Chapter12** practice file folder are not displayed in the dialog box, navigate to that folder now.

   TIP In practice, you would navigate to the network location in which you want to store the back-end database. Or you could avoid including a drive letter in the path to the back-end database location by entering the UNC path (\\<server>\<share>) of the storage location to the left of the file name in the File Name box. Either way, the location must be specified at this time in order for the links that the wizard establishes between the back-end and front-end databases to work.

6   Click **Split**.

   TIP The splitting operation for this practice file is very short, but for some working databases, the process can take quite a long time.

7   When a message notifies you that the database has been successfully split, click **OK** to close the message box and the wizard.

   The GardenCompany12_split file (the one you started with) is now the front-end file. Let's try working with the split database.

8   In the **Navigation** pane, right-click the **Garden Company** category, click **Category**, and click **Object Type** to display the **All Access Objects** category.

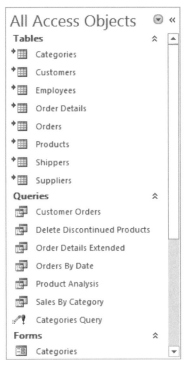

The Tables group now contains shortcuts to the tables in the back-end database, as indicated by the arrows to the left of the table icons.

You can now distribute the **GardenCompany12_split** database to anyone who needs to use it. Provided that person has a connection to the computer on which the associated back-end database is stored, the front-end database will automatically connect to the back-end to retrieve data as needed.

❌ CLEAN UP Close the GardenCompany12_split database.

12

Securing databases for distribution

When a database is used on your own computer or on your company's network, it is not difficult to control who has access to it. But if you send the database out into the world, on its own or as part of a larger application, you lose that control. There is no way you can know who is using the database or what tools they might have available to hack into it. If this is of concern to you, consider distributing your database as an Access Database Executable (.accde) file.

Suppose you want to make a database available for use by several organizations, but you don't want the organizations' members to be able to change the database objects. You can save the database as an .accde file and distribute that file instead of the .accdb file. Saving a database as an .accde file compiles and compacts the resulting database. Users of the .accde file can view forms and reports, update information, and run queries, but they cannot change the design of forms and reports.

TIP ACCDE databases also restrict what can be done with macros, modules, and VBA code. These topics are beyond the scope of this book.

You can't save a database in ACCDE format back to the source ACCDB format, so after saving a database as an .accde file, be sure to retain the original .accdb file in a safe place. If you need to change a form or report in the database, you will need to make the change in the original database and then save it as an .accde file again.

TIP When creating an ACCDE database that is accessed by multiple users, first ensure that no user has the database open. In File Explorer or Windows Explorer, navigate to the location of the file, and verify that there is no file of the same name with an .laccdb (Locked Access Database) extension. If you attempt to create an .accde file for an open database, you will be warned that the database has already been opened by someone else (the user name and computer name are provided) and told to try again later.

In this exercise, you'll create a secure database by saving it as a distributable .accde file. You'll then test the file.

SET UP You need the GardenCompany12 database you worked with in the preceding exercise to complete this exercise. Open the database (not the GardenCompany12_split database), and then follow the steps.

1 Close any open database objects, and then display the **Save As** page of the **Backstage** view.

2 In the **Advanced** area of the right pane, double-click **Make ACCDE**.

3 In the **Save As** dialog box, verify that the contents of the **Chapter12** practice file folder are displayed, change the name of the database to **GardenCompany12_accde**, and then click **Save**.

4 Close the database without exiting Access.

Let's verify that Access has created a database executable file.

5 Display the **Open** page of the **Backstage** view, and then display the contents of the **Chapter12** practice file in the **Open** dialog box.

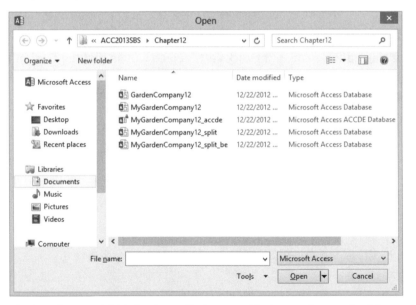

The icon for an ACCDE database displays a red lock over the standard Access icon.

TIP You might need to adjust column widths to display the file types.

12

6   Double-click the version of the **GardenCompany12** database that is identified as a **Microsoft Access ACCDE Database**. A somewhat scary security notice is displayed.

Microsoft Access Security Notice

A potential security concern has been identified.

Warning: It is not possible to determine that this content came from a trustworthy source. You should leave this content disabled unless the content provides critical functionality and you trust its source.

File Path: C:\Users\Joyce\Documents\ACC2013SBS \Chapter12\MyGardenCompany12

This file might contain unsafe content that could harm your computer. Do you want to open this file or cancel the operation?

More information

Open   Cancel

This security warning is displayed when you open an executable file that is from an untrusted publisher or that is stored in an untrusted location.

7   Because you trust the source of this file (you!), click **Open**.

8   In the **Navigation** pane, right-click each object. Notice that the **Design View** command is not available. Neither is it available on the **Home** tab or the **View Shortcuts** toolbar, meaning that you cannot make any design changes to the forms and reports in the **Garden Company** category.

> **TIP** If you change the Navigation pane category to All Access Objects, you can right-click tables and display them in Design view. To prevent the possibility of changes to table design in an .accde file, eliminate access to the Navigation pane as described in "Controlling which features are available" in Chapter 11, "Make databases user friendly," and then create the file.

❌ CLEAN UP Close the ACCDE database, and if you want, delete it.

Packaging and signing databases

If you want to convey to users of a database executable file that they can trust the file, use the Package And Sign tool to create an Access Deployment (.accdc) file. An .accdc file contains one database that has been compressed. The file is signed by using a digital signature, signifying that no changes have been made since the package was created.

TIP You can purchase a digital signature from a third-party company. For information, search for *digital signature* in Access Help.

To package the current database as a signed .accdc file:

1 With all database objects closed, display the **Save As** page of the **Backstage** view.
2 In the **Advanced** area of the right pane, double-click **Package and Sign**.
3 When a security message asks you to confirm that you want to use the installed certificate, click **OK**.
4 In the **Create Microsoft Access Signed Package** dialog box, specify a location for the package and assign a name. Then with **Save as type** set to **Microsoft Access Signed Package**, click **Create**.

To use the packaged file:

1 In File Explorer or Windows Explorer, navigate to the location in which the signed ACCDC database is stored.
2 Double-click the package, and when Access displays a security notice, click **Show Signature Details**.
3 Check the signature in the **Digital Signature Details** dialog box, and then click **OK**.

   TIP To trust all files originating from this publisher, you can click Trust All From Publisher to add the source to the Trusted Publishers list in the Trust Center. For information about the Trust Center, see "Changing default program options" in Chapter 13, "Work in Access more efficiently."

4 In the security notice box, click **Open**.
5 In the **Extract Database To** dialog box, navigate to the location to which you want to extract the database, and click **OK**.

You can then work on the database as you normally would.

12

Preventing database problems

Normal database use can cause the internal structure of any database in any database program to become fragmented, sometimes resulting in a bloated file and inefficient use of disk space. Fortunately, Access monitors the condition of database files as you open and work with them, but you still need to pay attention, particularly if the performance of the database seems slow or erratic.

You can take a variety of steps to help keep an Access 2013 database healthy and running smoothly. Your first line of defense against damage or corruption in any kind of file is to back it up. Database files can rapidly become very large, so you need to choose an appropriate place to store a backup copy, such as a DVD, another computer on your network, or removable media such as a USB flash drive or external hard disk.

TIP To back up a split database, you must back up the front end and back end separately. You might want to back up the back end (the data) on a regular schedule and the front end only after a design change.

In addition to regularly backing up the database, you can use the following Access utilities to keep it running smoothly:

- **Compact and Repair Database** Optimizes performance by rearranging how the file is stored on your hard disk, and then attempts to repair any corruption in tables, forms, and reports.

  TIP It's a good idea to compact and repair a database often. You might even want to have Access run this utility automatically each time the database is closed. To automatically run the utility, display the Current Database page of the Access Options dialog box, select the Compact On Close check box in the Application Options area, and then click OK.

- **Database Documenter** Produces a detailed report that contains enough information to rebuild the database structure if necessary.

- **Analyze Performance** Analyzes the objects in the database and offers three types of feedback: ideas, suggestions, and recommendations. You can instruct Access to optimize the file by following through on any of the suggestions or recommendations.

- **Analyze Table** Tests database tables for compliance with standard database design principles, suggests solutions to problems, and implements those solutions at your request.

In this exercise, you'll first back up a database. Then you'll run the Compact And Repair Database, Analyze Performance, and Database Documenter utilities.

 SET UP You need the GardenCompany12 database you worked with in the preceding exercise to complete this exercise. Open the database file FOR EXCLUSIVE USE, and then follow the steps.

1   Close any open database objects, and then display the **Save As** page of the **Backstage** view.

2   In the **Advanced** area of the right pane, double-click **Back Up Database**.

3   In the **Save As** dialog box, verify that the contents of the **Chapter12** practice file folder are displayed, and then click **Save**, which creates a copy of the database with the current date appended to the file name in the specified folder.

    TIP As with any file name, you can change the name to suit your needs.

    Now let's run the Compact And Repair Database utility.

4   Display the **Info** page of the **Backstage** view, and then click **Compact & Repair Database**.

    TIP You can also click the Compact And Repair Database button in the Tools group on the Database Tools tab.

    TROUBLESHOOTING If you don't have enough space on your hard disk to store a temporary copy of the database, you don't have appropriate permissions, or another user also has the database open, the Compact And Repair Database utility will not run.

    The utility takes only a few seconds to run, and the database will not look any different. If you have been using a database regularly and have not compacted it for a while, running the Compact And Repair Database utility can sometimes reduce the file size by as much as 25 percent.

    Next let's run the Analyze Performance utility.

5   Close any open database objects, and then in the **Forms** area of the **Navigation** pane, click **Home Page**.

6   On the **Database Tools** tab, in the **Analyze** group, click the **Analyze Performance** button to open the **Performance Analyzer** dialog box. Notice that each type of database object is represented by a page, and there are also pages for all objects and for the database as a whole.

The active page reflects the object that is selected in the Navigation pane when you start the utility.

7   Click the **All Object Types** tab, click **Select All**, and then with the check boxes for all the objects in the database selected, click **OK** to start the analyzer.

The Key tells you the nature of each item in the Analysis Results list.

TIP In previous versions of Access, Access Database Executable (.accde) files were called *Microsoft Database Executable (.mde)* files, hence the use of the MDE acronym in the first item in the Analysis Results list shown in this graphic.

8   Click each entry in turn, and read the information in the **Analysis Notes** area.

TIP Always scrutinize the suggestions. Some will help you refine the database and correct aberrations before problems develop; others are not valid in context. For example, the suggestion to create a relationship for the Products table and the suggestion to change the data type of the PostalCode field to Long Integer are not appropriate for this database.

9   Close the **Performance Analyzer** dialog box.

Finally, let's create a report of the structure of the database.

10   On the **Database Tools** tab, in the **Analyze** group, click the **Database Documenter** button to open the **Documenter** dialog box. Notice that this dialog box is identical to the **Performance Analyzer** dialog box, with a page for each type of object the utility can document and a page for all the existing database objects.

11   Click the **Tables** tab, and then click **Options**, which opens the **Print Table Definition** dialog box.

These print options are associated with tables.

TIP The options associated with each type of database object vary, but they all enable you to specify what items you want to include in the documentation for that type of object.

12   In the **Print Table Definition** dialog box, click **Cancel**.

13   Click the **All Object Types** tab, click **Select All**, and then click **OK** to start the documentation process and create the report, which Access displays in **Print Preview**.

The report for this simple database is more than 200 pages long.

14   Zoom in on the report to examine the kinds of things included in the documentation. Then use the page navigation bar to scroll through a few pages.

Table: Categories   Page: 1

Properties

DatasheetGridlinesBehavior:	Both	DateCreated:	8/27/2006 11:43:04 AM
DefaultView:	2	Description:	Categories of The Garden Company products.
DisplayViewsOnSharePointSi	1	FilterOn:	False
FilterOnLoad:	False	GUID:	{guid {636BCC1D-7244-45BE-967F-32AEF1BC1EE8}}
HideNewField:	False	LastUpdated:	12/22/2012 12:57:42 PM
NameMap:	Long binary data	OrderByOn:	False
OrderByOnLoad:	True	OrderOn:	False
Orientation:	Left-to-Right	RecordCount:	18
TotalsRow:	False	Updatable:	True

Columns

Name	Type	Size
Category ID	Long Integer	4
AggregateType:	-1	
AllowZeroLength:	False	

The report details the structure of every object in the database.

TIP You probably don't want to print this long report, but it is a good idea to create and print a report such as this one for your own databases, in case you ever need to reconstruct them. You can't save the report, but you can export it in a variety of formats by right-clicking the report, clicking Export, and then clicking the format you want.

⊗ CLEAN UP Close the Object Definition report and the GardenCompany12 database.

Key points

- You can assign a password to a database to prevent unauthorized users from opening it. Assigning a password automatically encrypts the database.

- Splitting a database can enhance database performance and safeguard data in a multiuser environment.

- If you save the database as an .accde file, people can use its forms and reports but not create new ones.

- Access automatically fixes many problems that can arise with a database. You can prevent problems by frequently using the utilities provided for that purpose.

- The simplest way to protect your database is to back it up regularly.

12

Chapter at a glance

Change

Change default program options,
page 350

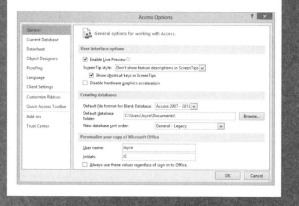

Customize

Customize the ribbon,
page 363

Manipulate

Manipulate the Quick Access Toolbar,
page 370

Work in Access more efficiently

13

IN THIS CHAPTER, YOU WILL LEARN HOW TO

- Change default program options.
- Customize the ribbon.
- Manipulate the Quick Access Toolbar.

If you use Microsoft Access 2013 only occasionally, you might be perfectly happy creating new databases by using the wide range of tools we have already discussed in this book. And you and the people who use your databases might be comfortable with the default working environment and behind-the-scenes settings of the Access program installed on your computers.

However, if you create a lot of databases of various types, you might find that you want to streamline the development process or change aspects of the program to make it more suitable for the users of the databases you create.

In this chapter, you'll take a tour of the pages of the Access Options dialog box to understand the ways in which you can customize the program. Then you'll manipulate the ribbon and the Quick Access Toolbar to put the tools you need for your daily work at your fingertips.

PRACTICE FILES To complete the exercises in this chapter, you need the practice file contained in the Chapter13 practice file folder. For more information, see "Download the practice files" in this book's Introduction.

Changing default program options

In earlier chapters, we accomplished most common database tasks by working with the default Access program settings. After you work with Access for a while, you might want to refine these settings to tailor the program to the way you work. Knowing which settings are where in the Access Options dialog box makes the customization process more efficient.

In this exercise, you'll take a closer look at the Access Options dialog box and explore several of the available pages.

SET UP You don't need any practice files to complete this exercise. Open a blank database, and then follow the steps.

1   Display the **Backstage** view, and then click **Options** to open the **Access Options** dialog box with the **General** page displayed.

The options on this page control the user interface appearance, the availability of Live Preview, the default file format and storage location, and user identification.

TIP As you work your way through this exercise, don't worry if the settings in your Access Options dialog box are different from ours. Settings can vary depending on changes you might have made while working through the exercises, or your system administrator might have configured some settings to comply with your company's policy. Also don't worry about the height of the dialog box; for screen shot purposes, we sized the dialog box to best fit its contents.

The options in the bottom area of the **General** page apply to all Microsoft Office programs, not just Access.

2   In the **Personalize your copy of Microsoft Office** area, click the **Office Background** arrow to display its list.

No Background
Calligraphy
Circles and Stripes
Circuit
Clouds
Doodle Circles
Doodle Diamonds
Geometry
Lunchbox
School Supplies
Spring
Stars
Straws
Tree Rings
Underwater

Choosing an option from this list adds a background effect to the top of all Office program windows.

3   Click away from the list or press **Esc** to close the list without choosing an option.

13

4   In the left pane, click **Current Database** to display the options that control the features available to the current database.

The options on this page apply only to the active database, not to all databases.

5   Scroll to the bottom of the page to view all the options.

You will probably use these options less frequently.

SEE ALSO For information about how to use several of the options on the Current Database page, see "Controlling which features are available" in Chapter 11, "Make databases user friendly."

13

6　In the **Navigation** area, click the **Navigation Options** button to open the **Navigation Options** dialog box.

In this dialog box, you can change the display and behavior of the Navigation pane.

7　Click **Cancel**. Then in the left pane of the **Access Options** dialog box, click **Datasheet**.

The options on this page affect the default appearance of gridlines, cells, and fonts in tables and query results in Datasheet view.

8   Display the **Object Designers** page. Scroll down to view all the options available.

The options on this page affect the way Design view looks and behaves when you are manipulating tables, queries, forms, and reports.

TIP Most of the settings on this page have no effect when an object is displayed in Datasheet or Layout view.

9   Display the **Proofing** page.

13

Access includes the same tools for checking spelling as the other Office 2013 programs.

10   In the **AutoCorrect options** area, click the **AutoCorrect Options** button to display the **AutoCorrect** dialog box.

The table lists entries that will automatically be replaced.

11   If you are not already familiar with AutoCorrect, scroll the list at the bottom of the dialog box, noticing the built-in replacements, and then close the dialog box.

12   Display the **Language** page.

You can make additional languages available for databases that will be used by international audiences, and specify the editing, display, and Help languages.

13   Display the **Client Settings** page, which controls default program behavior on the
      local computer. Scroll down to view all the options available.

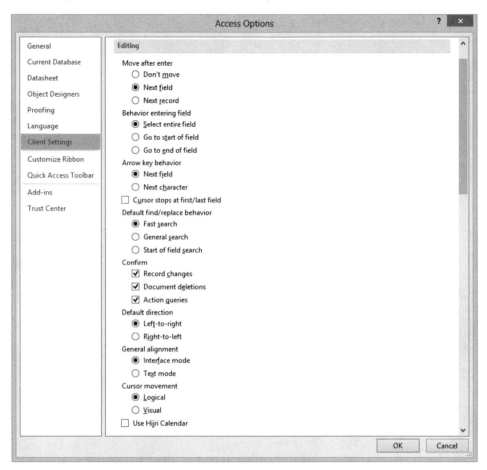

The options on this page affect default behaviors of Access on your local computer.

14   Skipping over **Customize Ribbon** and **Quick Access Toolbar**, which we discuss in later topics in this chapter, click **Add-ins**.

You can use the Manage options at the bottom of the page to add and remove add-ins.

TIP Don't worry if your Add-ins page looks different from ours. We have no installed add-ins on this computer. For information about add-ins, see the sidebar "Using add-ins" following this topic.

13

15   Display the **Trust Center** page.

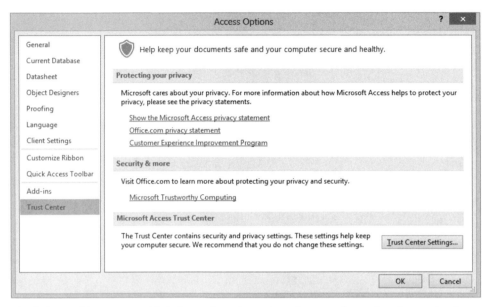

The links on this page provide information about the privacy and security of your databases.

16   In the **Microsoft Access Trust Center** area, click the **Trust Center Settings** button to display the **Trust Center**.

The Trusted Publishers page stores the names of any publishers whose digitally signed files you have specified are safe for Access to open.

TIP You cannot add publishers on this page. You add them in response to a message Access displays when you open a digitally signed file. For more information about digitally signing databases, see the sidebar "Packaging and signing databases" in Chapter 12, "Protect databases."

17 In the right pane, click **Trusted Locations** to display the locations from which Access won't block content.

The Access wizards are stored in a trusted user location, meaning that Access will not block them from running on your computer.

TIP From this page, you can also control the actions Access takes in response to databases that are provided by certain people or companies (publishers) or that contain ActiveX controls or macros.

18 Explore the other pages of the **Trust Center** dialog box, and then click **Cancel** to return to the **Access Options** dialog box.

❌ CLEAN UP Close the Access Options dialog box.

13

Using add-ins

Add-ins are utilities that add specialized functionality to a program (but aren't full-fledged programs themselves). Access includes two primary types of add-ins: Component Object Model (COM) add-ins and Access add-ins.

There are several sources of add-ins:

- You can purchase add-ins from third-party vendors—for example, you can purchase an add-in that creates forms that have controls automatically sized to fit their data.

- You can download free add-ins from the Office website or other websites.

- When you install a third-party program, you might install an add-in to allow it to interact with Microsoft Office 2013 programs.

TIP Be careful when downloading add-ins from websites other than those you trust. Add-ins are executable files that can easily be used to spread viruses and otherwise wreak havoc on your computer. For this reason, default settings in the Trust Center intervene when you attempt to download or run add-ins.

To use some add-ins, you must first install them on your computer and then load them into your computer's memory, as follows:

1 At the bottom of the **Add-ins** page of the **Access Options** dialog box, display the **Manage** list, click either **COM Add-ins** or **Access Add-ins**, and then click **Go** to open an **Add-Ins** dialog box corresponding to the type of add-in you chose.

2 In the dialog box, click **Add** or **Add New**.

3 In the dialog box that opens, navigate to the folder in which the add-in you want to install is stored, and double-click its name to add it to the list of those that are available for use.

4 In the list, select the check box of the new add-in, and then either click **OK** or click an option to load the add-in. (For example, you might be given the option of always loading the add-in when you start your computer.)

TIP You can also manage add-ins in the Add-In Manager dialog box that is displayed when you click the Add-Ins button in the Add-Ins group on the Database Tools tab.

Customizing the ribbon

In "Controlling which features are available" in Chapter 11, "Make databases user-friendly," we described options you can set for a specific database that determine what Access features are available for that database. However, you can also control what people can do with any database by customizing the Access program installed on a local computer.

Many people use Access to perform the same set of tasks all the time, and for them, the plethora of buttons on the ribbon is just a form of clutter. Would you prefer to have fewer commands displayed, not more? Or would you prefer to have more specialized groups of commands? Or do you want to make only specific commands available to users to prevent inadvertent changes to your databases?

Well, you can. Clicking Customize Ribbon in the left pane of the Access Options dialog box displays the Customize Ribbon page.

In the box on the left, you can list all the commands available in Access. In the one on the right, you can display the commands currently available on the ribbon.

You can customize the ribbon in the following ways:

- Turn off tabs you rarely use.

- If you use the commands in only a few groups on each tab, remove the groups you don't use. (The group is not removed from the program, just from its tab.)

- Move a predefined group by removing it from one tab and then adding it to another.

- Duplicate a predefined group by adding it to another tab.

- Create a custom group on any tab and then add commands to it. (You cannot add commands to a predefined group.)

- For the ultimate in customization, create a custom tab. For example, you might want to do this if you or the people who work with your databases use only a few commands from each tab and it is inefficient to flip between them.

Don't be afraid to experiment with the ribbon to come up with the configuration that best suits your Access databases and the type of work performed with them. For example, someone who only does data entry might need a different configuration than someone who creates queries to produce reports. If at any point you find that the new ribbon configuration is harder to work with rather than easier, you can always reset everything back to the default configuration.

TIP If you have upgraded from Access 2003 or an earlier version, you might have identified a few commands that no longer seem to be available. A few old features have been abandoned, but others that people used only rarely have simply been pushed off to one side. If you miss one of these sidelined features, you can make it a part of your Access environment by adding it to the ribbon. You can find a list of all the commands that do not appear on the ribbon but are still available in Access by displaying the Customize Ribbon page of the Access Options dialog box and then clicking Commands Not In The Ribbon in the Choose Commands From list.

In this exercise, you'll turn off tabs, remove groups, create a custom group, and add commands to the new group. Then you'll create a tab and move predefined groups of buttons to it. Finally, you'll reset the ribbon to its default state.

SET UP You need the GardenCompany13 database located in the Chapter13 practice file folder to complete this exercise. Be sure to use the practice database for this chapter rather than continuing on with the database from an earlier chapter. Open the database, and if you want, save your own version to avoid overwriting the original. Then follow the steps.

1 Display the **Customize Ribbon** page of the **Access Options** dialog box.

2 In the **Customize the Ribbon** list, clear the check boxes of the **External Data** and **Database Tools** tabs. Then click **OK** to remove all but the **File**, **Home**, and **Create** tabs.

You cannot remove the File tab.

3 Redisplay the **Customize Ribbon** page of the **Access Options** dialog box, and in the **Customize the Ribbon** list box, select the **Database Tools** check box.

Now let's work with groups.

4 In the **Customize the Ribbon** list box, click the plus sign adjacent to **Database Tools** to display the groups on this tab.

5 On the left, display the **Choose commands from** list, and click **Main Tabs**. Then in the list box, click the plus sign adjacent to **Database Tools** to display the groups that are predefined for this tab.

13

6   In the **Customize the Ribbon** list box, click the **Move Data** group, and then click **Remove** to remove the group from the **Database Tools** tab on the ribbon. Notice that the group is still available in the **Choose commands from** list box, so you can move it back to the **Database Tools** tab, or add it to a different tab, at any time.

7   If the **Home** group is not expanded in the **Customize the Ribbon** list box, click the plus sign adjacent to **Home** to displays its groups, and then click the word **Home**.

8   Below the list box, click **New Group**. When the **New Group (Custom)** group is added to the bottom of the **Home** group list, click **Rename**, enter Final in the **Display name** box, and click **OK**. Then click the **Move Up** button until the **Final (Custom)** group is above **Views** in the group list.

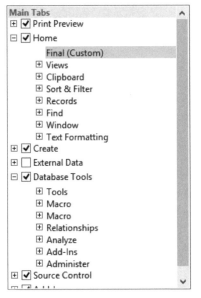

Because of its location in the hierarchy, the custom group will appear at the left end of the Home tab.

9   With **Final (Custom)** selected, display the **Choose commands from** list, and click **File Tab** to display only the commands available in the **Backstage** view in the list box below it.

10   In the **Choose commands from** list box, click **Encode/Decode Database**, and then click **Add**. Then repeat this step to add **Package and Sign**.

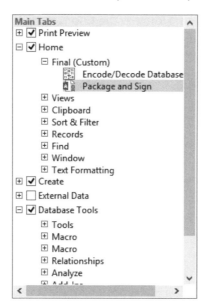

You can add commands to a custom group, but not to a predefined group.

Next let's create a custom Search tab.

11   In the **Customize the Ribbon** list box, remove the **Find** and **Sort & Filter** groups from the **Home** tab.

12   Click the word **Home**, and then below the list box, click **New Tab**. Notice that Access adds a new tab called **New Tab (Custom)** to the list, selects it for display on the ribbon, and assigns it one custom group.

13   For the purposes of this exercise, we don't need the custom group, so remove it.

14   Click **New Tab (Custom)**, and then click **Rename**. In the **Rename** dialog box, enter **Search** in the **Display name** box, and click **OK**.

TIP The name appears on the ribbon with the capitalization you use in the Rename dialog box. If you want Search to appear as SEARCH, enter it that way. However, bear in mind that entering the tab name with an initial capital letter visually identifies it as a custom tab.

13

15   With the **Search (Custom)** tab selected, display the **Choose commands from** list, and click **Main Tabs**. Then in the list box, expand the **Home** tab.

16   Add the **Sort & Filter** and **Find** groups from **Home** in the **Choose commands from** list box to **Search (Custom)** in the **Customize the Ribbon** list box.

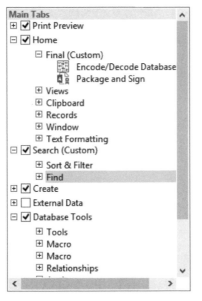

You have created a new tab that contains two predefined groups.

17   Close the **Access Options** dialog box.

The Home tab now has a Final group that contains two buttons.

18   Display the **Customers** table in **Datasheet** view, and then click the **Search** tab.

The custom Search tab contains all the commands for filtering, sorting, and finding records.

Let's restore the default ribbon configuration.

19   Display the **Customize Ribbon** page of the **Access Options** dialog box. Below the **Customize the Ribbon** list box, click **Reset**, and then click **Reset all customizations**.

20   In the message box that asks you to confirm that you want to delete all ribbon and Quick Access Toolbar customizations, click **Yes**. Then close the **Access Options** dialog box.

❌ CLEAN UP Close the Customers table. Keep the GardenCompany13 database open for use in the last exercise.

Customizing the status bar

You can easily add or remove controls from the status bar by right-clicking any blank area of the status bar and then, on the Customize Status Bar menu, clicking the control you want to add or remove.

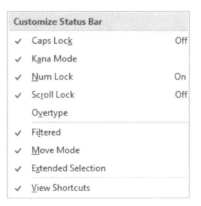

On the Customize Status Bar menu, a check mark indicates a control that is currently shown or will be shown when information of that type is available.

Manipulating the Quick Access Toolbar

By default, the Save, Undo, and Repeat/Redo buttons appear on the Quick Access Toolbar. If you regularly use a few buttons that are scattered on various tabs of the ribbon and you don't want to switch between tabs to access the buttons or crowd your ribbon with a custom tab, you might want to add these frequently used buttons to the Quick Access Toolbar. They are then always visible in the upper-left corner of the program window.

Clicking the Customize Quick Access Toolbar button at the right end of the Quick Access Toolbar displays a menu that lists commonly used commands. Check marks appear to the left of commands currently available on the Quick Access Toolbar. You can click these commands to remove them, and click other commands to add them.

Customize Quick Access Toolbar
New
Open
✓ Save
Email
Quick Print
Print Preview
Spelling
✓ Undo
✓ Redo
Mode
Refresh All
Sync All
Touch/Mouse Mode
More Commands...
Show Below the Ribbon

You can customize the Quick Access Toolbar by selecting or clearing buttons on the Customize Quick Access Toolbar menu.

As you add buttons to the Quick Access Toolbar, it expands to accommodate them. If you add many buttons, some of them might not be visible, which defeats the purpose of adding them. To resolve this problem, you can move the Quick Access Toolbar below the ribbon by clicking the Customize Quick Access Toolbar button, and then clicking Show Below The Ribbon.

Clicking More Commands on the Customize Quick Access Toolbar menu opens the Access Options dialog box with the Quick Access Toolbar page displayed. This page gives you more options for displaying commands on the toolbar.

In the box on the left, you can list all the commands available in Access. The box on the right displays the commands currently available on the Quick Access Toolbar.

You can customize the Quick Access Toolbar in the following ways:

- Define a custom Quick Access Toolbar for all databases, or define a custom Quick Access Toolbar for a specific database.

- Add any command from any group of any tab, including tool tabs, to the toolbar.

    TIP A quick way to add a command is to right-click it on the ribbon and then click Add To Quick Access Toolbar.

- Display a separator between different types of buttons.

- Move buttons around on the toolbar until they are in the order you want.

- Reset everything back to the default Quick Access Toolbar configuration.

If you never use more than a few buttons, add those buttons to the Quick Access Toolbar and then hide the ribbon by double-clicking the active tab or by clicking the Collapse The Ribbon button. Only the Quick Access Toolbar and tab names remain visible. You can temporarily redisplay the ribbon by clicking the tab you want to view. You can permanently redisplay the ribbon by double-clicking any tab or by clicking the Pin The Ribbon button.

KEYBOARD SHORTCUT Press Ctrl+F1 to minimize or expand the ribbon. For a list of keyboard shortcuts, see "Keyboard shortcuts" at the end of this book.

In this exercise, you'll add a few buttons to the Quick Access Toolbar for all databases, and then you'll test some of the buttons.

 SET UP You need the GardenCompany13 database you worked with in the preceding exercise to complete this exercise. Open the database, open the Employees table in Datasheet view, and then follow the steps.

1 Display the **Quick Access Toolbar** page of the **Access Options** dialog box. Then display the **Choose commands from** list, and click **All Commands**.

    TIP If you want to create a Quick Access Toolbar that is specific to the active database, display the Customize Quick Access Toolbar list on the right, and click For *<path of database>*. Then any command you select will be added to that specific toolbar instead of the toolbar for all databases.

2 In the **Customize Quick Access Toolbar** list box, click **Redo**. Then at the top of the **Choose commands from** list box, double-click **Separator** to divide the default **Save**, **Undo**, and **Redo** commands from the custom commands you are about to add to the toolbar.

3   Scroll about two-thirds of the way down the **Choose commands from** list box, click
         Quick Print, and then click **Add**.

         TIP You can also add the Quick Print button to the Quick Access Toolbar by clicking
         the Customize Quick Access Toolbar button and then clicking Quick Print.

4   Repeat step 3 to add the **Forms**, **Reports**, and **Tables** ribbon groups, so that you can
         use their commands without having to display the **Create** tab of the ribbon.

         TIP To quickly find a particular command in the Choose Commands From list box,
         click any command and then enter the first letter of the command you want. The list
         box scrolls to the first command that starts with that letter.

5   Rearrange these groups so that they appear in this order: **Tables**, **Forms**, and then
         Reports.

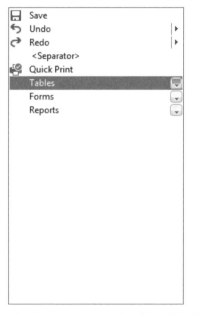

The down-arrows to the right of Tables, Forms, and Reports indicate
that clicking these buttons on the Quick Access Toolbar will display
the associated group's commands.

13

6   Close the **Access Options** dialog box. Notice that the **Quick Access Toolbar** now
     includes the default **Save**, **Undo**, and **Repeat/Redo** buttons, separated by a line from
     the custom **Quick Print** button and the **Tables**, **Forms**, and **Reports** group buttons.

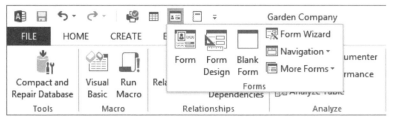

You have added a button and three groups to the Quick Access Toolbar.

Now let's test the new Quick Access Toolbar.

7   Verify that your printer is turned on, and then on the **Quick Access Toolbar**, click the
     Quick Print button.

8   Close the **Employees** table.

9   With **Employees** selected in the **Navigation** pane, on the **Quick Access Toolbar**, click
     the **Forms** button to display the commands in that group.

*All of the buttons in the Forms group are active because the Employees table is selected
in the Navigation pane.*

Let's restore the default Quick Access Toolbar configuration.

10   Display the **Quick Access Toolbar** page of the **Access Options** dialog box. Below
     the **Customize Quick Access Toolbar** list box, click **Reset**, and then click **Reset only
     Quick Access Toolbar**.

11   In the **Reset Customizations** message box, click **Yes** to return the **Quick Access
     Toolbar** to its default contents. Then close the **Access Options** dialog box.

❌ CLEAN UP Close the GardenCompany13 database.

Key points

- The Access environment is flexible and can be customized to meet your needs.

- Most of the settings that control the working environment are gathered on the pages of the Access Options dialog box.

- For efficiency and security, customize the ribbon to make only the database tools each user needs available.

- Provide one-click access to any Access command by adding a button for it to the Quick Access Toolbar, either for all databases or for a specific database.

13

Glossary

Access Database Executable (.accde) file An Access database file that has been compiled and compacted for distribution. The ACCDE format allows users to view forms and reports, update information, and run queries, but prevents them from changing database objects.

Access Deployment (.accdc) file An Access database file that has been compressed and digitally signed for distribution.

action query A type of query that performs an action on matched records, such as updating fields or deleting the records. See also *select query*.

add-ins Utilities that provide specialized functionality to a program but aren't full-fledged programs themselves.

aggregate function A function that performs a calculation, such as Sum or Avg (average), on multiple values and returns a single summary value.

append query A query that adds, or appends, records from one or more tables to the end of one or more tables.

application parts Predefined database objects that you can add to an existing database.

arithmetic operator An operator that is used with numerals: + (addition), - (subtraction), * (multiplication), or / (division).

back-end database The portion of a split database that contains the tables that store all the data. The back-end database is kept on a central computer. See also *front-end database* and *split database*.

binary file A file that contains encoded information that is interpreted by a computer according to the application that created it. In general, a binary file can be edited only by the application in which it was created. A binary file is not encrypted and is therefore not secure.

boolean A Yes/No data type used for fields that can have only two possible mutually exclusive values, such as True or False. This data type is named after George Boole, an early mathematician and logistician.

bound Linked, as when a text box control is linked to a specific field in a table. See also *unbound*.

Cascade Delete A deletion of data that is also implemented in related records.

combo box A control that combines a text box with a list box. With a combo box, the user can type an entry or choose one from a list.

comma-delimited text file A text file in which each field is separated from the next by a comma.

command button Any button with which users initiate an immediate action. You can add command button controls to forms and reports.

comparison operator An operator that compares two expressions, expressed as > (greater than), < (less than), = (equal to), >= (greater than or equal to), <= (less than or equal to), <> (not equal to), or like (pattern matching).

constant A value that is not calculated and does not change. For example, the number *210* and the text *Quarterly Earnings* are constants. An expression, or a value resulting from an expression, is not a constant.

control An object, such as a text box, combo box, or command button, that displays data or choices, performs an action, or makes a database object easier to use.

control property A setting that determines the control's appearance, what kind of data it can display, and its behavior. The properties for a selected control are displayed in the Property Sheet pane.

control source The object, such as a field, table, or query, to which a control is bound. See also *record source*.

crosstab query A type of query that displays data for summarized values from a field or table and then groups them by two sets of facts: one down the left side, and the other across the top of the datasheet.

data type A property that restricts entries in a field to a specific type of data.

database application A database that is made easier to use by the inclusion of queries, forms, reports, custom categories and groups, macros, and other tools.

database object One of the components of an Access database, such as a table, query, form, report, macro, or module.

database security Measures adopted to protect data from accidental or intentional corruption and to make it difficult for unauthorized people to gain access to private information; for example, passwords, encryption, and .accde files.

datasheet A table with data displayed in columns (*fields*) and rows (*records*). The first row contains column headings (*field names*).

Datasheet view The view in which you can review and modify the data in a table or returned by a query.

delete query A query that deletes records that match a specified pattern from one or more tables.

delimited text file A text file in which each field is separated from the next by a specific character, such as a comma or a tab.

delimiter A character, such as a comma (,), semicolon (;), or backslash (\), that is used to separate records and fields in a delimited text file.

design grid In Design view, the grid in which you can manually work with advanced filters and queries.

Design view The view in which you can review and modify the structure of a table, query, form, or report.

dialog box launcher On the ribbon, a button in the lower-right corner of some groups that opens a dialog box with features related to the group.

duplicate query A type of select query that finds records containing identical information in one or more specified fields. Can be created with the assistance of the Find Duplicates Query wizard.

empty string A string with the value "" (two quotation marks with nothing between them).

encrypting To encode (scramble) information in such a way that it is unreadable to all but those individuals possessing the key to the code.

exclusive use A setting that permits only one person to have a database open. Generally used when setting or removing a database password.

exporting The process of converting an Access table or database into a format that can be used by other programs. See also *importing*.

expression A combination of functions, field values, constants, and operators that can be used to assign properties to tables or forms, to determine values in fields or reports, as part of a query, and in many other places. Also known as a *formula*.

Expression Builder A tool used to create an expression. The Expression Builder includes a list of common expressions that you can select from to define the properties you want to target.

field An element of a table that contains a specific item of information, such as a last name. A field is represented in Access as a column in a database table. See also *record*.

field alias A label assigned to a field. You can change the labels Access assigns to make them more meaningful.

field names The names assigned to fields that appear as column headings in the first row of a database table.

field property A property that controls what data can be entered in a field, how it must look, and what Access should do with it.

filter A set of criteria that specifies what table data should be displayed.

fixed-width text file A common text file format that is often used to transfer data from older programs. The same field in every record contains the same number of characters. If the actual data doesn't fill a field, the field is padded with spaces so that the starting point of the data in the next field is the same number of characters from the beginning of every record.

flat database A simple database that can store information in only one table. Also known as a *flat file database*. See also *relational database*.

foreign key In related tables, the foreign key field in one table corresponds with the primary key field in the other table.

form An organized and formatted view of some or all of the fields from one or more tables or query results. Forms work interactively with the tables in a database and are often used to simplify data entry.

form selector The box at the intersection of the vertical and horizontal rulers when a form is displayed in Design view. You click the form selector to select the entire form.

front-end database The portion of a split database that contains the forms, queries, and reports people use to work with data. The front end can be copied to the local computer of any user who needs to work with the database. See also *back-end database* and *split database*.

function A named procedure or routine, often used for mathematical or financial calculations.

group On a ribbon tab, an area containing buttons related to a specific database object, element, or function. On the Navigation bar, a list that is part of a category.

grouping level The level by which records are grouped in a report. When you group on a field, the report adds a group header and footer around each group of records that have the same value in that field.

HTML A markup language used to create hypertext documents that are portable from one platform to another. HTML files are simple ASCII text files with embedded markup tags that control formatting and hypertext links. See also *XML*.

HTML tag A code that identifies an element in an HTML document, such as a heading or paragraph, for the purposes of formatting, indexing, and linking information in the document.

importing The process of converting external data into a format that can be used by Access. See also *exporting*.

input mask A property that controls the appearance, format, and type of data in a field.

label control A control that contains text as it will appear on a form or report.

linking The process of connecting to data in other programs so that you can view and edit it both in Access and the originating program.

logical operator An operator, such as AND, OR, or NOT, that is used in queries and filters to extract matching records from tables.

Lookup wizard An Access wizard with which you can create a lookup list.

main form A form that contains embedded subforms. See also *subform*.

main report A report that serves as a shell for one or more embedded subreports. See also *subreport*.

make-table query A query that combines all or part of the data from one or more tables into a new table.

many-to-many relationship A relationship between two tables in which records in each table have multiple matching records in the related table. For example, each sales invoice can contain multiple products, and each product can appear on multiple sales invoices. See also *one-to-many relationship* and *one-to-one relationship*.

Microsoft Database Executable (.mde) file The equivalent of an .accde file created by previous versions of Access. See *Access Database Executable (.accde) file*.

named range A group of related spreadsheet cells defined by a single name.

navigation control A control on a navigation form that consists of a placeholder for a navigation button and a subform or subreport control.

navigation form A form that presents the user with a set of navigation buttons that can be clicked to display and work with forms and reports. Database designers can use navigation forms to make it easier for users to access and manipulate data and more difficult for them to unintentionally change or delete it.

Navigation pane An area of the Access program window that enables the user to quickly open database objects.

normalization The process of ensuring that a set of data is stored in only one table. The rules that govern normalization are designed to minimize data redundancy and result in a database in which referential integrity can be enforced.

Null Nothing; a field with no entry.

one-to-many relationship In relational databases, a relationship between two tables in which a single record in the first table can be related to one or more records in the second table, but a record in the second table can be related to only one record in the first table. See also *many-to-many relationship* and *one-to-one relationship*.

one-to-one relationship In relational databases, a relationship between two tables in which a single record in the first table can be related to only one record in the second table, and a record in the second table can be related to only one record in the first table. See also *many-to-many relationship* and *one-to-many relationship.*

operator See *arithmetic operator, comparison operator,* and *logical operator.*

option button A control that allows a user to select from a fixed set of mutually exclusive choices.

parameter query A type of query that, when run, prompts for the values (criteria) to use to match records. Because the criteria are entered at run time, the same parameter query can be used to match different records. See also *action query, crosstab query,* and *select query.*

parsing The process of analyzing an imported document, such as an HTML document, and identifying anything that looks like structured data.

password A string of characters used to access information or log on to a computer. Passwords help prevent unauthorized people from accessing files, programs, and other resources. See also *secure password.*

populating To add data to a table or other object.

primary key One or more fields whose value or values uniquely identify each record in a table. A primary key field cannot contain a Null value. In related tables, the primary key field in one table corresponds with the foreign key field in the other table.

property A named attribute of a control, a field, or an object that you set to define one of the object's characteristics (such as size, color, or screen location) or an aspect of its behavior (such as whether the object is hidden).

publisher The person or entity who digitally signs a database or other file, thereby guaranteeing its source.

query A database object that locates specific information stored in a table and allows you to view and manipulate the results. The results of a query can be used as the basis for forms and reports.

Quick Access Toolbar A small, customizable toolbar that displays frequently used commands.

record All the related information about an item. A record in Access is represented as a row in a database table. See also *field.*

record selector The gray bar along the left edge of a form in Form view. You can select an entire record by clicking its record selector.

record source The source from which the data in a bound record originates. See also *control source.*

referential integrity A restriction on data in two related tables that does not allow an entry in one table unless it already exists in the other table.

relational database A type of database that stores information in related tables. Relational databases use matching values to relate data in one table to data in the other table. In a relational database, you typically store a specific type of data just once. See also *flat database.*

relationship An association between common fields in two or more tables.

report A database object used to display table information in a formatted, easily accessible manner, either on the screen or on paper. It can include items from multiple tables and queries, values calculated from information in the database, and formatting elements such as headers, footers, titles, and headings.

report selector The box at the intersection of the vertical and horizontal rulers when a report is displayed in Design view. You click the report selector to select the entire report.

results datasheet The presentation of the records matched by a query and any specified calculations in a table-like structure.

ribbon A user interface design that organizes commands into logical groups, which appear on separate tabs.

row selector The gray box at the left end of each row in the field definition area when a table's structure is displayed in Design view.

secure password A password that includes uppercase letters, lowercase letters, and symbols or numbers, and that is not a word found in a dictionary. Also called a *strong password*. See also *password*.

security warning A warning that appears when a database that contains one or more macros is opened.

select query A query that matches records from one or more tables and displays them in a results datasheet. Can contain specifications for which fields to display in what order and how to group (summarize) their values. See also *action query*.

signing The act of guaranteeing the source and content of a file by attaching a digital signature.

sorting A method of arranging data based on the order of specified information.

split database A database that has been organized into two parts: a back-end database that contains the tables that store all the data, and a front-end database that contains the forms, queries, and reports that people use to work with the data. See also *back-end database* and *front-end database*.

SQL database A database based on Structured Query Language (SQL).

subdatasheet A datasheet that is contained within another datasheet.

subform A form that is contained within another form. See also *main form*.

subquery A nested query that uses the results of one query as a field in another query. The nested query involves the use of a Structured Query Language (SQL) Select statement.

subreport A report that is contained within another report. See also *main report*.

syntax The required format in which expressions must be entered.

tab A component of the ribbon that contains buttons organized in groups

tabbed page The display area allocated to an open database object in the Access program window workspace. You click the tab to display the object's page. By default, database objects are displayed on tabbed pages. Alternatively, you can display objects in their own windows.

table A structured arrangement of one or more rows and one or more columns. The intersection of each row and column is a cell. All the items of information in a row constitute a record, and all the items of information in a column constitute a field.

tag A code in HTML or XML that provides instructions for formatting or defining the structure of a document.

template A ready-made pattern that can be used to create a specific type of database. Access 2013 comes with several templates, all of which can be customized.

text box control A control on a form or report in which text can be viewed, entered, or edited. A text box control is bound to a field in the underlying table.

unbound Not linked. An unbound control is not linked to a field in an underlying table; instead it might be used, for example, to calculate values from multiple fields. See also *bound*.

undocking To drag a toolbar, pane, or similar item so that it floats in the program window.

Universal Naming Convention (UNC) The system of naming files among computers on a network so that a file on a given computer will have the same path when it is accessed from any of the other computers on the network.

unmatched query A select query that locates records in one table that do not have any related records in another table. This query can be created with the assistance of the Find Unmatched Query wizard.

update query A query that changes the values in one or more fields of matched records in a table.

validation rule A field property that ensures that entries contain only the correct type, size, or range of data.

view The display of information from a specific perspective. Each Access object has two or more views, such as Datasheet view and Design view.

View Shortcuts toolbar A set of buttons at the right end of the status bar that provides convenient methods for switching the view of the active database object.

wildcard character A keyboard character that can be used to represent one or many characters in a search. The question mark (?) represents a single character, and the asterisk (*) represents one or more characters.

XML A format for delivering rich, structured data in a standard, consistent way. XML tags describe the content of a web document, whereas HTML tags describe how the document looks. Designers can use XML to create their own customized tags. See also *HTML*.

Keyboard shortcuts

Throughout this book, we provide information about how to perform tasks quickly and efficiently by using keyboard shortcuts. This section presents information about keyboard shortcuts that are built in to Microsoft Access 2013 and Microsoft Office 2013.

TIP In the following lists, keys you press at the same time are separated by a plus sign (+), and keys you press sequentially are separated by a comma (,).

Access 2013 keyboard shortcuts

This section provides a comprehensive list of keyboard shortcuts built into Access 2013. The list has been excerpted from Access Help and formatted in tables for convenient lookup.

Open, save, and print databases

Action	Keyboard shortcut
Display the New page of the Backstage view.	Ctrl+N
Display the Open page of the Backstage view.	Ctrl+O
Open the Save As dialog box for an unsaved object, or save a previously saved object.	Ctrl+S or Shift+F12
Open the Save As dialog box.	F12
Open the Print dialog box.	Ctrl+P
Open the Print dialog box from Print Preview.	P or Ctrl+P
Open the Page Setup dialog box from Print Preview.	S
Cancel Print Preview or Layout Preview.	C or Esc

Work in Design, Layout, or Datasheet view

Action	Keyboard shortcut
Cycle between open objects.	Ctrl+F6
Close the active object.	Ctrl+W or Ctrl+F4
Display the Property Sheet pane in Design view.	Alt+Enter
Open or close the Property Sheet pane (form or report Design view and Layout view).	F4
Switch to Form view from form Design view.	F5
Cycle through the upper and lower parts of the Query Designer, Navigation pane, access keys in the Keyboard Access System, and Zoom controls (query Design view, and the Advanced Filter/Sort window).	F6
Cycle through the field grid, field properties, Navigation pane, access keys in the Keyboard Access System, Zoom controls, and the security bar (table Design view).	F6
Open the Choose Builder dialog box (form or report Design view).	F7
Open the Expression Builder dialog box (query Design view).	Ctrl+F2
Open the Zoom box to enter expressions and other text in small input areas.	Shift+F2
Open the Visual Basic Editor from a selected property in the Property Sheet pane (form or report).	F7
Switch from the Visual Basic Editor to form or report Design view.	Alt+F11

Work in the Navigation pane

Action	Keyboard shortcut
Open or close the Navigation pane	F11
Open the selected database object.	Enter
Run the selected macro.	Enter
Open the selected table, query, form, report, macro, or module in Design view.	Ctrl+Enter
Display the Immediate window in the Visual Basic Editor.	Ctrl+G
Move up or down one line.	Up Arrow or Down Arrow
Move up or down one window.	Page Up or Page Down
Move to the last object.	End
Rename a selected object.	F2
With the Navigation pane active, display its Search box.	Ctrl+F

Work in the Property Sheet pane

Action	Keyboard shortcut
Open or close the Property Sheet pane (Design or Layout view).	F4
Move among choices in the control drop-down list one item at a time.	Down Arrow or Up Arrow
Move among choices in the control drop-down list one page at a time.	Page Down or Page Up
Move to the Property Sheet tabs from the control drop-down list.	Tab
Move among the Property Sheet tabs with a tab selected, but no property selected.	Left Arrow or Right Arrow
With a property selected, move down one property on a tab.	Tab
With a property selected, move up one property on a tab; or if already at the top, move to the tab.	Shift+Tab
Toggle forward or backward between tabs when a property is selected.	Ctrl+Tab or Ctrl+Shift+Tab

Work in the Field List pane

Action	Keyboard shortcut
Open or close the Field List pane.	Alt+F8
Add the selected field to the form or report detail section.	Enter
Move up or down the Field List pane.	Up Arrow or Down Arrow
Move between Fields Available lists in the Field List pane.	Tab

Edit controls in forms or reports in Design view

Action	Keyboard shortcut
Copy the selected control to the Clipboard.	Ctrl+C
Cut the selected control and copy it to the Clipboard.	Ctrl+X
Paste the contents of the Clipboard in the upper-left corner of the selected section.	Ctrl+V
Move the selected control to the right (except controls that are part of a layout).	Right Arrow or Ctrl+Right Arrow
Move the selected control to the left (except controls that are part of a layout).	Left Arrow or Ctrl+Left Arrow

Action	Keyboard shortcut
Move the selected control up (except controls that are part of a layout).	Up Arrow or Ctrl+Up Arrow
Move the selected control down (except controls that are part of a layout).	Down Arrow or Ctrl+Down Arrow
Increase or reduce the height of the selected control.	Shift+Down Arrow or Shift+Up Arrow
Increase or reduce the width of the selected control. (If used with controls that are in a layout, the entire layout is resized.)	Shift+Right Arrow or Shift+Left Arrow

Work with combo boxes or list boxes

Action	Keyboard shortcut
Open a combo box.	F4 or Alt+Down Arrow
Refresh the contents of a Lookup field list box or combo box.	F9
Move up or down one line.	Up Arrow or Down Arrow
Move up or down one page.	Page Up or Page Down
Exit the combo box or list box.	Tab

Set properties for a table in Design view

Action	Keyboard shortcut
Move from the field grid to the field properties area. Pressing F6 continuously also activates the Navigation pane, access keys in the Keyboard Access System, Zoom controls, and the security bar.	F6
With a tab selected, but no property selected, move between the General and Lookup tabs.	Left Arrow or Right Arrow
Move between the tabs when a property is selected.	Ctrl+Tab
Move to the first property of a tab when no property is selected.	Tab
Move down one property on a tab.	Tab
Move up one property on a tab; or if already at the top, select the tab itself.	Shift+Tab

Work with text and data

TIP Although many of these keyboard shortcuts also work in other Office programs, they are gathered here for convenience.

Select text in a field

Action	Keyboard shortcut
Change the size of the selection by one character to the right.	Shift+Right Arrow
Change the size of the selection by one word to the right.	Ctrl+Shift+Right Arrow
Change the size of the selection by one character to the left.	Shift+Left Arrow
Change the size of the selection by one word to the left.	Ctrl+Shift+Left Arrow

Select a field or record

TIP To cancel a selection, use the opposite Arrow key.

Action	Keyboard shortcut
Select the next field.	Tab
Select all records.	Ctrl+A or Ctrl+Shift+Spacebar

Extend a selection

Action	Keyboard shortcut
Extend selection from the current record to the previous or next record when Extend mode is not turned on.	Shift+Up Arrow or Shift+Down Arrow
Extend selection from the current column to the previous or next column when Extend mode is not turned on.	Shift+Left Arrow or Shift+Right Arrow
Turn on Extend mode; pressing F8 repeatedly extends the selection to the word, the field, the record, and all records.	F8
In Extend mode, extend a selection to adjacent fields in the same row in Datasheet view.	Left Arrow or Right Arrow
In Extend mode, extend a selection to adjacent rows in Datasheet view.	Up Arrow or Down Arrow
Undo the previous extension.	Shift+F8
Cancel Extend mode.	Esc

Move a column in Datasheet view

Action	Keyboard shortcut
Turn on Move mode.	Ctrl+Shift+F8
Move selected column(s) to the right or left in Move mode.	Right Arrow or Left Arrow

Move the cursor in a field

Action	Keyboard shortcut
Move the cursor one character to the right or left.	Right Arrow or Left Arrow
Move the cursor one word to the right or left.	Ctrl+Right Arrow or Ctrl+Left Arrow
Move the cursor to the end of the field, in single-line fields; or move it to the end of the line in multiple-line fields.	End
Move the cursor to the end of the field, in multiple-line fields.	Ctrl+End
Move the cursor to the beginning of the field, in single-line fields; or move it to the beginning of the line in multiple-line fields.	Home
Move the cursor to the beginning of the field, in multiple-line fields.	Ctrl+Home

Enter data in Datasheet or Form view

Action	Keyboard shortcut
Insert the current date.	Ctrl+Semicolon (;)
Insert the current time.	Ctrl+Shift+Colon (:)
Insert the default value for a field.	Ctrl+Alt+Spacebar
Insert the value from the same field in the previous record.	Ctrl+Apostrophe (')
Add a new record.	Ctrl+Plus Sign (+)
In a datasheet, delete the current record.	Ctrl+Minus Sign (-)
Save changes to the current record.	Shift+Enter
Switch between the values in a check box or option button.	Spacebar
Insert a new line in a Short Text or Long Text field.	Ctrl+Enter
Undo changes in the current field or current record; if both have been changed, press Esc twice to undo changes, first in the current field and then in the current record.	Esc

Refresh fields with current data

Action	Keyboard shortcut
Recalculate the fields in the window.	F9
Requery the underlying tables; in a subform, this requires the underlying table for the subform only.	Shift+F9
Refresh the contents of a Lookup field list box or combo box.	F9

Find and replace text or data (Datasheet view or Form view)

Action	Keyboard shortcut
Open the Find tab in the Find And Replace dialog box.	Ctrl+F
Open the Replace tab in the Find And Replace dialog box.	Ctrl+H
Find the next occurrence of the text specified in the Find And Replace dialog box when the dialog box is closed.	Shift+F4

Navigate records

Navigate in Design view

Action	Keyboard shortcut
Switch between Edit mode (with cursor displayed) and Navigation mode.	F2
Switch to Form view from form Design view.	F5
Cycle through the upper and lower parts of the Query Designer, Navigation pane, access keys in the Keyboard Access System, and Zoom controls (query Design view, and the Advanced Filter/Sort window).	F6
Cycle through the field grid, field properties, Navigation pane, access keys in the Keyboard Access System, Zoom controls, and the security bar (table Design view).	F6
Open the Visual Basic Editor from a selected property in the Property Sheet pane for a form or report.	F7
Open or close the Field List pane in a form or report.	Alt+F8
Switch from the Property Sheet pane to the design grid without changing the selected control (form or report Design view).	Shift+F7

Navigate in Datasheet view

Navigate between fields and records

Action	Keyboard shortcut
Move to the next field.	Tab or Right Arrow
Move to the previous field.	Shift+Tab or Left Arrow
Move to the first or last field in the current record, in Navigation mode.	Home or End
Move to the current field in the previous or next record.	Up Arrow or Down Arrow
Move to the current field in the last record, in Navigation mode.	Ctrl+Down Arrow
Move to the last field in the last record, in Navigation mode.	Ctrl+End
Move to the current field in the first record, in Navigation mode.	Ctrl+Up Arrow
Move to the first field in the first record, in Navigation mode.	Ctrl+Home

Navigate to another screen of data

Action	Keyboard shortcut
Move up or down one screen.	Page Up or Page Down
Move left or right one screen.	Ctrl+Page Up or Ctrl+Page Down

Navigate in subdatasheets

TIP You can navigate between fields and records in a subdatasheet with the same shortcut keys used in Datasheet view.

Action	Keyboard shortcut
Move from the datasheet to expand the record's subdatasheet.	Ctrl+Shift+Down Arrow
Collapse the subdatasheet.	Ctrl+Shift+Up Arrow
Enter the subdatasheet from the last field of the previous record in the datasheet.	Tab
Enter the subdatasheet from the first field of the following record in the datasheet.	Shift+Tab
Exit the subdatasheet and move to the first field of the next record in the datasheet.	Ctrl+Tab
Exit the subdatasheet and move to the last field of the previous record in the datasheet.	Ctrl+Shift+Tab

Action	Keyboard shortcut
From the last field in the subdatasheet to enter the next field in the datasheet.	Tab
From the datasheet to bypass the subdatasheet and move to the next record in the datasheet.	Down Arrow
From the datasheet to bypass the subdatasheet and move to the previous record in the datasheet.	Up Arrow

Navigate in Form view

Navigate between fields and records

Action	Keyboard shortcut
Move to the next or previous field.	Tab or Shift+Tab
Move to the last control on the form and remain in the current record, in Navigation mode.	End
Move to the last control on the form and set focus in the last record, in Navigation mode.	Ctrl+End
Move to the first control on the form and remain in the current record, in Navigation mode.	Home
Move to the first control on the form and set focus in the first record, in Navigation mode.	Ctrl+Home
Move to the current field in the previous or next record.	Ctrl+Page Up or Ctrl+Page Down

Navigate in forms with more than one page

Action	Keyboard shortcut
Move down one page; at the end of the record, moves to the equivalent page on the next record.	Page Down
Move up one page; at the end of the record, moves to the equivalent page on the previous record.	Page Up

Navigate in Print Preview

Action	Keyboard shortcut
Open the Print dialog box from the Print page of the Backstage view, or from datasheets, forms, and reports.	Ctrl+P
Open the Page Setup dialog box (forms and reports only).	S
Zoom in or out on a part of the page.	Z
View the next page (when Fit To Window is selected).	Page Down or Down Arrow
View the previous page (when Fit To Window is selected).	Page Up or Up Arrow
Move to the page number box. Then enter the page number, and press Enter.	Alt+F5
Scroll up or down in small increments.	Up Arrow or Down Arrow
Scroll up or down one full screen.	Page Up or Page Down
Move to the top or bottom of the page.	Ctrl+Up Arrow or Ctrl+Down Arrow
Scroll to the left or right in small increments.	Left Arrow or Right Arrow
Move to the left or right edge of the page.	Home or End
Move to the upper-left or upper-right corner of the page.	Ctrl+Home or Ctrl+End
Cancel Print Preview.	C or Esc

Navigate in the Query Designer

Action	Keyboard shortcut
Move among the Query Designer panes.	F6 or Shift+F6

Navigate in the top pane

TIP If multiple items are selected, pressing the Spacebar affects all selected items. Select multiple items by holding down the Shift key while clicking them. Toggle the selected state of a single item by holding down the Ctrl key while clicking it.

Action	Keyboard shortcut
Move among tables, views, and functions, (and to join lines, if available).	Tab or Shift+Tab
Move between columns in a table, view, or function.	Arrow keys
Choose the selected data column for output.	Spacebar or Plus key
Remove the selected data column from the query output.	Spacebar or Minus key
Remove the selected table, view, or function, or join line from the query.	Delete

Navigate in the query design grid

Action	Keyboard shortcut
Move among cells.	Arrow keys or Tab or Shift+Tab
Move to the last row in the current column.	Ctrl+Down Arrow
Move to the first row in the current column.	Ctrl+Up Arrow
Move to the upper-left cell in the visible portion of the grid.	Ctrl+Home
Move to the lower-right cell.	Ctrl+End
Move in a drop-down list.	Up Arrow or Down Arrow
Select an entire grid column.	Ctrl+Spacebar
Toggle between edit mode and cell selection mode.	F2
Toggle between insert and overstrike mode while editing in a cell.	Ins
Toggle the check box in the Show column. (If multiple items are selected, pressing this key affects all selected items.)	Spacebar
Clear the selected contents of a cell.	Delete

Navigate in the SQL pane

You can use the standard Windows editing keys when working in the SQL pane, such as Ctrl+Arrow keys to move between words, and the Cut, Copy, and Paste commands on the Home tab.

TIP You can only insert text; there is no overstrike mode.

Access web app keyboard shortcuts

Use the following keyboard shortcuts while working with Access web apps.

Customize a web app in Access

TIP Many of the shortcuts listed earlier in "Access 2013 keyboard shortcuts" are also available when customizing a web app.

Action	Keyboard shortcut
Advance through all tables and views (when not in Edit mode).	Tab
Move a table or view selector.	Arrow keys
Show or hide the Navigation pane.	F11
Advance through the controls in a view (when in Edit mode).	Tab
Move the selected control(s).	Arrow keys
Open or close the properties for the selected control.	F4
Show or hide the Field List.	Alt+F8

Work with a web app in a web browser

TIP You can also use any keyboard shortcut keys that are provided by the browser itself.

Action	Keyboard shortcut
Move between the table list, view selector, action bar, search box, and controls in views	Tab, Shift+Tab, or Arrow keys
Create a new item.	N
Delete an item.	Delete
Edit an item.	E
Save an item.	Ctrl+S
Cancel an action.	Escape
Edit a filter.	/
Close a popup view.	Escape

Office 2013 keyboard shortcuts

This section provides a comprehensive list of keyboard shortcuts available in all Office 2013 programs, including Access.

Work with menus

Action	Keyboard shortcut
Display the shortcut menu.	Shortcut key (lower right of most keyboards) or Shift+F10
Display the access keys.	Alt or F10
Display the program icon menu (on the program title bar).	Alt+Spacebar
With the menu or submenu visible, select the next or previous command.	Down Arrow or Up Arrow
Select the menu to the left or right; or, when a submenu is visible, to switch between the main menu and the submenu.	Left Arrow or Right Arrow
Select the first or last command on the menu or submenu.	Home or End
Close the visible menu and submenu at the same time.	Alt
Close the visible menu; or, with a submenu visible, close the submenu only.	Esc

Use Open and Save As in the Backstage view

Action	Keyboard shortcut
Display the Open page of the Backstage view.	Ctrl+O
Display the Save As page of the Backstage view.	Ctrl+S
Save new version of a file that has a file name and location.	Ctrl+S
Return to the file from the Backstage view.	Esc

Use the Open and Save As dialog boxes

Action	Keyboard shortcut
View the Open dialog box.	Ctrl+F12
View the Save As dialog box.	F12
Open the selected folder or file.	Enter
Open the folder one level above the selected folder.	Backspace
Delete the selected folder or file.	Delete
Display a shortcut menu for a selected item such as a folder or file.	Shift+F10
Move forward through options.	Tab
Move back through options.	Shift+Tab

Display and use windows

Action	Keyboard shortcut
Switch to the next window.	Alt+Tab
Switch to the previous window.	Alt+Shift+Tab
Close the active window.	Ctrl+W or Ctrl+F4
Move to a pane from another pane in the program window (clockwise). You might need to press F6 more than once. Note: If pressing F6 doesn't display the pane you want, try pressing Alt to place focus on the ribbon and then pressing Ctrl+Tab to move to the pane.	F6
When multiple windows are open, switch to the next window.	Ctrl+F6
Switch to the previous window.	Ctrl+Shift+F6
Turn on Resize mode for the active window when it is not maximized.	Ctrl+F8
Resize the window in Resize mode.	Arrow keys
Apply the new size.	Enter
Minimize a window to an icon (works for only some Microsoft Office programs).	Ctrl+F9
Maximize or restore a selected window.	Ctrl+F10
Copy a picture of the screen to the Clipboard.	Print Screen
Copy a picture of the selected window to the Clipboard.	Alt+Print Screen

Navigate on the ribbon

1   Press the **Alt** key to display KeyTips over each feature that is available in the current view.

2   Press the letter shown in the KeyTip over the feature that you want to use. Depending on which letter you press, you might be shown additional KeyTips. For example, if the **External Data** tab is active and you press **C**, the **Create** tab is displayed, along with KeyTips for the groups on that tab.

3   Continue pressing letters until you press the letter of the command or control that you want to use. In some cases, you must first press the letter of the group that contains the command.

TIP To cancel the action that you are taking and hide the KeyTips, press Alt.

Move around in text or cells

Action	Keyboard shortcut
Move one character to the left.	Left Arrow
Move one character to the right.	Right Arrow
Move one line up.	Up Arrow
Move one line down.	Down Arrow
Move one word to the left.	Ctrl+Left Arrow
Move one word to the right.	Ctrl+Right Arrow
Move to the end of a line.	End
Move to the beginning of a line.	Home
Move up one paragraph.	Ctrl+Up Arrow
Move down one paragraph.	Ctrl+Down Arrow
Move to the end of a text box.	Ctrl+End
Move to the beginning of a text box.	Ctrl+Home

Work with text

Action	Keyboard shortcut
Copy the selection to the Clipboard.	Ctrl+C
Cut the selection and copy it to the Clipboard.	Ctrl+X
Paste the contents of the Clipboard at the cursor.	Ctrl+V
Delete the selection or the character to the left of the cursor.	Backspace
Delete the selection or the character to the right of the cursor.	Delete
Delete all characters to the right of the cursor.	Ctrl+Delete
Undo typing.	Ctrl+Z or Alt+Backspace
Check spelling.	F7

Move around in and work in tables

Action	Keyboard shortcut
Move to the next cell.	Tab
Move to the preceding cell.	Shift+Tab
Move to the next row.	Down Arrow
Move to the preceding row.	Up Arrow
Insert a tab in a cell.	Ctrl+Tab
Start a new paragraph.	Enter
Add a new row at the bottom of the table.	Tab at the end of the last row

Work with panes

Action	Keyboard shortcut
Move to a pane from another pane in the program window. (You might need to press F6 more than once.) Note: If pressing F6 doesn't display the pane you want, try pressing Alt to place focus on the menu bar and then pressing Ctrl+Tab to move to the pane.	F6
When a menu or toolbar is active, move to a pane. (You might need to press Ctrl+Tab more than once.)	Ctrl+Tab
When a pane is active, select the next or previous option in the pane.	Tab or Shift+Tab

Action	Keyboard shortcut
Display the full set of commands on the pane menu.	Ctrl+Down Arrow
Move among choices on a selected submenu; move among certain options in a group of options in a dialog box.	Down Arrow or Up Arrow
Open the selected menu, or perform the action assigned to the selected button.	Spacebar or Enter
Open a shortcut menu; open a drop-down menu for the selected gallery item.	Shift+F10
When a menu or submenu is visible, select the first or last command on the menu or submenu.	Home or End
Scroll up or down in the selected gallery list.	Page Up or Page Down
Move to the top or bottom of the selected gallery list.	Ctrl+Home or Ctrl+End

Work with wizards

Action	Keyboard shortcut
Toggle the focus forward between controls in the wizard.	Tab
Move to the next page of the wizard.	Alt+N
Move to the previous page of the wizard.	Alt+B
Complete the wizard.	Alt+F

Work with dialog boxes

Action	Keyboard shortcut
Move to the next option or option group.	Tab
Move to the previous option or option group.	Shift+Tab
Switch to the next tab in a dialog box.	Ctrl+Tab
Switch to the previous tab in a dialog box.	Ctrl+Shift+Tab
Move between options in an open drop-down list, or between options in a group of options.	Arrow keys
Perform the action assigned to the selected button; select or clear the selected check box.	Spacebar
Open the list if it is closed and move to that option in the list.	First letter of an option in a list
Select an option; select or clear a check box.	Alt+ the underlined letter in an option

Action	Keyboard shortcut
Open a selected drop-down list.	Alt+Down Arrow
Close a selected drop-down list; cancel a command and close a dialog box.	Esc
Perform the action assigned to a default button in a dialog box.	Enter
Close a dialog box. If no dialog box is open, exits program.	Alt+F4

Use edit boxes within dialog boxes

TIP An edit box is a blank in which you enter or paste an entry.

Action	Keyboard shortcut
Move to the beginning of the entry.	Home
Move to the end of the entry.	End
Move one character to the left or right.	Left Arrow or Right Arrow
Move one word to the left.	Ctrl+Left Arrow
Move one word to the right.	Ctrl+Right Arrow
Select or cancel selection one character to the left.	Shift+Left Arrow
Select or cancel selection one character to the right.	Shift+Right Arrow
Select or cancel selection one word to the left.	Ctrl+Shift+Left Arrow
Select or cancel selection one word to the right.	Ctrl+Shift+Right Arrow
Select from the cursor to the beginning of the entry.	Shift+Home
Select from the cursor to the end of the entry.	Shift+End

Use the Help window

Action	Keyboard shortcut
Open the Help window.	F1
Close the Help window	Alt+F4
Switch between the Help window and the active program. (Cycles through all open programs.)	Alt+Tab
Go back to <program name> Home.	Alt+Home
Select the next item in the Help window.	Tab
Select the previous item in the Help window.	Shift+Tab
Perform the action for the selected item.	Enter

Action	Keyboard shortcut
In the Browse <program name> Help section of the Help window, select the next or previous item, respectively.	Tab or Shift+Tab
In the Browse <program name> Help section of the Help window, expand or collapse the selected item, respectively.	Enter
Select the next hidden text or hyperlink, including Show All or Hide All at the top of a topic.	Tab
Select the previous hidden text or hyperlink.	Shift+Tab
Perform the action for the selected Show All, Hide All, hidden text, or hyperlink.	Enter
Move back to the previous Help topic (Back button).	Alt+Left Arrow or Backspace
Move forward to the next Help topic (Forward button).	Alt+Right Arrow
Scroll small amounts up or down, respectively, within the currently displayed Help topic.	Up Arrow or Down Arrow
Scroll larger amounts up or down, respectively, within the currently displayed Help topic.	Page Up or Page Down
Stop the last action (Stop button).	Esc
Refresh the window (Refresh button).	F5
Print the current Help topic. Note: If the cursor is not in the current Help topic, press F6, and then press Ctrl+P.	Ctrl+P
Change the connection state.	F6, and then press Enter to open the list of choices
Switch among areas in the Help window; for example, switch between the toolbar and the Search list.	F6
In a Table of Contents in tree view, select the next or previous item, respectively.	Up Arrow or Down Arrow
In a Table of Contents in tree view, expand or collapse the selected item, respectively.	Left Arrow or Right Arrow

Index

Symbols

A

I

icons
    Access program, 10
    assigning to current database, 324
    asterisk, 66
    pencil, 66
    primary key, 78
image controls, 238
    effect of Size Mode property, 239
Import Objects dialog box, 288
import process, saving, 280
Import Specification dialog box, 291
Import Spreadsheet wizard, 293
Import Text wizard, 290
importing, 280
    by copying, 306, 308
    database objects, 281
    delimited text files, 282, 290
    Excel worksheets, 282, 293
    fixed-width text files, 282
    .html files, 285
    vs. linking, 295
    non-Access databases, 281, 283, 287
    Outlook folders, 283
    queries, 281
    with saved process, 281
    SharePoint lists, 283
    tables, 281, 380
    text files, 282
    .xml files, 286
inconsistent field values, avoiding, 183, 184
Indexed property, 176
indexing fields, 176
Info page (Backstage view), 332
Input Mask property, 165
Input Mask wizard, 168
input masks, 165
    defined, 380
    common characters, 166
    creating, 167
    custom, saving, 171
    for forcing case, 170
    literal characters, 166
    for phone numbers, 166, 167
    text, 167
Integer size (Number data type), 163

K

keyboard shortcuts
    for copying text, 306
    for Field List pane, 235, 259
    for moving controls, 145
    for navigating, 32
    for Navigation pane, 325
    for pasting text, 307
    for Property Sheet pane, 101, 234, 261
    for Save As dialog box, 161
    for selecting all controls, 148
keys
    foreign, 379
    primary, 381

L

label controls, 91, 142
    defined, 380
    captions, 106, 242
    as form titles, 239
    moving without text box controls, 236
labels, creating, 44
.laccdb files, 338
Language page (Access Options dialog box), 357
languages, making available, 357
Layout view (forms), 33, 228
    opening forms in, 100
Layout view (reports), 43, 144, 263

P

About the authors

Joyce Cox

Joyce has more than 30 years' experience in the development of training materials about technical subjects for non-technical audiences, and is the author of dozens of books about Microsoft Office and Windows technologies. She is the Vice President of Online Training Solutions, Inc. (OTSI).

As President of and principal author for Online Press, she developed the Quick Course series of computer training books for beginning and intermediate adult learners. She was also the first managing editor of Microsoft Press, an editor for Sybex, and an editor for the University of California.

Joan Lambert

Joan has worked in the training and certification industry for 16 years. As President of OTSI, Joan is responsible for guiding the translation of technical information and requirements into useful, relevant, and measurable training and certification tools.

Joan is a Microsoft Office Certified Master, a Microsoft Certified Application Specialist Instructor, a Microsoft Certified Technology Specialist, a Microsoft Certified Trainer, and the author of more than two dozen books about Windows and Office (for Windows and Mac). Joan enthusiastically shares her love of technology through her participation in the creation of books, learning materials, and certification exams. She greatly enjoys communicating the benefits of new technologies by delivering training and facilitating Microsoft Experience Center events.

Joan currently lives in a nearly perfect small town in Texas with her daughter, Trinity.

The team

This book would not exist without the support of these hard-working members of the OTSI publishing team:

- Jan Bednarczuk
- Rob Carr
- Susie Carr
- Jeanne Craver
- Kathy Krause
- Marlene Lambert
- Jaime Odell
- Jean Trenary

We are especially thankful to the support staff at home who make it possible for our team members to devote their time and attention to these projects.

Rosemary Caperton provided invaluable support on behalf of Microsoft Learning.

Online Training Solutions, Inc. (OTSI)

OTSI specializes in the design, creation, and production of Office and Windows training products for information workers and home computer users. For more information about OTSI, visit:

www.otsi.com

Microsoft

How to download your ebook

Thank you for purchasing this Microsoft Press® title. Your companion PDF ebook is ready to download from O'Reilly Media, official distributor of Microsoft Press titles.

To download your ebook, go to
http://aka.ms/Access2013sbs/files
and follow the instructions.

Please note: You will be asked to create a free online account and enter the access code below.

Your access code:

> ## NDDVBDG

Microsoft® Access® 2013 Step by Step

Your PDF ebook allows you to:

- Search the full text
- Print
- Copy and paste

Best yet, you will be notified about free updates to your ebook.

If you ever lose your ebook file, you can download it again just by logging in to your account.

Need help? Please contact:
mspbooksupport@oreilly.com
or call 800-889-8969.

What do you think of this book?

We want to hear from you!
To participate in a brief online survey, please visit:

microsoft.com/learning/booksurvey

Tell us how well this book meets your needs—what works effectively, and what we can do better. Your feedback will help us continually improve our books and learning resources for you.

Thank you in advance for your input!